BRITISH HISTORY
1815–1914

1815–1822 Britain in Europe

CASTLEREAGH AND HIS AIMS

C.P. Hill & J.C. Wright

Oxford University Press 1981

Oxford University Press, Walton Street, Oxford OX2 6DP

London   Glasgow   New York   Toronto
Delhi   Bombay   Calcutta   Madras   Karachi
Kuala Lumpur   Singapore   Hong Kong   Tokyo
Nairobi   Dar es Salaam   Cape Town   Salisbury
Melbourne   Wellington

and associate companies in
Beirut   Berlin   Ibadan   Mexico City

ISBN 0 19 913264 X

Phototypeset in Great Britain by Filmtype Services Limited, Scarborough.
Printed in Hong Kong

Contents

List of Maps

Acknowledgements

The publishers would like to thank the following for their permission to reproduce photographs:

Barnaby's Picture Library p.256, p.278; C. Batstone p.97; BBC Hulton Picture Library p.12, p.14, p.16, p.20, p.21, p.22, p.24, p.30, p.33, p.39, p.42, p.46, p.47, p.54 bottom left, p.54 bottom right, p.61, p.65, p.72, p.79, p.80 top, p.80 bottom, p.83, p.84, p.85 top, p.85 bottom, p.86, p.87, p.88, p.90, p.92 top, p.92 bottom, p.94, p.96, p.99, p.103, p.105, p.108, p.111, p.112 bottom left, p.112 bottom right, p.114, p.115, p.128, p.133, p.138, p.141, p.143, p.145, p.171, p.172, p.174, p.182, top left, p.182 top right, p.187, p.191, p.195, p.196, p.199 top, p.199 bottom, p.206, p.207, p.209, p.210, p.212, p.213, p.217, p.221, p.225, p.243, p.246, p.251, p.257, p.258, p.260, p.273, p.274, p.287; British Library Newspaper Library p.263; Canadian Tourist Board p.272 top; Communist Party Library p.53, p.70, p.140; Mary Evans Picture Library p.15, p.164, p.184 top left, p.184 top right, p.240, p.272 top; Illustrated London News p.50, p.81, p.130, p.169; Edward Leigh p.224 top, p.224 bottom; Mansell Collection p.25, p.41, p.58, p.73, p.74, p.76, p.82, p.102, p.204, p.234, p.235, p.293; National Portrait Gallery p.6, p.119, p.153; Punch p.160.

Preface

Our main purpose in this book is to provide a text appropriate to the needs of GCE Ordinary Level candidates who are studying British history between the Napoleonic and Great Wars. If students following general courses in Sixth Forms also find it useful, so much the better. We have tried to write a reasonably detailed account covering what seem to us the main themes of a century in which British people carried through, and endured, remarkable changes. The central narrative is political, yet there is also a measure of the economic and social history without which the politics cannot make sense. We hope we have provoked thought and enquiry, as well as offered knowledge, and we have done our best to keep in touch with recent scholarly work in this well-tilled field. Readers will find a fair proportion of illustrations of various kinds, and of maps tailored to the text; and an index which pays special attention to some of the central topics and personalities of the period. They will not find either examples of contemporary documents or sets of exercises. We have deliberately sacrificed both in order to provide more of the detailed narrative which Ordinary Level candidates deserve; the documents with regret, the exercises in the belief that good teachers will wish to provide their own.

We are greatly indebted to Mr S.R. James of the Nelson Thomlinson School, Wigton, Cumbria, to Dr Bruce Coleman of the University of Exeter, and to Dr W.R. Lambert, who have generously made time in busy lives to read our typescript and have improved our text in many places. They bear no responsibility for any errors, misinterpretations and other defects that may remain.

C.P. Hill and J.C. Wright.

Introduction

On 18 June 1815 Anglo-Prussian forces commanded by the Duke of Wellington and Marshal Blucher defeated the last of the French Emperor Napoleon's armies on the field of Waterloo, near Brussels. The battle was, in Wellington's words, 'the nearest run thing you ever saw in your life'. But it was peculiarly decisive. It clinched the victory of Britain and her allies over Napoleon, sending him into exile forever on the island of St Helena. It ended long years of war – for the British, from 1793 to 1815 with little interruption. It was followed by forty years in which British armies fought no great campaigns on the continent, and not for a century was there any conflict comparable in scale with the Napoleonic War. Waterloo also closed the period of a century and a half during which France had been the main threat to European peace.

Thus 1815 may be seen as a year of unusual importance in British and in European history. Yet history, the story of endless change, is a continuous process. Each new generation of human beings inherits from the past a legacy which it takes into the future. The legacy includes opportunities and problems, movements begun and ideas launched. Out of these men shape the future. The British people alive in 1815 inherited a complicated legacy. What they, and their successors during the next hundred years, did with it provides the material of this book. Among the main elements of that legacy the following may be suggested as pointers to British history between 1815 and 1914:

The growth of population. Since the 1780s the population of Britain had been rising fast. By 1811 it was nearly 12 millions, and by 1821 over 14 millions – a rate of increase of 16 per cent, the fastest known in any ten-year period of our history. The number of people living in Britain almost doubled during the first half of the nineteenth century.

The consequences of the French Wars. The wars had brought dislocation of trade and industry; inflation and high prices; much poverty and high poor rates; heavy taxation and over-investment in agriculture to make Britain self-supporting in food. With peace came demobilisation and much unemployment; trade depression and continued poverty; heavy taxation to meet the interest on the National Debt, which had practically quadrupled during the wars; laws to protect farming by keeping food prices high; and widespread discontent among the poor who had to pay most of the taxes.

The Industrial Revolution. From about the 1780s a series of technological changes, of which the most significant was probably the adaptation of James Watt's steam engine for use in cotton mills (first recorded in 1785), had set going a transformation in British industry. A historian can describe this 'Industrial Revolution' as 'probably the most important event in world history, at any rate since the invention of agriculture and cities'. Its effects dominated nineteenth-century British history. For most people they brought, in food, clothes and housing, higher standards. But in 1815, part way through its early course, it meant for many thousands – especially in the pits and mills and foundries in the coalfields of the north and midlands – factory discipline and slums.

The Agricultural Revolution. In the countryside – where the first census (1801) showed just under eighty per cent of British people living – the wars and the needs of a rising population accelerated changes already under way. These included more varied crop rotation, scientific stockbreeding, and enclosure of land to replace the 'open fields' – bringing more, and more varied, food. In 1815 the social consequences of these changes were still being felt, among them poverty and under-employment for the farm labourer, particularly in southern England where better-paid jobs in factories were not at hand.

The aftermath of the French Revolution. The great French Revolution of 1789 had meant to nearly all Englishmen the Fall of the Bastille, the Jacobin Reign of Terror with its remorseless instrument 'Madame Guillotine', and the dictatorship of 'Boney'. The war was to them its chief legacy. Yet it left also a legacy of ideas, memorable in the slogan 'Liberté, Egalité, Fraternité'. These ideas, of nationalism and liberalism, were to inspire revolutions throughout Europe and indeed the world during the nineteenth century – nationalism meaning the demand for national independence and liberalism that for the freedom of the individual. Liberalism was to be loudly proclaimed by Radical orators in Britain soon after Waterloo.

Parliamentary Reform. The second half of the eighteenth century had seen the beginnings of a movement for parliamentary reform in Britain. The French wars had stifled it; it would come to life again after 1815. A growing middle class of merchants and professional men would not remain content to be ruled by aristocratic landowners. Working-class discontent also would demand an outlet. Parliamentary reform would bring other changes, for example in the role and importance of political parties.

The Evangelical Movement. In 1815 the religious movement called the 'Evangelical Revival' was firmly established among the upper and middle classes. Reacting against the 'atheism' of the French Revolution and demanding stricter standards of conduct from all, it had got the Slave Trade abolished in 1807; and its influence was to be strong in Victorian England both upon the Court itself and on the course of social reform.

The 'condition of the people'. Before 1815 politicians concerned themselves only a little about the condition of the people: mostly at local
level, and mainly to prevent disorder or to cope with poverty out of the
rates. After 1815, as population and great cities grew and society
became more complex, so this concern extended, if only slowly. 'The
condition of the people' question – involving factories and mines,
houses and drains, health, law and order, education and drink – became
a central issue of British politics, yet for the most part only during the
second half of the nineteenth century.

The British Empire and Ireland. In the second half of the eighteenth
century the British had lost one empire (the Thirteen Colonies which
became the United States) and gained another (great territories in India
and Canada). In 1800 the Act of Union destroyed the Dublin Parliament and incorporated Ireland in the United Kingdom. So on the other
side of the Irish Sea was a continuing problem; while far across the
globe was a range of opportunities, to test – and sometimes to bedevil –
British statesmen throughout the century after Waterloo.

Britain and Europe. In the French Wars Britain, safeguarded against
invasion by the Navy, had nevertheless in her own interest joined the
coalition against the conqueror Napoleon. This pattern continued into
the peace settlement in 1815, with Britain taking part in a united,
concerted effort by the great powers (the Concert of Europe) to deal
with Europe's problems.

1
Postwar resettlement and its problems

1 The instability of Europe and Castlereagh's policy

In 1815 the greatest war that Europe had yet known came to an end, and the representatives of the victorious Allies met to draw up a peace settlement. The treaties arranged since Napoleon's first abdication in April 1814 were updated into the Treaty of Vienna which was to fix the direction of European history until the first World War: not before 1919 was there to be a major revision of the territorial settlement made at Vienna. Britain's part in these negotiations was an influential one. More than any other Power she had, by her efforts and example through twenty-three years of nearly continuous war, made victory possible. She had, as her representatives, Lord Castlereagh and the Duke of Wellington, both with long experience and sound understanding of European affairs. She was therefore able not only to influence the general policy of the Allies but also effectively to safeguard her own particular interests.

Castlereagh had been Foreign Secretary since 1812 and had done much to keep the Fourth Coalition together. Like every other British Foreign Secretary, he saw as his main task the maintenance of the security of Britain against attack and as his main danger a Europe dominated, as it had been under Napoleon, by one or more great powers. He appreciated that Britain needed a prolonged period of peace in which to recover from the war and to develop her overseas trade. He also realised that it was Britain who would suffer most from a settlement which, by trying to please all, would provide new causes for future disputes. Thus his policy was first to construct a workable peace settlement and then to keep that settlement in working order. The one he achieved in the Vienna Settlement, the other he attempted in the Quadruple Alliance and the Congress System.

Much of the Vienna Settlement was clearly a triumph for Castlereagh. France was restrained but not so humiliated that she later sought a war of revenge. She returned to her frontiers of 1790, handed over a war indemnity of 700 million francs, restored looted art treasures, abolished the Slave Trade, and paid for an army of occupation of 150,000 for up to five years. Her Bourbon king, Louis XVIII, was restored. The Austrian Netherlands were joined with Holland to form a new Kingdom of the Netherlands better able to meet possible French threats to an area always vital to British interests, if only as a base for

Lord
Castlereagh

Vienna
Settlement

invasion. Britain gained important possessions overseas of great commercial and strategic value – Malta, Ceylon, Heligoland, Mauritius, Trinidad, Tobago, St. Lucia and the Ionian Islands, while the unwilling Dutch were made to sell Cape Colony for £6m. The lenient treatment of France was central to Castlereagh's plans; without it he considered that a lasting peace was impossible. Louis XVIII and his Foreign Secretary Talleyrand, for their part, were anxious for the rest of Europe to forget their mistrust of France as soon as possible and were more than ready to co-operate with Britain. Over the other changes made by the Vienna Settlement Castlereagh had less control and Russia, Austria and Prussia gained new territories to strengthen themselves against France whom they continued to regard as the main danger.

Lord Castlereagh (1769–1822)

Holy Alliance   While the details of the Settlement were still being worked out two quite separate Alliances were proposed to deal with future problems. In September 1815, Tsar Alexander I invited all European monarchs to join a Holy Alliance in which they bound themselves to deal with affairs

6

of state according to the teachings of Christian doctrines. Castlereagh's opinion of this proposal was expressed in a letter to Lord Liverpool, the Prime Minister, when he called it 'a piece of sublime mysticism and nonsense', yet he had no wish to offend the Tsar. The Prince Regent replied to Alexander promising co-operation but, like the Pope and the Sultan, signed no agreement. Castlereagh's suspicions were justified. The Holy Alliance soon became dominated by the Austrian minister Metternich who, by 1822, was using it as a means of suppressing liberal and nationalist ideas not only in the Austrian Empire but throughout Europe. Castlereagh himself had little sympathy for these ideas but did not see the Holy Alliance as the most likely way of preserving peace.

The second proposal seemed much better suited to British interests. **Quadruple Alliance** This was the Quadruple Alliance which was formed in November 1815 by Britain, Austria, Russia and Prussia with the original intention of safeguarding part of the Vienna Settlement. The Allies agreed to combine against any revolution within France which might threaten her neighbours, and to exclude the Bonaparte family from any position of power. What was more important was contained in Article VI of the Alliance, drafted by Castlereagh, whereby 'to secure the execution of the present Treaty, the Powers have agreed to renew their meetings at fixed periods .... for consulting upon their common interests'. From this early attempt to replace conflict by discussion came the Congress System.

At this stage, Castlereagh hoped that regular meetings of the Quadruple Alliance would deal with attempts by any Power to break the Vienna Treaty and so threaten the stability of Europe. He was prepared to commit Britain to intervention in European affairs in order to uphold that Treaty, however unpopular his policy was at home. What happened was that his European allies preferred regular meetings of the Holy Alliance to deal with internal threats to their own despotic rule. They expected British support for a Europe permanently run on the ideas and methods of the *Ancien Régime*. In this scheme Castlereagh could not and would not co-operate. The Tory government of Lord Liverpool, reactionary by modern standards, was liberal compared with those of its European contemporaries; it was increasingly influenced by business men who hoped for a more progressive Europe in which they could trade freely, not one tied by restriction and privilege; it would certainly not vote money for a British army to fight other powers' battles on the continent. Castlereagh's chief critic, Canning, put the general view that 'this system of periodic meetings .... will involve us deeply in all the politics of the continent, whereas our true policy has always been not to interfere except in great emergencies and then only with commanding force'. Abroad, liberals could see no difference between the Quadruple Alliance and the Holy Alliance as instruments of reaction. From the very start of the Congress System, therefore, Castlereagh had little choice of action. He had to take a firm stand against using British forces to help put down revolutions in other countries, and he had to rely on the personal influence he still had with his old wartime allies to keep the so-called Balance of Power.

Before this happened, Castlereagh had dealt with some of the problems still existing after the Anglo-American War of 1812–14. It was agreed that the rival navies on the Great Lakes should be scrapped, and in 1818 the undefended frontier between Canada and the U.S.A was continued along the Forty-ninth Parallel as far as the Rockies. Many issues were still to arise (pp.69, 132–4) but at least the pattern of negotiation had been set.

Congress System – Aix

Meanwhile, in Europe, the first Congress had opened at Aix-la-Chapelle in September 1818. France was given a seat at the conference table and, on Wellington's advice, the army of occupation was withdrawn. The Tsar suggested that France should be admitted to the Quadruple Alliance, which Castlereagh felt made nonsense of its original aims; in spite of his opposition, she was brought into a new Quintuple Alliance. Proposals for action against the Barbary Pirates and the Slave Trade brought further disagreements, the one because it would have given the Russian Fleet a chance to dominate the Eastern Mediterranean, the other because it would have given the British Fleet the controversial 'right of search' on the high seas. The real turning point for Castlereagh came in the proposal that revolutions anywhere should be put down by all other states acting in concert, and that there should be periodic congresses to regulate European affairs. Castlereagh opposed the suggestions and, for the moment, they were dropped. It was clear that the interests of Britain and of the other Powers had begun to diverge.

Troppau

In 1820 a revolt in Spain widened the split. Russia, Austria, Prussia and France were all for intervention. Castlereagh was against and, in a State Paper of May 1820, attacked the principles behind the Holy Alliance, saying 'When the territorial balance of Europe is disturbed Britain can interfere with effect, but she is the last government which can be expected to commit herself on any question of an abstract character'. A further rising in Naples led to the second congress at Troppau in October 1820 to which Britain and France sent only observers and not delegates with full powers. Here the representatives of Austria, Russia and Prussia signed the Troppau Protocol, a document which asserted that 'states which have undergone a change of government due to revolution *ipso facto* cease to be members of the European alliance. If immediate danger threatens other states the Powers bind themselves, if need be by arms, to bring back the guilty party into the bosom of the alliance'. France accepted the Protocol, but Castlereagh saw his worst fears confirmed and he formally protested. The congress was adjourned to Laibach in January 1821 and here Austria was authorised to put down the revolt. Stewart, the British observer, again made it clear that Britain opposed intervention.

8

The final congress was called for the autumn of 1822 at Verona. Since Laibach there had been an anti-Austrian revolt in Piedmont, the Greeks had risen against the Turks, the South American colonists had broken away from Spain, and there were more disturbances in Spain itself and in Portugal. Castlereagh continued to plan alternatives to wholesale intervention but, in August 1822, he committed suicide through overwork and depression. By the time the congress met George Canning was Foreign Secretary.

As a key figure in Liverpool's post-war government Castlereagh was highly unpopular, and, to a country anxious for peace, he seemed too keen to involve Britain in a European role. He was also an uninspiring speaker in debate and made no effort to explain his policies outside the cabinet. Like Salisbury later, he felt that the proper place for diplomacy was behind locked doors, not in public debate. Thus he suffered by comparison with Canning who knew the value of good publicity and a witty speech. They had fought a duel in 1809: it was typical of Castlereagh that it took him three pages to set out his challenge, and typical of Canning to reply that he would rather fight than have to read it. Nevertheless, Britain owed much to Castlereagh – 'the most creative and imaginative of nineteenth-century British foreign secretaries', as Norman Gash calls him. The overseas territories gained at Vienna were vital to our expanding economy, whilst his strong sense of European unity, with the major Powers committed to the maintenance of peace, was the most sensible policy for Britain at the time. Few of his countrymen appreciated what he was trying to do, and, for this, he had largely himself to blame.

2 Distress at home from Waterloo to Peterloo

After Waterloo Britain was at a peak of power and reputation in Europe and the world. But at home the years which followed victory were hard and bitter. Poverty and misery were widespread, and distress led easily to disturbance in an age when few had the vote, trade unions were feeble, and there were no effective police. Industry was in depression, unemployment high. Strikes, riots, machine-breaking and rick-burning, clashes between troops and demonstrators were frequent; plots and rumours of revolution on the French Jacobin model were rife. It was a time of desperation among the labouring poor and of fear among the rich and the middle class, when many sober citizens thought the entire framework of society about to collapse.

The underlying causes of this state of affairs were two. One was the steepest rise ever known in the rate at which Britain's population has grown. Between 1801 and 1831 it went up by over 4 millions, an increase of about 35 per cent. Everywhere for most people this caused great and continuing hardship, by pressure on food supplies and prices and on water resources. It also added greatly to the average man's chances of becoming unemployed – helped in this by the arrival in Britain of large numbers of Irish peasants willing to accept starvation wages. The second cause was the economic dislocation produced by a war which lasted over twenty years, and by its sudden ending. Prices had almost doubled during the war, and yet wages, at any rate on the land, had not kept pace. Food supplies had been erratic, and local shortages sometimes severe. Some industries, notably agriculture and iron and the other metal trades, prospered in wartime; others, more dependent on overseas trade, fared less well. Yet on balance the war and its accompanying inflation stimulated the British economy. When it stopped, hardship came quickly, checked only by a brief post-war boom in exports of cotton goods, hardware and the like. Government expenditure was halved during 1815. A rapid demobilisation threw about 300,000 soldiers and sailors on to the labour market. The consequences were disastrous – a vast trade depression, the shutdown of countless firms, the halt of business expansion and widespread unemployment. The countryside, where most people still lived, suffered at least as much as the towns. Expenditure on poor relief rose from £4,000,000 in 1803 to almost £8,000,000 in 1818.

Effects of Industrial Revolution

Upon the hard-hit nation there fell also the impact of the Agrarian and Industrial Revolutions. In the year of Waterloo Britain was about half-way through the most radical economic and social transformation her people had ever seen, and the generation alive in 1815 was the principal victim of that great series of changes. By 1815 indeed the worst effects of enclosures were probably over: after that date nearly all were of wasteland, and some areas (e.g. Devon) were hardly touched by them. As a cause of poverty and unemployment in rural England they were far less important than the huge unchecked growth of population. Yet they had in many areas disrupted the lives of villagers, particularly by depriving the poorer farmers of their pasture and so of their animals, and had helped to turn them into ill-paid and landless labourers. The coming of machinery had robbed many of them of the bye-industries like spinning and weaving which were traditionally combined with farming. From places within reach of the new industrial areas many thousands had gone to the factories in search of higher wages, for the countryside was necessarily the reservoir from which these drew their workers. In the factory towns they found themselves living in close-packed slums, in cellars or 'jerry-built' houses; working under the strict discipline essential to full use of the new machines; and thus becoming, in the countryman William Cobbett's words in *Rural Rides* 'poor creatures compelled to work fourteen hours a day, in a heat of eighty-four degrees, and liable to punishment for looking out at a window of the factory'.

Uprooted, often bewildered and brutalised by their living and working conditions, such people provided splendid combustible material for agitation in the early nineteenth century. Not all the ills of their plight were new ones. Thus child labour, whereby children of six or seven toiled full days in mill or mine, had also been customary in the old domestic industry. The hovels of eighteenth-century villages were not notably superior to nineteenth-century slum dwellings, and their inhabitants' expectation of life was certainly no greater. But there were novel elements in the situation created by the Industrial Revolution which caused distress on a larger scale and made disturbance and violence far more likely than before. The coming of factory industry in itself created a new problem of mass unemployment, with whole towns and villages suddenly thrown out of work because trade depression had struck local industry, whether textile mill or iron foundry. By contrast with the days of cottage industry, large numbers of 'hands', as workers were now beginning to be called, were employed together in one place, a situation which made mass action, whether strike or riot, far more likely and practicable. Finally, there were many groups of industrial craftsmen whose livelihood was directly threatened by technical progress and who tried deliberately to halt that progress. In 1811–12 bands of Nottinghamshire weavers, allegedly under the leadership of 'General' Ned Ludd from a headquarters in Sherwood Forest, had smashed a thousand stocking frames which their employers were using to make low-grade goods. The authorities had taken the Luddites very seriously, making frame-breaking a capital offence. The movement spread to the West Riding of Yorkshire and to Lancashire, and some twenty people were executed for various offences before it died away. The legend of Luddism and of its martyrs remained strong after 1815.

Two economic measures passed by Parliament made matters worse. **The Corn Laws**
Most of its members were landowners, and they put through the Corn Law of 1815 in order to protect farmers from the flood of foreign corn which poured into British ports when war ended and sent British wheat prices tumbling down. The law, which totally forbade the import of foreign corn until the price of British corn reached 80s. per quarter[1], was not very successful in helping farmers at this time, for the inflated prices of the war years did not return, and it was no longer profitable to cultivate marginal land. But it made bread prices very high for the poor, preventing them spending their money on other necessities, and it was thus a powerful cause both of popular discontent and of a decline in trade. The following year Parliament took another step which also hit the poor. This was the abolition of income tax, introduced (at 2/- in the £ on incomes of £200 and more) in 1798 by the Prime Minister, William Pitt the Younger, with the pledge that it would be withdrawn immediately the war ended. Against the government's wishes the Commons forced its ending in 1816. To replace it, the government made big increases in indirect taxation, such as customs and excise duties – which fell relatively far more heavily on the poor than on the

[1]A quarter of grain is a measure of capacity=8 bushels=2.91 hectolitres.

'General' Ned Ludd.

better-off[1]. Almost half the entire public expenditure at this time went to pay the interest on the National Debt, which during the war had

[1]Among the multitude of items taxed at this time were not merely wine, tea, cider, malt and dogs, but also paper and newspapers, glass, bricks and stone, hair-powder, cocoa, stage-coaches, windows, coats of arms and candles.

soared from £248 million to £834 million. The 'fundholders', those who held investments in the National Debt, came from among the well-to-do. So in effect taxation was transferring income from the poor to the rich.

Against this sombre background it is scarcely surprising that in 1816 a wave of popular discontent swept across Britain. In rural East Anglia barns were burned and threshing machines smashed; farm labourers armed with pikes and guns established a reign of terror, ended only by calling in troops. There were strikes on Tyneside, processions of unemployed throughout the Midlands, riots and violence in south Wales and around Glasgow. The climax came in the winter, with a series of mass meetings at Spa Fields in London; the last of these turned into a riot, some of whose members, waving the tricolour flags made notorious during the French Revolution, looted a gunsmith's shop and made for the Tower of London, firing at passers-by as they went. A handful of troops restored order easily enough by nightfall. But the events of the year frightened the well-to-do, chilling their sympathies for the sufferings of the poor.

Some of the disturbances were certainly a revival of Luddism, as at Nottingham and Loughborough, where factories were burned down. A few may have reflected propaganda among out-of-work craftsmen and discharged soldiers by the Society of Spencean Philanthropists, the followers of Thomas Spence (d. 1814), an earnest revolutionary schoolmaster from Tyneside who had advocated equal distribution of land. But most simply expressed the need of desperate men for some solution of their problems. The particular solution most widely demanded was reform of Parliament, by the giving of votes to a far greater proportion of the population than the perhaps one in ten English men who had them at this time[1]. This became the central cry of those popular leaders who came to the fore in these years, like Henry Hunt and William Cobbett. Hunt, a wealthy gentleman-farmer, tall and handsome, wearing a white top-hat and possessing a voice of enormous power, was the great orator of the reform movement. He did much to spread the cause among workingmen at meetings across the land – and much, too, by his vanity and wildness of phrase, to frighten away middle-class supporters. William Cobbett (1763–1835), son of an innkeeper and farmer of Farnham in Surrey, imprisoned in 1810 for attacking flogging in the army, had published reforming news and opinion in a *Weekly Political Register* since 1804, and in 1816 he started a cheaper *Register* at 2d. His enemies called it 'Twopenny Trash'; by the end of the year it was selling 60,000 copies a week. Cobbett's direct and outspoken style made him, in his contemporary William Hazlitt's words, 'unquestionably the most powerful political writer of the present day'. Many of his glaring prejudices – for example, against the

[1]In Scotland it may have been as few as one in a hundred men.

Bank of England, clergymen, and paper money – no doubt made him more supporters than enemies among the poor. His writing, particularly in the *Register*, was most effective in spreading the gospel of parliamentary reform throughout the country at a time when the law hindered the formation of national political associations.

William Cobbett (1762–1835), the enemy of the rich

The Blanketeers   In January 1817 a missile shattered the windows of the Prince Regent's coach as he was returning from the state opening of Parliament. Yet the main focus of concern for the authorities this year lay to the north, with two episodes which in their upshot proved pathetic yet in their origins looked formidable. One, in the spring, was the so-called 'march of the Blanketeers'. Some six hundred weavers set out to march from Manchester to London, each with a blanket on his back, to present a petition to the Prince Regent asking him to help relieve the depressed state of the cotton industry. Special constables, yeomanry and troops turned most of them back on the border of Derbyshire, and only one man reached London. The second episode, in June, was more sinister. This was the Pentrich Revolution, when a small group of Derbyshire labourers, quarrymen and ironworkers, led by Jeremiah Brandreth, were encouraged into futile rebellion by an *agent provocateur* planted in their ranks by the government, one 'Oliver the Spy'. Three were executed outside Derby Gaol, many others transported or impris-

Oliver the Spy

1817 – plotters at the White Horse, Pentrich, Derbyshire

oned. The government claimed that these wretched yokels were part of a general plan for a nation-wide rising whose aim was to set up a republic. Like the Blanketeers, the Pentrich men themselves had believed that hundreds of thousands were waiting to rise in their support in London.

A good harvest in 1817 brought food prices down; trade revived and 1818 was a better year. But conditions worsened in 1819, and that August brought the notorious affair of the Peterloo Massacre. A great crowd, reckoned at 60,000, in holiday mood and dressed in their Sunday best, with many women and children in their ranks, marched in orderly fashion to St. Peter's Fields in Manchester to hear 'Orator'

Peterloo

15

The Peterloo Massacre (1819)

Hunt speak on reform. The local magistrates, responsible for law and order, decided to arrest Hunt. The Manchester and Salford Yeomanry, unskilled volunteers[1], charged into the densely-packed crowd and got hemmed in. The magistrates in panic called on the 15th Hussars to go to their rescue. Within minutes the field was empty; eleven people, including two women, were dead and several hundreds injured. The affair, at once nicknamed 'The Massacre of Peterloo', produced an outcry of protest throughout the north, with rumours of armed insurrection and vengeance. The responsibility for what had happened lay with the local magistrates. Yet the government at Whitehall, half believing in the possibility of revolution, thanked them and the soldiers for their 'prompt, decisive and efficient measures for the preservation of the public tranquillity'. The sheer horror of the episode passed into the legend of English history.

3 Civil disorder and government reaction

Liverpool's Ministry

The Prime Minister from 1812 to 1827 was Lord Liverpool. An experienced politician and a good speaker, notably honest by contrast

[1]Who, according to one historian, 'consisted almost exclusively of cheesemongers, ironmongers and newly enriched manufacturers'. R. J. White, *From Waterloo to Peterloo*, 1957.

with his eighteenth-century predecessors, he controlled his Cabinet more by amiability than by forcefulness. The strong man of the government was Lord Castlereagh, leader of the House of Commons as well as Foreign Secretary. At the Home Office, the department responsible for coping with the disturbances, was Lord Sidmouth, who was inclined to panic. Other important members of the government included Lord Eldon, who as Lord Chancellor was hostile to almost any change in the law; Robert Peel, appointed as Secretary for Ireland at the age of 24; and, from 1816, George Canning, former Foreign Secretary. Finally there was the Duke of Wellington, Arthur Wellesley, unique in his fame as the conqueror of Napoleon, no politician, resolute in his devotion to firm government, a formidable personality of whom everyone from the Prince Regent downwards seems to have been frightened. He joined the Cabinet in 1816, a step which led many reformers to believe that a military despotism was about to begin.

These men, and their supporters in Parliament, called themselves Tories. But party lines were still very blurred in a political world containing many independent M.P.s and with no party organisation like that of the twentieth century. The nominal opposition, the Whigs, were notably feeble at this period, few in number, divided among themselves, and often at least as fearful of social upheaval as the Tories. Lord Grey, a great Northumberland landowner and a leading Whig, once warned a radical friend that if Hunt gained power 'I shall not precede you many months on the scaffold.' It was important, in the circumstances of the post-war years, that the great majority of M.Ps. were landowners, and that the power of the House of Lords was strong in resisting change[1]. Moreover, all members of the government had lived through the French Revolution and the long years of the Revolutionary and Napoleonic Wars, and many of them had held high office then. The Terror and the guillotine, the tales told by French *emigré* noblemen and the threat of invasion were indelibly stamped upon their memories. Liverpool himself, indeed, as a young man of 18 had witnessed the Paris mob's attack on the Bastille on July 14th 1789, and reminded Parliament of it from time to time. Such men were scarcely likely to welcome reform of Parliament, still less revolution, in which they would clearly be the first victims. Such memories also made many middle-class men Tory in outlook, champions of the established constitution.

Yet there was much more in their hostility to reform than mere selfishness or crude concern for the interests of their own class. They lived at a time when people's assumptions about what governments could do, and ought to do, were notably different from those which have developed since. It was the duty of statesmen to uphold law and

[1]Yet by no means all the Cabinet belonged to the landed aristocracy. Eldon was the son of a Tyneside coal-heaver, Peel of a Bury mill-owner, Sidmouth of a fashionable doctor; Canning's mother was an actress; and Liverpool himself was only a second-generation peer.

order, to safeguard property, to defend the nation against external enemies, and often to become unpopular in doing these things. But it was not at all their task to cure unemployment, still less to provide a system of social security. Partly this was because nearly everybody believed, with Dr Johnson,

> How small, of all that human hearts endure,
> That part which Laws of Kings can cause or cure.

Laissez-faire Liverpool and his colleagues shared the ideas of most thoughtful men of their day. In economic matters, they accepted in general the notion of *laissez-faire*, the French catch-phrase which had come to summarise the view that trade and industry flourished best if left alone by governments, the view given its most famous expression by the Scottish philosopher Adam Smith in his book *The Wealth of Nations* (1776). The Liverpool government was not entirely consistent about this; for it had, after all, put through the Corn Law of 1815 in order to help the agricultural industry. Yet for the most part its members believed that politics could do little to help remove economic ills, and that attempts to do so were a defiance of the 'laws of economics' and would be disastrous to everyone, workmen as well as employers. It followed therefore that workmen were wasting their time in demonstrating in favour of parliamentary reform. Likewise such demonstrations were contrary to divine providence and the Christian religion. The Evangelical Movement, growing strongly at this time and very influential among contemporary M.P.s[1], preached the duty of Christian people to obey their rulers; so did Methodism, now expanding at its fastest. Thus Britain's rulers talked of rioters and strikers as 'poor deluded people' – deluded by radical agitators into defying both economic and religious law.

Government policy As rulers, they were gravely handicapped by the lack of an efficient peace-keeping force. There was no nationally-organised civilian police, and only a few local areas, such as Nottingham (to cope with Luddites), had developed their own. The yeomanry and militia, middle-class volunteers, were useful for patrol work, but, as Peterloo had shown, not convincing in a tight corner. Many places had special constables, many had elderly watchmen; neither was of much use against a riotous mob. It is not at all remarkable in such circumstances that disorder spread fast, particularly in the newly-crowded industrial towns of the North and Midlands. What is surprising is that there was not far more disorder – and that a widespread revolution did not occur. Nevertheless, the government did not hesitate to take a tough line throughout these years. They backed the local magistrates whose task it was to deal with disorder immediately it broke out, by providing regular soldiers: in 1817 27,000 troops were stationed in the manufacturing districts, the principal trouble-spots. They used, very haphazardly, spies, informers

---

[1] See below, p.101 William Wilberforce, lately (1807) successful in overthrowing the British Slave Trade, was the most celebrated Evangelical politician of the day.

and *agents provocateurs*, thereby adding greatly to the government's unpopularity but not much to its effectiveness. They enforced the existing laws very firmly: thus under the Game Laws they transported (see p.24) farm labourers caught poaching and under the Combination Acts (see p.26) they prosecuted workmen who formed unions in an effort to get higher wages. They put through Parliament a series of new measures whose object was to check disturbances and also to thwart the possibility of a planned and violent revolution. Habeas Corpus was suspended in 1817, and the Gagging Act of the same year forbade all public meetings except under licence from a magistrate. The most important new legislation, however, came after Peterloo, when mass meetings of protest at the action of the Manchester magistrates were held throughout the North, with the result that panic-filled letters from terrified manufacturers and other property-owners flooded into White-hall. The government deliberately congratulated the magistrates on what they had done, Liverpool believing that he had 'no alternative but to support them'; and they followed this up with the Six Acts of December, 1819. These limited the right of holding public meetings; gave magistrates power to seize publications thought blasphemous or seditious; extended the newspaper stamp duty to all pamphlets and newspapers; legalised warrants to search for arms; speeded up procedure in certain types of trial; and prohibited organised military drilling by civilians. While the last three of these laws might reasonably be regarded as proper in a time of considerable disorder, the first three aimed deliberately to stop the public expression of radical opinion, whether by Cobbett and other journalists or by Hunt and other orators.

The government accompanied the Six Acts by the arrest of the leading Radicals, and in the spring of 1820 Hunt was sentenced to two years' imprisonment. About the same time they crushed the Cato Street Conspiracy. A tiny group of extremists headed by Arthur Thistlewood, a bankrupt ex-officer, had planned to break in upon a Cabinet dinner, murder all its members, and proclaim a 'Britannic Republic'. A spy, George Edwards, had infiltrated their ranks, and they were seized at their London headquarters, a stable in Cato Street, as they were assembling their pistols, cutlasses, pikes and home-made bombs. Thistlewood and four others were executed. There is no convincing evidence that he and his accomplices were linked with any national plan, although they themselves – and Sidmouth – seem to have believed that simultaneous risings might be expected elsewhere.

In fact Cato Street and the year 1820 marked the end of the grim post-war spell. The disturbances died down and the fears of violence and revolution faded away, not to be revived until the Reform crisis of 1830–2 and the Chartist agitation of the 'Hungry Forties'. Why did this happen? Partly, no doubt, it resulted from the steps taken by the government. The banning of meetings, the attack on the press and the firm handling of disturbances all weakened any radical movement and

The arrest of the Cato Street conspirators (1820)

checked local disorder. Partly also it may be that the tragedy of the Peterloo Massacre itself deeply affected public opinion – on the one hand arousing the conscience of the ruling class, on the other turning the minds of working people towards parliamentary reform rather than violence, so leading all men to more moderate attitudes. As E.P. Thompson puts it, 'Never since Peterloo has authority dared to use equal force against a peaceful British crowd'. However this may be, two further and quite different short-term factors made the 1820s far calmer than the years between Waterloo and Peterloo. One was a general improvement in trade which started about 1820, bringing with it more employment, especially in the factory areas producing for the export market, and lower wheat prices, which meant cheaper bread. Life became more bearable for the poor, and prospects more difficult for reform agitators. The second was an event unique in modern British history, the Queen's Trial.

The Queen's Trial

George III, the 'old, mad, blind, despised, and dying King' of Shelley's sonnet *England in 1819*, died early in 1820, and the Prince Regent succeeded to the throne as George IV. He had been estranged from his wife, Caroline of Brunswick, ever since their marriage in 1795. Neither of them was an attractive character. George IV was selfish, extravagant and immoral, blindly reactionary in politics and deeply unpopular with his subjects. Caroline was an unbalanced exhibitionist whom one historian has described as 'flamboyant, dirty and highly-sexed', with manners 'largely of the farmyard and the taproom', and

George IV (1762–1830)

had long been a figure of scandal in continental Europe, where she had lived in exile since 1814. George, despite his own failings, had while Prince Regent pressed his ministers to secure him a divorce. The whole affair was highly embarrassing to Lord Liverpool, a pious Evangelical,

The trial of Queen Caroline (1820)

not least because it provided a splendid opportunity for the Whig Opposition to badger the government. When the old king died Caroline, posing as a much-wronged woman, came back to England to claim her crown. Her entry to London was a triumph, with the mob cheering itself hoarse, releasing their pent-up feelings against the extravagances of the court in these days of poverty. The government, at George's behest, introduced a bill of divorce accusing her of adultery and scandalous conduct. Henry Brougham, a great Whig advocate, defended her with skill and wit in the trial before the Lords; the press and the cartoonists had a field day, poking ribald fun at the king's corpulent figure and disreputable history. Eventually the government had to drop the bill as its majority in the Lords steadily fell. The excitement quickly vanished. Caroline lost her popularity, by trying to force her way into the coronation service in Westminster Abbey and by accepting a pension of £50,000, and died soon afterwards. Nevertheless this unsavoury and absurd episode in English history had important consequences. It helped to take people's minds away from their troubles; it strengthened the Whigs, making them a more effective parliamentary opposition; and it may also have helped to turn the government towards more constructive policies.

2
A search for solutions

1 Foundations of change – the Liberal Tories

In 1822 Lord Castlereagh, his mind deranged by overwork, cut his throat. George Canning, who succeeded him as Foreign Secretary, was the leading figure in the cabinet for the next five years. The son of an actress, Canning was regarded by many (for example, the Whig Lord Grey) as therefore unfit to become Prime Minister; he nevertheless did so when Liverpool had a stroke in 1827, but died himself later the same year. His cutting wit and his liberal opinions in foreign affairs and in matters of trade, and also on the great question of Catholic Emancipation (the claim of Roman Catholics to sit in Parliament), made him enemies as well as friends. The replacement of Sidmouth at the Home Office by Robert Peel (1822) and the appointment of William Huskisson as President of the Board of Trade (1823) made the government more efficient and more up-to-date in outlook. During the years up to 1830 this group of ministers, the so-called Liberal Tories, carried through important measures which marked a clear departure from the reactionary policy of the post-war years. Throughout the nineteenth century reforms came about when a majority in Parliament passed laws embodying proposals which groups outside Parliament, 'pressure groups' as we call them today, had been demanding for years. Important examples of this process occurred in the 1830s and 1840s, dealing with such problems as slavery in the British Empire, conditions in factories and mines, the Corn Laws (pp.69–76); and, above all, the structure and membership of Parliament itself (pp.35–44). In the 1820s, under the Liberal Tories, there were earlier signs.

Most obvious among these were the activities of Robert Peel in the field of law and order. Reformers had long been criticising the English system of criminal law. Its penal code was at once ferocious and inefficient, backward by comparison with that of other European countries. About two hundred offences (nobody seems to have known exactly how many) carried the death penalty; among them were murder, treason, forgery, horse-stealing, pilfering five shillings from a shop, destroying textile machinery, breaking river-banks, impersonating Greenwich pensioners and cutting down hop-vines. In practice many offenders got off scot-free, with juries deliberately returning incorrect verdicts of 'not guilty', while others added murder to their

Penal Reform

minor crimes. Vast numbers of criminals went undetected or uncaptured, for there was no effective system of police. Many of those who were caught were sentenced to the hulks, the rotting prison-ships on the Thames, or 'sent to Botany Bay', that is, transported to penal settlements in Australia. The numerous prisons in England itself, under local control without central supervision, were for the most part dreadful places run by brutal gaolers who made their living from fees extorted from the prisoners; squalid and disease-ridden, with young offenders contaminated by contact with hardened convicts, they bred as much villainy as they checked.

A prison ship in Portsmouth Harbour. This sketch was made in 1828

Peel, humane as well as firm, a superb administrator, made reform of the criminal law government policy. From 1823 onwards he began to make the penal code more rational. By removing the death penalty from over 100 offences, he set in train a process which eventually meant that after 1861 nobody was hanged except for murder or treason. A series of Gaol Acts (1823–5) started the reform of prisons and transportation, putting prisons under the scrutiny of the Home Secretary, establishing a regular pattern of discipline in them and a code for classifying and separating prisoners of different types. He also reorganized the rules about juries and began to tackle Chancery, the court notorious for delays, with cases commonly lasting twenty years or more. Most of Peel's work was only a beginning. Moreover, on the great question of the restriction of the death penalty, Peel was dragging behind much contemporary opinion. In 1831 English criminal laws remained, in the opinion of London jurymen, 'the most sanguinary of any in Europe'. By 1840 the Whigs had drastically reduced the use of capital punishment to less than one-eighth of the 1830 figure.

Probably the most important, and certainly the best-remembered, of Peel's reforms in the 1820s was his creation (1829) of the Metropolitan Police. A civilian force, wearing blue frock coats and top hats, and armed only with wooden truncheons[1], these 'Peelers' or 'Bobbies' rapidly won approval after initial doubts and popular hostility. From their headquarters at Scotland Yard they covered the Metropolitan area of London, and during the next thirty years other large towns and cities followed the London pattern – partly at least because its success had driven many criminals out of the capital to seek victims elsewhere. In 1856 Parliament insisted on co-ordination between local police forces

The First Police Force

A group of 'Peelers'

[1]The top hats, however, had iron frames.

and made them all subject to Home Office inspection, with grants from taxation dependent on efficiency. From the start the main purpose of Peel's police was to *prevent* crime, thus laying firm foundations for law and order.

Free Trade William Huskisson, like Canning, was M.P. for the great commercial city of Liverpool, whose merchants were among the leading supporters of Free Trade at that time. To them, and to their neighbours of Manchester with their swelling exports of cotton goods, free trade meant above all the lowering of international tariff barriers. Canning and Huskisson signed a series of reciprocity treaties with foreign governments whereby each country lowered its import duties on some goods from the other. He reorganised and simplified the tangle of British customs duties, and reduced those on some metal and textile raw materials and also on some semi-manufactured goods. He modified the Navigation Code, which since the seventeenth century had tried to keep trade with British colonies in British ships, and allowed the colonists some direct trade with Europe; while he admitted some colonial goods (e.g. wheat from Canada and rum from Jamaica) into the United Kingdom at rates lower than those on similar foreign goods. Such measures, though modest in scale, pointed to future developments, and they pleased the merchants of the 1820s. Another plan of Huskisson's, the introduction of a 'sliding scale' of corn duties, was not so well liked. The Corn Law of 1815, with its total prohibition of imported foreign corn until the price of British corn reached 80s. a quarter, was to be replaced by a variable scale of duties: if home prices fell foreign corn would pay more tax, if they rose it would pay less. The landlords, very strong in Parliament, did not welcome this, and Huskisson resigned office in 1828. Tragically, he was knocked down and killed when he stepped into the path of a locomotive at the opening in 1830 of the Liverpool – Manchester Railway, of which he had been a prominent supporter.

Trade Unions Huskisson and Peel were together responsible for yet another pointer to the future – laws which attempted to regulate the development of trade unions. In 1799 and 1800, in the crisis of the French Wars, Parliament had passed the Combination Acts, making 'combinations in restraint of trade' illegal. These Acts had been only erratically enforced by local magistrates, and as industry had expanded during the first quarter of the nineteenth century, so trade unions had grown in number. Francis Place, whose tailor's shop in the Charing Cross Road was a centre of London radicalism, and Joseph Hume, a Radical M.P., got a parliamentary committee of enquiry set up in 1824. Place claimed that making trade unions illegal drove them underground and led to violence, and even that if they were legalised they would cease to attract members. He coached working-class witnesses to give evidence to the committee, and the Combination Acts were repealed – with the immediate consequence of a widespread outbreak of strikes, the birth of many new unions, and a certain amount of violence. Peel, worried about law and order and also anxious to safeguard individual workmen and employers from the abuse of collective power, and Huskisson, concerned for trade and industry, between them in 1825 produced another Combination Act. This permitted trade unions to exist but forbade anyone to use violence, threats, molestation or obstruction to make others stop work, or join a union, or to force employers to alter their mode of carrying on business. This act, though severely limiting the effective powers of unions, at least recognized their existence and gave them minimal legal protection. It was the basis of trade union law for the next fifty years.

In 1828 Wellington became Prime Minister. His government was driven by the House of Commons to accept measures setting large numbers of the king's subjects free from religious disabilities. One, in 1828, was the Repeal of the Test and Corporation Acts, two seventeenth-century laws which had nominally – though often not in practice – excluded dissenters from holding local and national political office. This was a grievance felt mainly by Protestant Nonconformists. The second measure, the Catholic Emancipation Act of 1829, raised far more delicate and complicated political problems. Lawyers and, no doubt, criminals, were much interested in Peel's legal reforms; merchants in Huskisson's steps to help trade; trade unionists in the Combination Acts. Yet if M.P.s had been asked in the 1820s what they considered the biggest political issue of the day many would certainly have replied 'Catholic Emancipation'.

The demand that Roman Catholics should, on equal terms with Protestants, enjoy the right to sit in Parliament and hold important offices of state was at that time a highly sensitive issue. For very large numbers of British people were deeply prejudiced against Roman Catholics, regarding their beliefs as superstitious nonsense, their worship as idolatrous, and many of their practices and societies as sinister. Many M.P.s took the view stated to the House of Lords in 1825 by the Duke of York, then heir to the throne, that it would be utterly wrong to allow Roman Catholics to make laws for the established Church of England, as would happen if they were allowed to sit in Parliament. Moreover the Roman Catholic question was above all a question involving Ireland, where about six-sevenths of the people were followers of the Pope. Roman Catholics had been given the right to vote in 1793 – but their representatives had to be Protestants, for all M.P.s were required to swear an oath avowing the supremacy of the Protestant religion. In 1800 the Act of Union with Ireland had been passed: the separate Irish Parliament which then existed had been abolished, and instead Ireland had been given 28 seats in the Lords and 100 in the Commons at Westminster. William Pitt the Younger, then Prime Minister, had intended to accompany the Union by a grant of Catholic Emancipation, but George III declined to agree. Thus the Union

Catholic Emancipation

appeared to the vast majority of Irishmen to be imposed by England and marred from the start by a broken promise.

In the 1820s English opinion was much divided about Catholic Emancipation. A majority of the Commons was in favour, including most of the Whigs as well as Canning, Castlereagh, and many Tories; among the Tory opponents was Peel, whose tough pro-Protestant line while Chief Secretary for Ireland (1812–18) had earned him the inevitable nickname of 'Orange' Peel. The king and the Lords, including most of the Bishops, were hostile. In Ireland a popular Catholic lawyer, Daniel O'Connell (1775–1847), who combined a flair for political organisation with considerable powers of oratory[1], launched the Catholic Association (1823) as a nation-wide movement to secure Emancipation. Using parish priests as local agents and asking the peasants for regular contributions (the so-called 'Catholic Rent') as small as a farthing a week he accumulated £15,000 by 1825 (which he invested in British government securities). When the authorities banned the Association, he re-started it under another name. More important, he began to organise the peasants to vote in by-elections for candidates who would support Emancipation.

Chance played into his hands. In 1828 Wellington appointed a popular Protestant Irish landlord, Vesey Fitzgerald, as President of the Board of Trade when Huskisson resigned. Following what was then (and until 1919) the rule for new cabinet ministers, Fitzgerald had to offer himself for re-election to his constituents in County Clare. O'Connell himself stood against him and won, backed by the influence of the priests, though as a Roman Catholic he knew that he could not take his seat. The result put the government in a fix, for clearly O'Connell would follow the same tactics throughout Ireland at a general election. Wellington, fearing a civil war in Ireland if he tried to maintain the existing law, beat a retreat, persuading Peel, who at first wished to resign, to follow him. So in 1829 the Catholic Emancipation Act was passed, despite the angry resistance of a group of extreme Protestant M.P.s in Wellington's own party, the so-called 'Ultra-Tories'. Henceforward Roman Catholics could sit in Parliament, and occupy nearly all offices of state (not, however, those of Lord Chancellor or Viceroy of Ireland). To keep O'Connell from complete control of the Irish vote, the qualification for voting in Ireland was raised from 40 shillings freehold to £10. The Catholic Association was suppressed once more; as a sop to the more extreme English Protestants, monastic orders of men were to be abolished in Ireland; and by a piece of petty spite, O'Connell himself was forced to stand for re-election in County Clare.

The impact of this episode on British politics was very great. First, it split the Tories, leaving many Ultra-Tories deeply embittered in the

---

[1] He uttered memorable phrases. Peel's smile was 'like the silver plate on a coffin'; the Whigs of the 1830s were 'base, bloody and brutal'.

belief that Wellington and Peel had ratted on their party and their promises[1]. Peel, a man of sensitive conscience, resigned his Commons seat for the University of Oxford and was defeated in a fierce by-election there; for the remainder of his career, especially in the Corn Law crisis of 1845–6, right-wing Tory distrust was to haunt him (below, p.75). The Ultras took their revenge in 1830 by helping to turn Wellington out of the premiership – thus opening the way to parliamentary reform. Secondly, the events of 1829 gravely weakened all those who were hostile to reform of any kind. If Catholic Emancipation could be passed, anything was possible. And O'Connell's movement had shown how to do it, as an organised group bringing pressure to bear on Parliament. It was an example not lost on British reformers. Thirdly, the political landscape in Ireland itself had changed sharply. The way was open for the growth of an Irish party, predominantly Catholic. This in the later years of the nineteenth century would hold the balance of power in the House of Commons, and at times seem to control British politics.

2 The pursuit of an independent foreign policy – Canning and his successors

On the death of Castlereagh, the direction of British foreign policy passed to his old rival George Canning. Canning already had considerable experience in public life. As a young man, he had shown ability in handling propaganda during Pitt's last years in office. He had served briefly as Foreign Secretary from 1807 to 1809 and fought a duel with Castlereagh. In 1812 he had been Lord Liverpool's first choice as Foreign Secretary but, by demanding also to be made Leader of the House of Commons, had lost both posts to Castlereagh. Back in the cabinet in 1816, he was known to dislike diplomacy by congress and to favour a more vigorous policy against the Holy Alliance, but he kept his views to cabinet meetings. In any case, by 1822, Castlereagh himself was beginning to adopt a more flexible approach. In plans drawn up before his death for the Verona congress, he had taken the first steps away from non-intervention by proposing to recognise the rebelling Spanish colonies and even an independent Greece, and it was along these lines that Canning's own policy developed.

What Canning brought to the Foreign Office was not so much a new policy as new methods and a new style. As each problem developed his actions became more positive; increasingly he was prepared to intervene rather than to protest where British interests were at stake. Never committed to the idea of a Concert of Europe, he was more ready to act,

George Canning

[1]One Duchess, the wife of a leading Ultra, kept in a glass case a number of stuffed rats, appropriately named after politicians who had 'betrayed the Protestant cause.'

George Canning (1770–1827)

if the situation warranted it, in isolation. To some extent, this reflected pressure from commercial interests at home, keen to develop colonial and international trade. Because smaller countries fighting for constitutional government or independence were often involved, he emerged as the champion of liberalism against the Holy Alliance, even though the only major reforms he actively supported were Catholic Emancipation and the abolition of Slavery. Part of his reputation came from a tendency to play up his own successes and from an adroit use of publicity. He wrote articles regularly for the press, published a large number of his own despatches, and made speeches in Parliament clearly aimed at an international audience. Whereas Castlereagh had represented a Britain still recovering from war, Canning was able to profit from an atmosphere of growing prosperity and expansion. His actions mark an intermediate stage between the non-intervention of Castlereagh and the gunboat diplomacy of Palmerston.

The Verona congress, the last of the post-war congresses, was in session from October to December 1822. It was called to discuss the risings in Spain, the Spanish colonies, Portugal and Greece. The Powers themselves were divided over the Greek revolt against Turkey. They were divided over the Spanish colonies' bid for freedom, with Britain making a strong case against intervention. They were divided over Spain where there was a liberal revolt against the despotic king Ferdinand VII. At the congress, the other Powers authorised France to send in an army to support Ferdinand, and this decision led directly to a walk-out by Wellington who was Britain's representative. Canning took no action when the French army entered Spain except – and this was a sign of things to come – to threaten war if France tried to occupy Spain permanently, to seize any of her colonies or to invade Portugal. The Verona congress broke up. The experiment of trying to regulate European affairs by regular reunions of the Great Powers was over.

Spain

Since 1812 the Spanish South American colonies of Buenos Aires, Colombia and Mexico had been fighting for recognition of their independence from Spain. Castlereagh had already decided that British support was both morally right and economically profitable; since the end of the Napoleonic War there had been rapid growth in trade between Britain and the colonies. His only fears were that the new republics might be dominated by the United States, and that, if the issue were brought out into the open in Europe, it would lead to a further split among the Powers. In April 1823 the issue became unavoidable. The Holy Alliance Powers saw in the South American rebellions the same revolutionary spirit which had overrun Europe, and declared their intention of recapturing the colonies by force. In October, Canning informed Polignac, the French ambassador, that Britain would not tolerate such a move. He insisted that there must be no military action, no interference with British trade, and no further involvement without consultation with the United States. Canning's warnings were reinforced by the American President Monroe who announced, in what came to be called the 'Monroe Doctrine', that 'the American continents are henceforth not to be considered as subjects for future colonisation by any European Powers', and that any interference in either North or South America would lead to war. This was aimed not only at Spain but also at Russia which had recently laid claim to territory in Alaska. In Britain, the decision by Liverpool and Canning to recognise the independence of the colonies greatly offended George IV and some of their diehard colleagues, but otherwise it was a highly popular move. It supported the underdog. It offered great economic advantages and gave Britain a special relationship with South America that remained for the rest of the century. The new republics became in effect British economic colonies, and British investment in South

Spanish South American Colonies

America came to exceed that in India. The decision also prevented Latin America from being dominated either by the French and Spanish Bourbons or by the United States. Finally it dealt a near mortal blow to the Holy Alliance. Canning gave himself full credit for the way he played his cards, though, with the British navy as trumps, it was a hand he could hardly have lost. He told the Commons 'I resolved that if France had Spain it should not be Spain with the Indies. I called the New World into existence to redress the balance of the Old'. It was a memorable statement, though not one Castlereagh would have used; he would have seen through the second sentence at least as rhetoric rather than fact.

Portugal

Canning's success in helping the Spanish colonies led to his playing an active part in the affairs of Portugal and the Portuguese colony of Brazil. First the King of Portugal, John VI, was persuaded in 1825 to agree that Brazil should become an independent empire under his elder son Pedro. Then, on John's death in 1826, his younger son Miguel sought Spanish help to overthrow the new constitutional government of Pedro's daughter Maria. Canning immediately sent troopships with some 4,000 men to sail up the Tagus to prevent this threat to the independence of Britain's oldest ally. It was a positive and popular move even though Miguel was later to come to power. The committed opponent of Parliamentary reform at home was now firmly established as the champion of liberalism abroad.

Greek Independence

The Greek revolt posed far more complicated problems. As in Latin America, Britain had a thriving trade in the Eastern Mediterranean and wished to see political stability in that area. When the Greeks rose against the Turks in 1821 Castlereagh planned to work closely with Metternich to safeguard Turkish power against Russian expansion in the Balkans. Canning did not have the same close relationship with the Austrian Chancellor. He was, at first, unwilling to back either side and would have preferred mediation by the Powers rather than active intervention – a policy of which Castlereagh would have approved. He was aware, however, of a strong pro-Greek movement in Britain, stronger still after the death of Byron at Missolonghi in 1824; and when the Sultan enlisted the help of his viceroy of Egypt, Mehemet Ali, and Egyptian troops under Ibrahim invaded the Morea, the Greek leaders turned to Britain for help. In 1825, a Greek delegation met Canning to ask for protection, and offered the Greek crown to the Duke of Sussex or to any other person acceptable to Britain.

By now it was clear that Russia had every intention of helping the Greeks. The new Tsar Nicholas I saw them not as revolutionaries but as fellow-members of the Orthodox Church whom it was his duty to protect. Canning could no longer afford to stand by while Russia unilaterally won the war and dictated a peace which would certainly be against British interests. When public opinion was further outraged by Ibrahim's brutal treatment of the Greeks Canning decided to forsake

32

Pitt's original policy of support for Turkey and to aim instead at working with Russia and thereby controlling her. Wellington was sent to St Petersburg for consultations and a joint ultimatum was despatched to Turkey. It demanded that a self-governing Greek state, though still nominally under Turkish rule, should be set up or else an allied naval force would be sent to attack Ibrahim. To increase the pressure on Turkey, France was persuaded by Canning, now Prime Minister, to join with Britain and Russia. Since Austria and Prussia were firmly against help to any revolutionaries, the old Quintuple Alliance, split four to one over Spain and the Spanish colonies, was now split three to two. The proposals were formally signed by the allies at the Treaty of London in 1827. Predictably Turkey resented this interference and rejected the treaty but Canning died before the news reached London.

The effects of his death were immediately apparent. The control of foreign policy passed to Wellington who was uncompromisingly pro-Turk and who failed to see what Canning had appreciated, that a strong independent Greece could be to Britain's advantage. The post of Foreign Secretary was briefly held by the Earl of Dudley. When Turkey rejected the treaty he failed to give clear orders to the allied fleet; Codrington, its pro-Greek admiral, was ordered to use force 'if necessary'. Not surprisingly he clashed with Ibrahim's fleet in Navarino Bay in October 1827 and sank it. With its defeat went Turkish hopes of reconquering Greece and Canning's hopes of controlling Russia. At home the short-lived Goderich ministry fell and Wellington became

The sinking of the Egyptian and Turkish fleets at Navarino, 1827

Prime Minister. Through the King's Speech he described Navarino as an 'untoward event' and a strong Turkish state as 'necessary to the well-being of this country'. The Turks were therefore encouraged to think that Britain might now actively support them but, when Russia did declare war in April 1828, Wellington and Aberdeen, his Foreign Secretary, drew back.

Canning's worst fears had now been realised. Though it was a French force which drove the Egyptians from the Morea, it was Russia who alone defeated the Turkish armies and who alone dictated peace at the Treaty of Adrianople in 1828. By this she gained important trade concessions in the Levant and set a precedent for further protection of Orthodox subjects in the Ottoman Empire – both ominous signs for Britain. The final settlement of Greece was left to a conference to be held in London, and, before this could be held, the Whigs won the election of 1830 and Palmerston became Foreign Secretary. It was clear to him that anything but a fully independent Greece would invite constant Russian interference. He tackled the situation realistically and with decision. He put forward the idea of a fully independent Greece ruled by a constitutional monarch and guaranteed by the Powers; this he hoped would be the most likely way of bringing peace and stability to the area. In 1832, at the London conference, the new Greek state was recognised with Otto of Bavaria as king. For the moment the Greek question appeared to be solved. But the wider issue of Russian expansion at the expense of Turkey was to prove for British politicians the most persistent problem of the nineteenth century. Canning's attempt to control the inevitable break-up of the Turkish empire was no longer workable. From now on Britain was committed to the less flexible and often embarrassing policy of propping up what came to be known as 'the sick man of Europe'.

The Greek revolt saw the end of the Quintuple Alliance. Where Castlereagh had tried to work in concert with other Powers Canning made clear his personal dislike of Metternich and his preference for a more free-handed foreign policy. He had the personality, the popular support and the opportunities to follow a more independent line than Castlereagh. For him it was not enough to boycott congresses – the protest of the 'empty chair'. The reactionary Powers, particularly Austria and Russia, were prepared to dominate Europe in their fight against liberalism and nationalism. By 1832, however, a wedge had been driven between the two largely by Canning's actions over Portugal and Greece. The Congress System which Castlereagh had helped to create was thus finally destroyed by Canning.

3 The turning point – the Great Reform Act

In November 1830 the Duke of Wellington, the Prime Minister, told the House of Lords that in his opinion 'the legislature (i.e. Parliament) and the system of representation possessed the full and entire confidence of the country'. But in June 1832 the Great Reform Act was passed, amid widespread popular rejoicing, making drastic changes in both the system of representation and the membership of Parliament. What happened in the short interval between those two dates? Why and how did it happen?

In 1830, as for centuries past, Britain was ruled by King, Lords and Commons. By now the balance of power within the three had tilted decisively towards the Commons; and when we speak of 'the Reform Act of 1832' we are in fact referring to a law dealing only with the House of Commons. The other two partners in the British Constitution were certainly not powerless about 1830. George IV, who died in that year, had much influence in the choice of ministers, and his notorious hostility to Catholic Emancipation had not been without influence on public opinion; while his brother, William IV, who succeeded him on the throne, played an important role in the Reform crisis itself because of his powers to dissolve Parliament and to create peers. But in general royal authority had diminished and the monarchs were well on the way to becoming figureheads. The House of Lords, indeed, was still very strong in 1830. All bills had to be passed by the Lords before becoming law. The King had also to agree, yet no monarch had refused to sign a bill since Queen Anne over a hundred years before; whereas the Lords in the nineteenth century threw out great numbers of bills, many of them social reforms which would have benefited millions of people. In the words of E. L. Woodward: 'From the relief of little boys tortured by chimney-sweeps to the relief of millions of Catholics, from dislike of the Factory Acts to the defence of the monopoly of a few theatres, the House of Lords was an obstacle to changes reasonable in themselves and demanded by the country as a whole'. Moreover many peers played important parts in the government of the country. They formed a high proportion of the membership of cabinets: thus the Whig Cabinet of 1830, the one which carried the Reform Act of 1832, contained a duke, a marquess, three earls, two viscounts and two barons among its thirteen members. They owned vast areas of the British countryside and as landlords exerted influence on the lives and government of its people. Tenants, shopkeepers, clergymen, poachers, solicitors, horse-dealers, corn merchants, schoolteachers – all could be and often were dependent on the favour of aristocratic landlords.

Yet the House of Commons was the centre of real political power. Its control of taxation and financial policy was complete. The great debates on major issues took place there; most of the leading parliamentary figures were to be found in it, including, more often than not, the Prime Minister.[1] The principle which later generations have taken for

---

[1] Although in these years Lord Liverpool (1812–27), the Duke of Wellington (1828–30) and Earl Grey (1830–4) were important exceptions.

granted, that no British government can survive without a majority in the Commons, was firmly established. In 1830 the House of Commons had 658 members, of whom 45 represented Scotland and 100 Ireland. 188 sat for the counties, 465 for boroughs (nearly all with two members apiece), 5 for universities. Most members were landed gentlemen, for the property qualification even for a borough member was land worth £300 per annum, though they were often lawyers or merchants as well as landowners. In 1830 M.P.s could not be women, Quakers or Jews – and only since the previous year, as we have seen, could they be Roman Catholics. At elections there was no secret ballot. Polling took place on the 'hustings', a platform set up in the town square. Elections were not completed on a single day, but might go on for up to a fortnight, as every voter had to prove his claim when he came to the poll.

The unreformed Commons

There was no uniform franchise (right to vote). County members were elected by all those who had freehold land worth 40 shillings per annum. The boroughs had a variety of qualifications for voting. In 'scot and lot' boroughs any man paying poor rates could go to the poll; in 'potwalloper' boroughs, of which there were very few, any man who had lived for the last six months in the borough and 'had a family and boiled a pot there'. There were 'corporation' boroughs and 'freeman' boroughs (between them over half the total in England), in which respectively members of the corporation (usually a self-electing body) and those who had become freemen (usually by inheritance, by marrying a freeman's daughter, or simply by cash down) had a vote. Finally there were 'burgage' boroughs, where the vote was attached solely to particular pieces of property. The distribution of seats was most uneven, corresponding neither to population nor to geography. Every English county had two members except Yorkshire which had four; Welsh counties and Scottish counties had one each, Irish two each. Those boroughs which had M.P.s did so because long ago – in general before the seventeenth century – they had been given royal charters entitling them to send members to Parliament. Finally, altogether in 1831 some 419,000 men had the vote, in a total United Kingdom population of about 24,000,000.

This system, a mass of absurdities in twentieth-century eyes, had long been attacked on a variety of grounds, and condemned as unrepresentative, corrupt, out-of-date, inefficient, and unfair. Most critics directed their fire at the boroughs. There open voting, the small size of most electorates, and the decay of many places with the passage of time had created strange situations. Fifty-six of them, including nearly all the English corporation boroughs, had fewer than 50 electors each. Two of them had perished – Old Sarum near Salisbury, now a heap of stones, and Dunwich in Suffolk, which had fallen into the sea – but still sent their two M.P.s; Old Sarum was so notorious that tourists went to look at it. Among the others, in Marlborough, for example, the corporation, whose members had the franchise, was said to have consisted usually of the Marquess of Ailesbury's steward, butler, footmen and dependents; while in Gatton, a scot and lot borough, the vote went with six houses and the representation was sometimes put up for sale. Such places were called 'pocket' boroughs, in the pocket of a landlord; or 'rotten' boroughs, with a handful of voters ready to sell themselves to the highest bidder. By contrast the scot and lot borough of Westminster, the potwalloper borough of Preston, and several freeman boroughs (London, Bristol, Leicester, Liverpool and Nottingham) each had over 5000 voters, too numerous to bribe with certainty of success, yet ready enough to enjoy a good and drunken time at the candidates' expense. The Liverpool by-election of 1831 caused by Huskisson's death cost the winner over £80,000. County elections, with their large numbers of voters, were more prestigious and could be even more expensive; the Yorkshire election of 1807 is said to have cost over £250,000 all told. Polling was done only in the county towns, and candidates found themselves paying big bills for voters' transport, lodging, and 'treating'. Not surprisingly at many elections a good proportion of country seats were not contested; instead two dominant local aristocratic families would agree to take one seat each. As a whole the system put immense power into the hands of the aristocracy. In 1827 a well-informed Tory reckoned that 276 M.P.s held their seats through direct nomination by some great landlord or wealthy borough owner.

In the late eighteenth century the Whigs under Charles James Fox had associated themselves with a demand for reform, but the French Revolution had wrecked any chances of success. The system had not got much worse in the nineteenth century, yet its defects had become clearer to a large number of people. In particular the oddities of the distribution of parliamentary seats became more objectionable as new industrial areas began to develop on the coalfields and as big commercial cities grew fast. It became far more difficult to defend a pattern which gave Cornwall 44 seats, while the whole of Scotland had only 45; which gave the total area of Middlesex, London, Westminster and Southwark, by far the most densely-populated part of the country, merely 8; and left Birmingham, Manchester, Leeds and Sheffield, each of them by 1831 with over 80,000 people, entirely without separate representation.

Various groups of people, large and potentially strong, began to demand parliamentary reform in the early nineteenth century, as memories of the French Terror and Napoleon faded and liberal ideas on politics and social reform gained ground. One was the urban middle class. Merchants, the new factory owners and a growing number of professional men were beginning to ask for a share in political power, notably in order to promote the commercial and industrial interests of the areas where they made their wealth – the kind of men who supported Huskisson's ideas on trade. They wanted to break into the

The demand for reform

landlords' virtual monopoly of the Commons, and were specially critical of the unfair distribution of seats; there was much talk in the 1820s of disfranchising some of the most corrupt boroughs and giving their seats to the big industrial towns. In the counties many farmers and smaller landowners, suffering from agricultural depression in the 1820s, wanted reform. Now, too, many working-class men, above all in the factory and mining areas, saw the reform of Parliament as the key to improved conditions. As we have noticed, this challenge, voiced by men like Cobbett and Hunt, was widely taken up in the grim years after Waterloo. Workingmen's cry for reform was strongest in bad times; it quietened down during the better times of the 1820s, only to rise again when a depression came along in 1829–30.

Both middle and working-class groups found leaders among a small number of politicians known as Radicals because they wanted political change 'from the roots'. They were a collection of independents, not a party; some were in Parliament, some outside; they agreed upon little beyond the demand for reform of the Commons. They formed a rather ineffectual front for much widespread and ill-organised activity, with the formation of political clubs and many large meetings up and down the country. Usually the middle-class reformers wanted only moderate change – the abolition of the most rotten of the boroughs, the redistribution of seats to a number of the industrial towns, the vote for the owners of a middling amount of property. The working-class leaders wanted much more, and talked of the secret ballot, annual parliaments and votes for all men. Late in 1829 the Birmingham Political Union was formed, with the deliberate purpose of combining middle-class and workingmen supporters of reform in a single body. Its leader was Thomas Attwood, a country banker with an enthusiasm for currency reform; within a year it had 6,000 members, and its example had been followed in other areas. If circumstances occurred in which middle and working-class people throughout Britain together put pressure on the established system, change might easily occur. Such circumstances came about in 1830.

Times were hard in 1829–30. The harvests in both years were bad, there was a depression in business and much unemployment, poor rates were high. The death of George IV brought an election in July, 1830[1], in which reform of Parliament was the main issue. Wellington failed to increase his support, and some of Canning's former followers, notably Lords Melbourne and Palmerston, went over to the Whigs. That summer farm labourers throughout south-eastern England set fire to hayricks and destroyed threshing machines as a protest against low wages and bad conditions, in what came to be called 'the Last Labourers' Revolt', under the alleged leadership of a mysterious Captain Swing; and there were great strikes in industrial Lancashire.

---

[1]Until 1867 the law required that a general election had to be held within six months of the death of the sovereign.

Swing, the rick-burner. Pointing to his dying wife and homeless children, 'Swing' is explaining his case to the clergyman

These episodes, with their threat to property, shook the confidence of the ruling class. The July Revolution of Paris, which drove the Bourbon King Charles X into exile, stimulated political excitement in England, with reformers drawing the obvious moral. This was the sombre background against which Wellington made his extraordinary statement of complete confidence in the British parliamentary system. It is scarcely surprising that it provoked an outcry of protest, uniting reformers of all shades of opinion against him. The Ultra-Tories now took their revenge for Catholic Emancipation, and joined the Whig opposition to defeat him. The new King, William IV, sent for the Whig leader, Lord Grey, to form a government. The Whigs in the 1820s had been spasmodic champions of reform, blowing hot and cold by turns, much divided among themselves. But Grey, a cautious and dignified Northumberland landowner who forty years before had been an ardent reforming follower of Charles Fox, was now sure that the time was right. It was clear that his cabinet would have to introduce a reform bill. The real question was not whether reform would come, but how extensive it would be.

The bill was introduced in March 1831, in an atmosphere of great political excitement inside and outside Parliament. In the months before, Melbourne, the Whig Home Secretary, had taken a hard line against the farm labourers, crushing the Swing movement sternly. They had killed nobody, indeed done little more by way of violence than throw an unpopular farmer or two into their own duckponds; but 19 of them were executed (16 for arson) and nearly 500 transported. The Whigs were anxious to champion property at least as vigorously as the Tories. Yet when the reform bill came it was a great deal more far-reaching than most politicians had prophesied. Grey said at the time 'The principle of my reform is to prevent the necessity for revolution', and this entailed pretty drastic changes in the system. So when Lord John Russell read out the government's proposals in the Commons there were gasps of horror and ironical jeers from the Tories, especially at Schedule A, the list of boroughs condemned to lose both seats. The Whig proposals for the *redistribution of seats* meant that 108 English and Welsh boroughs would between them lose 168 M.P.s: the seats thus released would be transferred to the counties, to districts of London, and to some large industrial towns. The *franchise* was to be considerably widened. In the *counties* the 40 shilling freeholders were to keep the vote, and £10 copyholders and £50 short leaseholders were also to get it; in the *boroughs* all the old franchises were swept away (except that existing electors were to keep their votes for life if they actually resided in the borough) and replaced by a uniform £10 household qualification. Broadly these proposals admitted the middle class to a share in political power. Peel, against the bill, warned the Whigs that they were opening the gates for the future: 'others will outbid you, not now, but at no remote period – they will offer votes and power to a million of men . . . . and will carry your principles . . . . to their natural consequences'. But the historian Macauley, then a new young Whig member, saying 'The danger is terrible. The time is short', saw the bill as a safeguard against revolution. After nine days of intense debate the bill was carried by a single vote (302 to 301). But amendments were carried against it in committee. Parliament was dissolved, and another general election held, in May 1831.

The Struggle for the Bill The result of this election, fought on the single question of parliamentary reform, was a foregone conclusion. The Whigs won a great majority. In particular, they swept the field in the more 'open' constituencies, especially the counties and the bigger boroughs, where the number of voters was large and public opinion effective. In England nearly all the seats the Tories kept were in boroughs with small electorates, the traditional 'rotten' and 'pocket' boroughs. The message of public opinion was plain. Nevertheless the Lords threw out the Reform Bill when, after passing the Commons, it came to them in September 1831. As a result, that autumn witnessed an outburst of popular feeling throughout much of the land. At a meeting in Taunton

REFORM is become absolutely necessary — the Representation is corrupt — we have now Representatives of Green mounds, of Stone Walls, even of a Pig-sty, while many of our most populous manufacturing towns remain unrepresented.

Lord John stalking over the Boroughmongers; or, the Rotten Representation in Danger. See Report of Speech house of Commons March 1, 1831

the Whig clergyman Sydney Smith ridiculed the peers by comparing their efforts to defeat reform with those of a certain Mrs Partington of Sidmouth, who had tried in the great storm of 1824 to sweep back the Atlantic Ocean with her mop. But in the larger towns and industrial areas excitement turned to disorder and riot. Already in Merthyr Tydfil in June, 25 people had been killed when rioters and troops clashed. In

The Bristol Riots, 1831. The charge of the Dragoons

October there was trouble in Derby, and in Nottingham, where the castle, the property of the Duke of Newcastle, a notorious borough-owner, was burned down. Later the same month there were three days of rioting in Bristol: the Bishop's Palace, the Custom House and parts of the centre of the city were sacked and destroyed by drunken mobs. Britain seemed nearer to revolution than at any time in modern history. There was talk of forming an armed 'National Guard' on the French Revolutionary model. The Birmingham Political Union planned a scheme for a 'semi-military' organisation of citizens both working and middle class, to prepare against the fall of Grey's ministry.

In December 1831 the Reform Bill was introduced a third time. The Commons passed it in March 1832 but the Lords remained unwilling to yield, believing, as one Tory opponent put it, that 'the Bill once passed, good night to the Monarchy and the Lords and the Church.' In May 1832 Grey resigned. When Wellington could not form a government (Peel firmly declined to join him), Grey refused to return to office until William IV promised to create – if necessary – sufficient peers to outnumber the Tory majority in the Lords. Meetings throughout the land, petitions from the political unions, threats not to pay taxes, a run on the banks and pressure from frightened bankers, stagnation of trade, an increase in the sales of guns and other weapons, tales of secret drilling and rumours of every sort – all this did not frighten the Iron Duke, but this threat to increase the peerage drove the Lords to surrender. In June 1832 the Great Reform Act was passed.

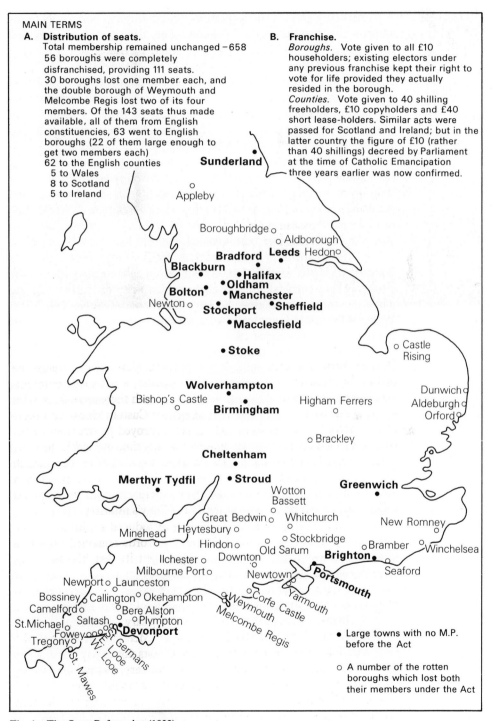

MAIN TERMS

A. Distribution of seats.

Total membership remained unchanged –658
56 boroughs were completely
disfranchised, providing 111 seats.
30 boroughs lost one member each, and
the double borough of Weymouth and
Melcombe Regis lost two of its four
members. Of the 143 seats thus made
available, all of them from English
constituencies, 63 went to English
boroughs (22 of them large enough to
get two members each)
62 to the English counties
5 to Wales
8 to Scotland
5 to Ireland

B. Franchise.

Boroughs. Vote given to all £10
householders; existing electors under
any previous franchise kept their right to
vote for life provided they actually
resided in the borough.
Counties. Vote given to 40 shilling
freeholders, £10 copyholders and £40
short lease-holders. Similar acts were
passed for Scotland and Ireland; but in the
latter country the figure of £10 (rather
than 40 shillings) decreed by Parliament
at the time of Catholic Emancipation
three years earlier was now confirmed.

Sunderland

Appleby

Boroughbridge

Aldborough

Bradford Leeds Hedon

Blackburn

Halifax

Oldham

Bolton Manchester

Newton Stockport Sheffield

Macclesfield

Stoke

Castle Rising

Wolverhampton

Bishop's Castle

Dunwich

Birmingham

Higher Ferrers Aldeburgh

Orford

Brackley

Cheltenham

Merthyr Tydfil Stroud

Greenwich

Wotton Bassett

Great Bedwin Whitchurch

New Romney

Minehead Heytesbury

Hindon Stockbridge

Bramber Winchelsea

Ilchester Downton Old Sarum

Brighton

Milbourne Port Newtown Seaford

Newport Launceston

Bossiney Callington Okehampton Corfe Castle Yarmouth Portsmouth

Camelford Bere Alston Weymouth

St.Michael Saltash Plympton Melcombe Regis

Fowey St. Germans

Tregony Devonport

W. Looe

St. Looe

St. Mawes

● Large towns with no M.P. before the Act

○ A number of the rotten boroughs which lost both their members under the Act

Fig. 1 The Great Reform Act (1832)

43

It marked a great turning-point in British history, both in its terms
and in the manner of its passing. The new franchise increased
the number of voters in England and Wales by nearly 80 per cent; in
Ireland by 84 per cent; in Scotland over fourteen-fold. The great
majority were middle class citizens, well enough off to be regarded as
having a stake in the country. Even though for the next seventy years
the landowners continued to provide most of Britain's ruling men,
others had secured a share in political power. But the working class, for
all their shouting and agitation in 1830–2, got no immediate reward –
no secret ballot, no votes for all men, no annual parliaments. In a sense
the middle class now formed part of the garrison, who might at a later
stage resist further change. On the other hand, the way in which the
Act had been passed was at least as important as its detailed terms. The
unreformed Parliament had reformed itself. Grey's purpose had been
attained: revolution had been avoided. Reform had come peacefully –
though there had been many times in 1830–2 when contemporaries
doubted this. But what had been done once could be done again. The
vital step had been taken, and the way was open for further change
when the time seemed ripe. So later reform acts (1867, 1884, 1918,
1928, 1969) would gradually extend the vote to the entire adult
population over the age of 18.

In the shorter term the Reform Act of 1832 had one unexpected
consequence for British political life. Minor clauses of the Act required
official registers of electors to be made and kept up-to-date, and limited
the time of polling in a constituency to two days. The parties quickly
realised the need to make sure that all their supporters' names appeared
on the register (and also to object as smartly as possible to known
opponents whom they might hope to erase from the lists). This led
them to employ local agents and to other steps which stimulated the
role of party in British politics. Further, the founding of political clubs
(the Carlton by Conservatives in 1832 and the Reform by Whigs in
1836) opened the way to the growth of central party organisations: the
Conservative Central Office was started in 1852. Such developments
were at first limited to registration and to 'getting out the vote'; yet they
were bound eventually to become concerned with propaganda to win
over the voters, and with deciding on policies to put before them. Thus
the Great Reform Act meant that after 1832 parties became much more
important in British politics than they had been before that date.

3
Whigs and Chartists
middle class and working class

1 Whig solutions

In December 1832, at the first general election after the Reform Act, the Whigs, strongly backed by the new middle-class voters, enjoyed a handsome victory. They and the two groups which supported them, the Radicals and O'Connell's Irish party, won over 450 seats out of the total 658; the Tories with some 180 were a shadow of their former selves, and many thought them on the way to extinction. The Whigs remained in office, with one brief interval, until 1841; Lord Melbourne replaced Lord Grey as Prime Minister in 1834. Their ministries carried through a series of important reforms. These made government more efficient, and set in train great social changes which have become part of the normal pattern of British life.

Yet these changes fell far short of what many reformers expected to follow the triumph of 1832. They aroused violent controversy and lowered the popularity of the government, so that by the later 1830s Melbourne was struggling desperately to cling to power, with his Commons majority crumbling away. A shrewd, cynical and rather lazy politician, he enjoyed office. But he had no enthusiasm whatever for reform, saying just before the election of 1832, 'when the new parliament meets we shall be pressed to go further in reform. There is no knowing to what one may be led by circumstances, but at present I am determined to make my stand here and not advance any further'. His authority in Parliament was not as strong as it seemed, for neither the Radicals nor the Irish could be relied on for votes, while the Tory Opposition, under the skilful leadership of Robert Peel, steadily gained ground at elections. Moreover he had trouble with William IV ('Silly Billy'), who in 1834 dismissed him and sent for Peel, who formed a ministry but lost the election which followed early in 1835. The King had to recall Melbourne. But the Whig majority in the Commons fell sharply, and after 1835 they did little by way of reform. The government's financial policy was ill-managed, and in 1841 Peel pictured its Chancellor of the Exchequer 'seated on an empty chest by the pool of bottomless deficiency, fishing for a budget'. Contemporaries certainly did not see the 1830s as years of Whig triumph.

The 'Whig Reforms' themselves reflected the fact that most middle-class people wanted only limited change. For they had seen the mobs in action in 1831-2, and they feared the working class – a fear which

Lord Melbourne

Lord Melbourne (1779–1848)

some events of the later 1830s did much to strengthen. The reforms, important though they were for the future, were far from radical. The Lords threw a fair number of proposals out. Those that became law were for the most part bi-partisan, backed by many Whigs and Tories alike. Peel's influence did much to win Tory votes in the Commons for them and to persuade the big Tory majority in the Lords to pass them.

Abolition of Slavery   The first major reform, the abolition of slavery in the British Empire (1833), was a victory for religion rather than for the Whigs. It was the climax of the work of a pressure group dominated by men of Evangelical faith like William Wilberforce, the hero of the Abolition of the Slave Trade in 1807, who lived just long enough to see this second triumph. The methods used by its supporters were copied by later movements. Most notable among them was the organisation throughout the land of enormous petitions: huge rolls of paper containing many thousands of signatures were borne along the Strand to the Houses of Parliament accompanied by long processions of supporters, and strong men, staggering under their weight, carried them into Parliament. The Emancipation Act of 1833 declared that all slaves under six years of age in the British dominions should be free[1]; those over that age must serve as apprentices to their former masters for seven years if they were field slaves and five if houseworkers. Compensation of £20,000,000 was granted to the slaveowners, the sugar planters of the West Indies and

[1]Strictly, British dominions *except* India, Ceylon, Mauritius and St. Helena.

the Boer farmers of South Africa. The planters continued to treat their apprentices like slaves, and so in 1838 Parliament abolished the entire system. It was a noble humanitarian reform. It also dealt a severe blow to the prosperity of sugar-growing in Jamaica, and contributed to the Great Trek of the Boers in South Africa (below, pp.292–3).

A second major reform of the same year 1833 was a Factory Act. **Factory Reform** There had been earlier Factory Acts, attempting to control child labour in textile mills; this was to prove the first effective one. Like the Emancipation of Slaves, it had its origins in a campaign outside Parliament which eventually forced the government to take action. This time the evil attacked was in England, not in far-off lands. Child labour was not new. Throughout the centuries children had been fully employed to watch sheep, glean corn and spin and card wool in weavers' homes. What led to a movement against it in the 1820s was the growth of the new power-driven factories in the textile districts, especially the West Riding of Yorkshire and south Lancashire. Here large numbers of children from about six years old were employed for long hours in filthy conditions and inadequate ventilation, doing dangerous jobs like tying broken threads while the machines were moving. The attack was launched by Richard Oastler, a Yorkshire land agent who published in 1830 a series of letters passionately denouncing the 'Yorkshire Slavery' endured by children in woollen mills, and it gained support in Parliament from a curious alliance of Tories and Radicals. Millhands

Richard Oastler (1789–1861)

backed Oastler, partly because many of them genuinely wanted to rescue their children from the terrible conditions they endured, yet partly also because control and reduction of child labour could obviously lead to an improvement in adult working conditions, in particular to a shortening of working hours. Thus arose in the textile areas of northern England what came to be known as the Ten Hours Movement, demanding a maximum working day – not uncommon in other industries – of ten hours. A few millowners were sympathetic, like John Fielden of Todmorden and the Gregs of Styal near Stockport. The majority were bitterly hostile. They argued that if government interfered with the 'economic laws' which determined hours (and wages) industry would collapse and everybody, masters and workers alike, would be ruined; and that with the reduction of child labour foreign competition would get the better of British industry, bringing both lower wages and widespread unemployment.

A Tory M.P., Michael Sadler, put before the Commons in 1832 a Ten Hour Bill, to apply to all textile workers under eighteen. This was referred to a select committee, and the evidence laid before this – of children deformed by their work or maimed in machinery, flogged by overseers, working in busy times from four or five o'clock in the morning to nine or ten o'clock at night, utterly exhausted, pale and stunted in their growth, with no time for schooling – made legislation inevitable. Sadler lost his seat in the election of 1832, and Lord Ashley (later Lord Shaftesbury) took over the leadership of the factory cause in the Commons. The outcome was a government-sponsored measure, the Factory Act of 1833, which applied to all textile factories except lace and silk mills. No children under nine were to be employed; a maximum of nine hours per day was fixed for those from nine to thirteen and of twelve hours from thirteen to eighteen. Night work was forbidden for all under eighteen. Government inspectors of factories were to be appointed, responsible to the Home Office. The Act was very difficult to enforce; only four inspectors were appointed at first, and local magistrates were unwilling to impose fines stiff enough to deter millowners from defying the law. Yet it was a beginning, the first of a long series of laws stretching on into the twentieth century which made factories tolerable and humane, a process in which the inspectors were gradually to play the vital role.

The New Poor Law

1834 brought a third major reform, the Poor Law Amendment Act. This 'new Poor Law' was probably the most important measure the Whigs introduced (apart from the 1832 Act itself), and it was certainly the most unpopular. A high proportion of the population in the nineteenth century were likely to be very poor indeed, around starvation level, at some stage in their lives. Clearly, as with child labour, there was nothing new about the problem of poverty; yet here also developments of the last fifty years – the astounding rise in population, the enclosures, the industrial changes, the long French Wars, the post-war depression – made it more evident. During most of that time poor relief over most of England and Wales had been administered under the Speenhamland System (named after the Berkshire parish where it began) or similar schemes, whereby a high proportion of the able-bodied working class was receiving outdoor relief from parish rates to subsidise wages. This was expensive, costing almost £7 million in 1832, and ratepayers were protesting strongly. Farmers and labourers alike had come to look upon such relief as normal, the former because they could pay lower wages, the latter seeing relief as their right irrespective of the amount of work they did. There was clearly widespread under-employment in the countryside, and great distress among farm labourers. The 'Last Labourers' Revolt' of 1830–1 had led the Whigs to appoint a commission to investigate the poor law.

The long and detailed Report of this commission was a landmark in British history. Most of its members believed that extreme poverty was normally the reward of idleness, not the result of circumstances outside the workman's control, and that change was needed to drive the able-bodied poor to find work. Only 'paupers' – a word of reproach – should obtain relief, and they should do so on hard terms. So the Poor Law Amendment Act of 1834, based on this Report, forbade outdoor relief except for the old and sick. Relief was instead to be given in workhouses, and conditions in these were to be 'less eligible' – that is, less desirable – than the lowest-paid type of employment outside. Parishes were to be grouped together in unions, each of which was to provide a workhouse. Control of the workhouse was to be in the hands of local Boards of Guardians, elected by ratepayers. The whole scheme was to be supervised by a body of three commissioners, set up by the central government and with its headquarters at Somerset House in London. The man whose name became particularly associated with the new Poor Law was Edwin Chadwick (1800–90), very prominent in compiling the Report and then appointed as Secretary to the 'Three Bashaws of Somerset House', as the commissioners were soon nicknamed.

The Act went through Parliament smoothly, with support from most Tories as well as Whigs, and the pattern of poor relief it created lasted into the twentieth century. The Guardians were not abolished until 1929; while the new-built workhouses themselves, long and austere-looking, often until recently called 'unions', are still readily identifiable features of many local landscapes. From the start the poor hated these new 'Bastilles' to which many thousands of them were condemned during the nineteenth century. There were immediate riots against them in Kent and Sussex, while in the industrial depression of 1837–8 Poor Law officials were stoned out of some northern towns such as Todmorden, and there was mob violence in Bradford and Dewsbury. Conditions varied from one workhouse to another, depending on the local Guardians or Workhouse Master. The majority were grim places harshly run, with families separated, meals taken in silence, and tedious work like picking oakum imposed. Things improved in the early 1840s with the relaxation of some rules. Moreover there is considerable evidence that in a good many places outdoor relief continued despite the act and the efforts of the central commissioners to stop it. When economic conditions got better during the second half of the century the fear of the workhouse was lifted from many of the poor. Yet for millions of Victoria's subjects its shadow never disappeared.

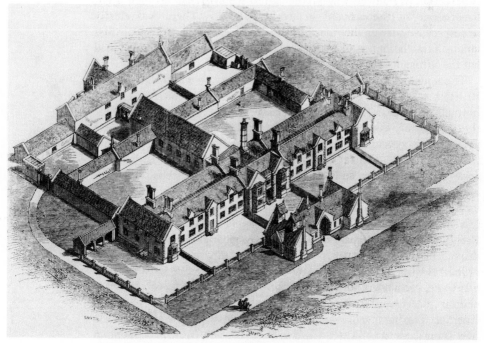

The Andover Union Workhouse, notorious for its appalling conditions in the 1840s

Municipal reform

A fourth major reform of quite a different sort came in 1835 with the passage of the Municipal Corporations Act. This gave to 178 old-established chartered boroughs town councils elected by all male ratepaying householders who had lived in the boroughs for three years. In some degree this followed the pattern of the Parliamentary Reform Act of 1832 and gave power over town government to the middle-class citizens. By doing so it transferred control of borough politics (still important in parliamentary elections too) from Tories and Anglicans to Whigs, radicals and nonconformists. The old corporations, like many of the parliamentary boroughs, had grown corrupt. The new elected councils took over their property. The ratepayers' interests were safeguarded by the proviso that the borough accounts had to be audited annually. In many towns, notably the bigger industrial ones of the north and midlands, public-spirited citizens had already got special

50

bodies of Improvement Commissioners (some 300 all told) set up to deal with particular problems like water supplies and street cleaning; and these duties too the new town councils could take over. Unchartered towns might also adopt the same pattern of government. The Act came only slowly into operation in the towns; yet its long-term importance was immense. It provided a standard pattern of town government, with elected members responsible to ratepayers, and gradually through the years which followed it enabled the people of English and Welsh cities to provide for themselves the great range of social services – police, health, cleansing, lighting, paving and countless others – essential to their growing needs. Rural England and Wales were left in the hands of the justices of the peace, in effect the local gentry, until county councils were set up in 1888.

To these major reforms of the 1830s several lesser measures must be added in view of their importance as pointers to the future. The Whig government was the first to give public money to education when (1833) it granted £20,000 to the two religious organisations (the National Society, wholly Anglican, and the British and Foreign Society, mainly nonconformist) which ran schools for the children of the poor. In the field of law and order, so desperate a problem in the 1830s, the Whigs in some ways went further than Peel had gone in the 1820s: more crimes were freed from the death penalty, the Prisons Act (1835) set up a central prison inspectorate, the Rural Police Act (1839) made it possible to extend the pattern of the Metropolitan Police to the country districts. Factory Reform was decisively helped by the Registration Act (1836) which made the registration of births compulsory, and thus in future made it harder for parents or employers to evade the laws about child labour. The same act appointed registrars of births, marriages and deaths throughout the country; permitted civil marriages; and required medical certificates to state the cause of death. Finally in 1840 came the Penny Post, proposed by a midland schoolmaster, Rowland Hill. Hitherto the Post Office had charged postage according to distance and required payment to be made by the sender. This was costly and inefficient; it penalised the poor, hindered business, and encouraged fraud. The fee for a letter from London to Edinburgh was 1s. 4½d. Hill reckoned that the real cost, given a reasonable number of letters to carry, was about 1/36 of a penny. He suggested prepayment by an adhesive stamp of a fixed charge, whatever the distance inside Britain, beginning at one penny. The government reluctantly accepted the plan. The number of letters posted rose from 76 million in 1839 to 642 million in 1847. The Post Office prospered mightily; the gains in human happiness and commercial efficiency were far beyond calculation. It also enabled political pressure groups like the Anti-Corn law League (founded 1839) to send out propaganda cheaply and efficiently.

Thus in many ways the Whig achievement of 1832–41 was great, setting a framework for later nineteenth century development. Yet the

Other reforms

The Penny Post

British electorate showed little gratitude to Melbourne. When William IV died in 1837 his successor was his 18-year-old niece, Victoria, who quickly became devoted to the kindly and amusing Melbourne. In 1839, when the government's majority fell to five, the Prime Minister resigned and advised the Queen to send for Peel. But Peel, whom Victoria found shy and cold in manner (as she said in her *Journal*, 'how different, how dreadfully so, to that frank, open, natural, and most kind, warm manner of Lord Melbourne's') insisted that the Queen replace her Whig Ladies of the Bedchamber by Tories. Victoria refused; the Whig ministers supported her over this Bedchamber Question; and Melbourne hung on to office until he lost a vote of confidence and finally resigned in 1841.

2 Chartist failure

The People's Charter

Many people in the 1830s were more concerned about what the Great Reform Act had failed to do than about what it had done. They saw that the vote still belonged only to property-owners and occupiers, to only one in seven adult males in the United Kingdom, and therefore to the middle and upper classes; that the electors still had to vote on open hustings, and so ran the risks of eviction from their houses by their landlords and of violence from gangs of hired bullies; that the M.P.s themselves still came almost exclusively from 'the wealthy and leisured classes'; that constituencies still varied widely in size (thus even after 1832 Totnes with 179 voters and Liverpool with 8600 each returned two members); and that bribery in cash (two guineas a head at Yarmouth) and in kind (the Tories distributed what became notorious as 'blue beef' at Bristol) remained widespread. A handful of these critics were middle-class Radical politicians, but most of them were working-class men who considered they had been tricked by Whigs and Tories in the Reform crisis, and the later 1830s witnessed the spectacular outburst of the most exciting British working-class movement of the nineteenth century. This was Chartism, which took its name from the Charter of Six Points issued by the London Working Men's Association in 1838. The Six Points were radical demands for further political reforms – for (1) votes for all men (2) the secret ballot (3) equal electoral districts (4) the abolition of the property qualifications for M.P.s (5) payment of M.P.s and (6) annual parliaments. These political demands became a rallying cry for the hopes and dreams of millions of working men during a period of hardship and distress. Three times – in 1838–9, in 1842 and in 1848, all years of severe economic depression – Chartist activities presented a direct challenge to the existing political system and also, it seemed, to law and order, striking fear into the hearts of the propery-owning classes.

CHARTIST
DEMONSTRATION!!

"PEACE and ORDER" is our MOTTO!

TO THE WORKING MEN OF LONDON.

Fellow Men,—The Press having misrepresented and vilified us and our intentions, the Demonstration Committee therefore consider it to be their duty to state that the grievances of us (the Working Classes) are deep and our demands just. We and our families are pining in misery, want, and starvation! We demand a fair day's wages for a fair day's work! We are the slaves of capital—we demand protection to our labour. We are political serfs—we demand to be free. We therefore invite all well disposed to join in our peaceful procession on

MONDAY NEXT, April 10,

As it is for the good of all that we seek to remove the evils under which we groan.

The following are the places of Meeting of THE CHARTISTS, THE TRADES, THE IRISH CONFEDERATE & REPEAL BODIES:

East Division on Stepney Green at 8 o'clock; City and Finsbury Division on Clerkenwell Green at 9 o'clock; West Division in Russell Square at 9 o'clock; and the South Division in Peckham Fields at 9 o'clock, and proceed from thence to Kennington Common.

Signed on behalf of the Committee, JOHN ARNOTT, *Sec.*

Henry Mitchener, Printer, 3, Edward Street, Hampstead Road.

Notice of a Chartist demonstration

Chartism was not an organised movement. It was more a kind of banner under which men with very varied grievances joined forces from time to time. In the mid 1830s hundreds of radical clubs, political

Causes of Chartism

unions and workingmen's associations grew up throughout the land. Widespread in the industrial areas, weak in the countryside, Chartism was strongest of all among handicraft workers whose wages had been driven down to starvation level by the coming of steam-powered factories, like the framework knitters of Nottingham and the handloom weavers of the West Riding; and in the middle-sized industrial towns which were growing particularly fast at this time, such as Bradford, Bolton and Stockport. Here was the militant core of the Chartist Movement. Yet there were other elements in Chartism. One was working-class tradition, notably the memory of what had happened at Peterloo. Another was the demand for Factory Reform; many a supporter of the Ten Hours Movement, like Richard Oastler himself, took part in Chartist meetings. A third was the resentment of skilled artisans (like Francis Place and William Lovett), often well-educated, politically ambitious, yet excluded from political life. A fourth, highly important in many northern towns, was a violent hostility to the New Poor Law and its 'Bastilles'. At bottom, almost everywhere, was the pressure of hunger and poverty and bad conditions. Thus the Charter became in the contemporary writer Thomas Carlyle's famous words 'the cry of pent-up millions suffering under a diseased condition of society'; or, as one of its leaders put it, the right to vote was 'a knife and fork question, a bread and cheese question'.

Feargus O'Connor (1794–1855)

William Lovett (1800–77)

Its leaders, most of them middle-class in their origins, were as various as its causes. Prominent among them were J. R. Stephens, a former Methodist minister who preached violent revolt; Thomas

Attwood, the banker and currency reformer who had started the Birmingham Political Union; Joseph Sturge, a wealthy Quaker corn merchant; George Julian Harney, the nearest Chartism got to producing a socialist revolutionary; and John Frost, draper and sometime Mayor of Newport. Perhaps the most attractive among them was William Lovett, the Cornish cabinet-maker who became the leading spirit of the London Working Men's Association. Certainly the most important was the Irishman Feargus O'Connor, a powerful mob-orator and founder in 1837 of the radical newspaper, the *Northern Star*. Published in Leeds and selling at its peak about 50,000 copies a week, this paper gave O'Connor wide influence throughout the country.

The Six Points became a national issue in the winter of 1838–9, when **Main events** the Chartists held huge meetings of many thousands, often by torchlight, in the great cities like Birmingham and Glasgow or on the open moorlands of Lancashire and Yorkshire. In February 1839 a National Convention of Chartist delegates from all the industrial areas met in London, seeing itself as a kind of 'People's Parliament'. It appointed Lovett as its secretary, talked of proclaiming a 'sacred month' or general strike, and set about preparing a monster petition to present to Parliament. The government took military precautions; while, as a humane warning, Sir Charles Napier, in command in the north, invited the Chartist leaders to witness an artillery demonstration. In May the Convention, sharply divided between 'moral force' men led by Lovett and those who were prepared if necessary to use 'physical force', adjourned to Birmingham. Here in July there were riots in the Bull Ring in the city centre, quelled by the Metropolitan Police called in for the occasion. Later that month a National Petition asking for the adoption of the Six Points was presented to the Commons, who by 235 votes to 46 refused to consider it. The Convention, many of whose members had gone home, eventually dissolved itself in August. The great movement had fizzled out. There was one tragic tailpiece that November, when an armed band of miners marched upon Newport, probably with the ultimate object of freeing a Chartist speaker held prisoner in Monmouth Gaol. A single volley from soldiers dispersed them and they fled back to the hills. Their leaders, including John Frost, were arrested and sentenced to death; the sentences were commuted to transportation for life.

So ended the crucial year of Chartism. Support for the movement fell away sharply, yet there were two later demonstrations of its appeal to working men. In 1842, a year of severe unemployment, there were strikes and riots throughout the industrial areas in which Chartists took the lead. Again a petition, this time with three million signatures, was carried to the Commons, and again rejected. In Lancashire there occurred the so-called 'Plug Plot', when strikers went round the factories removing the plugs from boilers in order to cut off the source of power. Six years later, in 1848, the 'Year of Revolutions' in nearly every country in Europe, Feargus O'Connor, who had been elected M.P. for Nottingham in 1847, made a third attempt to launch the Charter. He announced a Chartist meeting on Kennington Common, to be followed by a march to Westminster to present a petition with some six million signatures to Parliament. The government took the affair very seriously. They enrolled 150,000 special constables; sent the Queen to the Isle of Wight; put the Duke of Wellington (now almost 79) in command of London's defences; and forbade the Chartists, who numbered perhaps 20,000, to cross the Thames bridges. O'Connor was allowed to bring the petition in three cabs. It was found to contain fewer than two million signatures, many of them bogus, such as Victoria Rex, the Duke of Wellington, Punch and Flatnose. The whole episode was a fiasco, and Chartism was for practical purposes dead, though the movement lingered on in name for another ten years. O'Connor went out of his mind and died in 1855.

Reasons for failure

Chartism accomplished nothing – except that it became a working-class legend. Five of the Six Points were achieved later[1]. In its own day it failed utterly, for all the enthusiasm it awoke among millions of humble men. Why was this? One reason certainly was the tough line taken by both Whig and Tory governments towards it. Neither Melbourne nor Peel showed the slightest hint of compromise with Chartist demands. Both, aided by the new police, stood firmly for law and order. This policy was warmly backed by landowners and tenant farmers. Melbourne arrested most of the Chartist leaders, including Lovett and O'Connor, in 1839; while Peel's government in 1842 took 400 men into custody in Nottingham alone. Moreover, the Chartists failed to win any substantial support from the middle class. The alliance which had brought the Reform Act in 1832 had disappeared. The respectable folk, the professional men, merchants, tradesmen and others who had just got the vote were not at all anxious to share it with 'the labouring classes' anyway, and the mass meetings and the wild threats of revolution terrified them.

There were great weaknesses within the Chartists' own ranks. As the arguments within the Convention of 1839 over the use of 'physical force' showed, they were never a united movement. They could usually shout together for the Six Points but when it came to action they were divided. Local pressures were strong. The Leeds textile workers wanted different things from the craftsmen whom Lovett led in the London Working Men's Association. Some Chartists really wanted Factory Reform, others cheap bread, many were above all else against the Poor Law and its workhouses. Great numbers followed O'Connor; some 70,000 people subscribed to his Land Company, launched in 1845 for establishing smallholdings in rural areas (though by mid-1848 there

---

[1]Adult male suffrage by a series of Reform Acts from 1867 to 1969; secret ballot in 1872; broadly equal electoral districts gradually over the nineteenth and twentieth centuries; abolition of the property qualification for M.P.s in 1858; payment of M.P.s in 1911.

were only about 250 actual smallholders). But others abandoned the movement with William Lovett in the early 1840s and gave their energies to promoting working-class education or temperance or some similarly peaceful 'non-political' cause. It is just to say that Chartism was not well-served by its leaders, even though it found its martyrs in such men as John Frost of Newport. Feargus O'Connor in particular, despite his skills as journalist and orator, was a liability to those he led. A vain and boastful intriguer, at once jealous and contemptuous of other leaders, he was ready enough to threaten violence but not to use it when the crisis came.

One deeper cause must be taken into the reckoning of the decline and fall of the Chartists. Although the People's Charter was a political document, containing six demands for the radical reform of the system of government, it is plain that the reasons why so many thousands of men clamoured for it were overwhelmingly social and economic. The right to vote, the secret ballot, the payment of members of Parliament and the abolition of the property qualifications – the ordinary Chartist wanted these things not for their own sake but as means to such ends as a regular job and decent wages, the abolition of the workhouse test, the ten hour day. These were ends which he thought only a 'People's Parliament' could bring him. He was most conscious of these needs in bad times. 'Poverty', as O'Connor said, 'was the parent of Chartism'. Chartism was in effect a barometer of depression. 1838–9, 1842, 1847–8 were hard times. By contrast, the middle forties, when support for the Charter fell away, saw a great spell of railway building, which stimulated trade and provided employment. The handloom weavers and other 'out-workers' were rapidly declining in numbers as steam-driven industry expanded. In many areas the 'New Poor Law' became far less of a grievance because much outdoor relief continued. Then the years after 1848 brought a spell of industrial prosperity in which working men shared – and Chartism vanished. Its rise and fall were in great measure determined by events outside the movement itself.

3 Self-interest abroad – Palmerston 1830–41

British foreign policy from 1830 to 1865 was dominated by the remarkable Henry Temple, Lord Palmerston. Alive for eighty vigorous years, he spent nearly fifty of them in office, a record which no other British politician has come anywhere near breaking. Like Gladstone and Churchill, he began his political career as a backbencher in one party and rose to the leadership of another. From 1809 to 1828 he was the Tory Secretary at War. His first major speech on foreign affairs was in 1829 when, as a Canningite and out of office, he criticised Wellington's policy towards Greece. In 1830 he went over to the Whigs and Grey, thinking perhaps that foreign powers might be less suspicious of

Lord Palmerston

an ex-Tory than of a Whig or Radical, made him Foreign Secretary. Palmerston never looked back. He was responsible for foreign policy under Grey and Melbourne from 1830 to 1841 and under Russell from 1846 to 1851, he influenced it while Home Secretary under Aberdeen from 1853 to 1855, and he controlled it as Prime Minister from 1855 to 1858 and from 1859 to 1865.

Henry John Temple, Lord Palmerston (1784–1865)

Gladstone once described how a Frenchman, wishing to be complimentary, told Palmerston that if he were not a Frenchman he would wish to be an Englishman, and that Palmerston's reply had been – 'If I were not an Englishman I should wish to be an Englishmen'. It was a typical Palmerstonian remark, popular with his countrymen and irritating to foreigners. Well aware that he represented the world's richest economic power, he had, as his overriding priority, to protect the trading and commercial interests of the British middle classes. As a second, less important priority, he considered that, since the 1832 Reform Act had given this country a constitutional government to be envied, Britain should throw her 'moral weight into the scale of any people who are striving for freedom'. The fact that he opposed any further change in the British constitution led to his being called a conservative at home and a liberal abroad, but this was not the contradiction it sounded. His general strategy was to keep a balance of power in Europe and to support whichever side it was at that moment in British interests to support. His policy thus appears at times impulsive and inconsistent whereas his methods were much more predictable. He bullied weaker powers, relied heavily on a declining but still effective navy, made skilful use of the press, and was an expert in what is now called brinkmanship. In Cobden's words, 'he liked to drive the wheel close to the edge.' He had, like Peel, an immense capacity for work and so an immense grasp of detail. He told Queen Victoria that her ministers 'must be minutely acquainted with all the details of the business of their offices' and his treatment of the Foreign Office staff was notoriously harsh. Drivers of horse-drawn omnibuses pointed him out to passengers as he stood at his desk in the window of his Piccadilly home. "E earns 'is wages' said one. 'I never come by without seeing 'im 'ard at it'. The Court and many of his colleagues disliked him; a sharp tongue earned him the name of Lord Pumicestone; and, for someone with great responsibilities, he often seemed flippant. For most of his career, however, he perfectly expressed the views of the majority of his countrymen. Only occasionally and at the very end did he seem to speak for Palmerston rather than for Britain.

The first problem that he had to face concerned Belgium. For **Belgium** centuries, British foreign policy had tried to prevent possible enemies controlling Antwerp and the mouth of the Scheldt, both vital to British trade. The joining of Belgium and Holland in the new kingdom of the Netherlands in 1815 was engineered by Castlereagh with this in mind. He hoped that the new state would be strong enough to resist interference by, say, France or Prussia but not powerful enough by itself to be a threat. From the start, however, the Belgians felt themselves to be exploited by the Dutch, and in 1830, fired by the July Revolution in Paris, they revolted. The Dutch king appealed to the powers for help. Wellington, fearing a French invasion of the Netherlands, called a conference in London. At this point the Whigs took over and Palmerston became involved.

Where Wellington might have worked to repair this first big breach in the Vienna Settlement, Palmerston accepted from the start that the break-up of the Kingdom of the Netherlands was inevitable, and that British interests could still be protected by two buffer states instead of one. A union between France and Belgium had to be prevented or the Belgian coast would again be in French hands as it had been under Louis XIV and Napoleon. To secure a truly independent and viable Belgium took Palmerston nearly nine years of hard work and skilful diplomacy. First, he recognised the break-up of the Netherlands by admitting a Belgian deputation to the conference, and by making a start on defining the boundaries of the new Belgium. Then, when the Duc de Nemours, the second son of the French king Louis Philippe, was suggested by both the French and the Belgians as the first Belgian king, Palmerston persuaded them not only to withdraw him as a candidate, but to accept Queen Victoria's uncle, Leopold of Saxe-Coburg, in his place and as head of a constitutional government. Next, when the Dutch in protest invaded Belgium, he sent a naval force to protect Antwerp, and saw to it that an army sent in by the French was withdrawn once the Dutch had retreated. He was quite blunt about it – 'The French must go out of Belgium, or we shall have a general war . . . . in a given number of days'. Two more Anglo-French actions were needed before the Dutch finally gave in, but France gained nothing for her help. Finally, in 1839, Palmerston arranged, by the Treaty of London, for Belgian neutrality to be guaranteed by Holland and the five major powers. So modern Belgium was created with Palmerston as its chief architect. He was lucky in that Austria, Russia, and Prussia, who might have supported Holland, had other problems of their own at the time, but, for a first attempt at protecting British interests, it was an impressive start to a new career.

Mehemet Ali   A second major achievement followed in the Middle East. Mehemet Ali, the ruler of Egypt, had never received Syria which the Sultan had promised in return for his help against the Greeks. In 1831, therefore, his son Ibrahim invaded and overran Palestine and Syria and threatened Constantinople. Palmerston was not only too busy with the Belgian question, he was not sure which side to support. The Sultan asked Britain for help but the navy was engaged in coercing the Dutch. Thus the Russians were able to step in by themselves, defeat Ibrahim, and sign the Treaty of Unkiar-Skelessi with Turkey in 1833. A secret clause, which soon became public, said that, in wartime, only Russian warships would be allowed to move through the Straits. What worried Palmerston far more was that Russia and Turkey agreed to consult each other on foreign policy, so that 'the Russian ambassador becomes chief cabinet minister of the Sultan'. Britain's failure to act he now felt to have been a tremendous blunder. He set out to undo the special relationship which Russia now had with Turkey by renewing Canning's policy of joining with Russia to prevent her from again acting unilat-

Mehemet Ali (1769–1849)

erally. In 1839, an attempt by the Sultan to drive Ibrahim from Syria
failed. Russia was only too ready to join in and, this time, France, who
saw Mehemet Ali as a useful Middle East ally, seemed ready to escalate
the war by helping him defend Syria and Egypt. Palmerston was quick
to act and, as with Belgium, he put forward his own solution. Mehemet
Ali was to give up Syria in exchange for becoming hereditary Pasha of
Egypt. If he did not accept, he would be 'chucked into the Nile' in
which, incidentally, he might have been drowned forty years before had
the British not fished him out after the battle of Aboukir Bay. The
French reaction, under the chief minister Thiers, was furious and they
began to mobilize for war, but at that point Syria itself rebelled against
Mehemet. At once Palmerston sent arms (for which he demanded
payment) while the navy under Charles Napier and with the help of a
small Austrian flotilla, captured Beirut and Acre and forced the

Egyptians out. This prompt action, and the fact that Thiers had been replaced by the more pro-English Guizot, defused a dangerous situation so that, in 1841, Palmerston was able to get the same five powers who had signed the Belgian Treaty to sign the Straits Convention; by this, no warships at all could enter the Dardanelles in time of peace. It was a diplomatic triumph. Russia had lost whatever influence she had gained over Turkey in 1833 and a confrontation with France had ended with the French backing down. Britain had again played the part of international arbiter and the value of British trade within the Turkish empire increased to £12 million by the end of the decade. Aden became a British protectorate when its ruler sought help from Egyptian attack. True, Britain was now committed to supporting Turkey and, sooner or later, this would lead to trouble with Russia. But, for the time being, there was a balance of power in the Eastern Mediterranean favourable to British interests.

The Opium War   The third important issue with which Palmerston was involved was the first war with China – the Opium War of 1840–2. The search for new markets was, he felt, part of foreign policy, and, unlike Cobden and Bright (p.71), he was prepared to use force to find them. 'It is' he said 'the business of Government to open and secure the roads for the merchants'. The import of tea from China through the single port of Canton was, by the 1830s, already big business. It was paid for mainly with opium brought by British merchants from India, and the trade increased when, having been limited to the East India Company, it was opened to individual traders in 1834. The Chinese authorities, who had no great wish to trade with any foreigner in any commodity except perhaps silver, particularly wanted to suppress opium smoking. Fortified no doubt by the fact that they made up about a third of the world's population, they decided to teach the British a lesson. Their man on the spot, Commissioner Lin, imprisoned two hundred merchants and released them only after £1.25 million worth of opium had been dumped into the sea. The next year he attacked two British ships in an attempt to arrest an English sailor accused of murdering a Chinese villager. Four of his junks were sunk and the brief war had begun. A British naval squadron seized Canton and Chusan. The Chinese were brave but somewhat unrealistic in that their war plans included using monkeys with fireworks attached and banning the export of rhubarb in the hope that Britain would succumb to nationwide constipation. The peace terms were signed at Nanking in 1842 when Peel was in power, but most people accepted that it was 'Palmerston's war and Palmerston's peace'. The five ports of Canton, Amoy, Foochow, Ningpo and Shanghai were opened to all foreign, not merely British, trade; what Palmerston called 'the desert island of Hong Kong' was ceded to Britain; and China had to pay the cost of the war and of the seized opium. British trade interests appeared to have won a vast new market but, in fact, the volume of trade in that area did not greatly increase and two more wars were required before the Chinese were resigned to trading with the West. Their determination to suppress opium smoking never wavered but this was an issue which Palmerston chose to ignore.

He showed himself to be a good disciple of Canning in his policy during this period towards Spain and Portugal. In both countries there were young queens, Maria in Portugal and Isabella in Spain, whose advisers seemed in favour of limited constitutional reform. Both were under attack from their uncles, Miguel and Carlos, who were strongly anti-liberal. Palmerston wanted the Iberian peninsula to be at peace and thought this more likely under the queens. He sent warships to help them; he was behind the creation of the British Legion for Spain, an unofficial force of 8,000 volunteers, and he supported an equally unofficial navy under Charles Napier to fight Miguel. Finally, he persuaded France to join with Britain, Spain and Portugal in the Quadruple Alliance of 1834 which he called 'a capital hit and all my own doing' and which he saw as a counterpoise to the old Holy Alliance powers who were busy putting down revolutions in other parts of Europe. Reformers hailed him, as they had hailed Canning, as the champion of liberalism in Europe. In fact, the Anglo-French part of the Alliance soon collapsed during the Mehemet Ali crisis, while liberals in Spain and Portugal gained little from it.

Spain and Portugal

By the summer of 1841, however, Palmerston's reputation as the protector of British interests was assured. France, even twenty-five years after Waterloo, was still feared and distrusted and she had been isolated and humiliated over Mehemet Ali. The Opium War was widely popular. British traders and British subjects, wherever they were in the world, felt more secure. When the King of Naples excluded British merchants from a share of the local sulphur trade, the Royal Navy was sent in 1840 to blockade the port of Naples, and compensation was duly paid. Then, in 1841, the Whigs resigned and, for the next five years, Palmerston was in opposition. He was already much more than a leading politician and, in both public and private life, was becoming something of a legend. There were still twenty-four years to go.

4
The first Conservative
Sir Robert Peel

1 Peel's career before 1830

Sir Robert Peel

Sir Robert Peel, who became Conservative Prime Minister in 1841, was born in the cotton town of Bury in 1788. His father, also named Robert, was a wealthy mill-owner, humane enough to have promoted in 1802 an act attempting to control the employment of workhouse children in factories. He had bought a landed estate at Drayton near Tamworth in Staffordshire and he had given his son the traditional education of the landed gentry, sending him to Harrow and Oxford. His 21st birthday present from his father was a seat in Parliament for an Irish rotten borough, and in 1812, at 24, he was appointed Chief Secretary for Ireland, second only to the Viceroy in responsibility for the destinies of six million people.

Few Prime Ministers have been so splendidly endowed by nature and by fortune. A tall handsome young man with reddish-gold hair, he had a brilliant mind, gaining a 'double first' in Classics and Mathematics at Oxford. In the Commons he at once proved himself an outstanding speaker, and in Ireland a tough and hard-working administrator. He had inherited from his father not only wealth and a Lancashire accent, but also honesty and courage, qualities of immense importance in the crises of his career. A humane man, who cared intensely about personal distress and about poverty, he was also a politician born to lead, a natural statesman. Yet there were, too, characteristics in him which men found repellent. Perhaps because of his rich endowment, he was over-sensitive to criticism, awkward and sometimes arrogant in manner; he did not suffer fools readily and was not good at managing men. This blend of qualities made him a dominant figure in Parliament – and a difficult party leader.

Robert Peel became a Tory in politics like his father. Toryism in the early nineteenth century meant loyalty to the monarchy and the House of Lords; devotion to the Church of England; and the maintenance of law and order. To these principles Peel adhered throughout his career. He added to them two other elements. One was his readiness to accept the changing ideas of the time about economic matters – to see that industry and commerce, especially overseas commerce, were at least as important to Britain as agriculture; and, in particular, that free trade, the removal of customs barriers, was essential if Britain's exports were to grow. The second was simpler – the recognition that in politics as in

Sir Robert Peel (1788–1850)

war the moment sometimes comes when men have to abandon positions they have long defended. Twice – in the 1820s and in the 1840s –

circumstances were to put this element in Peel to severe test.

Peel in the
1820s

Peel's work in Ireland (1812–18) foreshadowed his later career in two ways. He was a firm champion of the Protestant cause and an opponent of Catholic Emancipation; and the Peace Preservation Act of 1817 created a civilian police force to maintain order in disturbed districts of Ireland. Back in England he presided over the Currency Committee (1819), which recommended a return to cash payments, suspended by the Bank of England as a consequence of war in 1797; a step backed by the leading economists of the day, but disliked by many Tory landowners. His appointment as Home Secretary (1821) in Liverpool's ministry signalled his arrival at 33 (Sidmouth, whom he succeeded, was 63) in the highest ranks of government. In that office he launched important reforms in the law and the penal code (above, pp.24–6), and he supported Huskisson's trade treaties. Yet on the biggest issue of the day, Catholic Emancipation, he took the Protestant line of resistance to change. When he joined Wellington's government in 1828, both men were pledged against the admission of Roman Catholics to Parliament; but when the Duke next year believed it his duty to grant Emancipation, Peel was most reluctant to stay in office and did so out of loyalty to his chief. His sensitive conscience compelled him to resign his seat as M.P. for the University of Oxford, and he was defeated in a bitterly fought by-election. Some Tories, the 'Ultras', never forgave him for what they saw as betrayal; many more were always ready to distrust him; while Peel himself, a proud man, remained sensitive to the damage done to his reputation.

2 Peel and Conservatism in the 1830s

Catholic Emancipation split the Tories. The Reform Act of 1832 came near to destroying them, and Peel's main task while in opposition during the 1830s was to rebuild the party. He fought to the end against the reform bills in the Commons, yet he firmly declined to join Wellington's absurd attempt to form a Tory government. Once the Act was passed Peel accepted it, saying that he considered 'that question [Reform of Parliament] as finally and irrevocably disposed of'. He went on to develop a policy of constructive opposition, helping the Whigs to pass measures of which he approved, and thus displaying his own party as a possible alternative government. It was highly successful, thanks in great part to Peel's own mastery of the Commons. As the old Radical William Cobbett, now M.P. for Oldham, said, 'If he would put himself at the head of the movement we would turn these fellows [Melbourne's Whig ministry] out in twenty-four hours'.

The Tamworth
Manifesto

When in 1834 William IV made him Prime Minister for what became known as Peel's Hundred Days, he published for his election campaign at Tamworth a statement of the attitude of his government towards the issues of the time. In this Tamworth Manifesto he appealed 'to that class which is much less interested in the contentions of party, than in the maintenance of order and the cause of good government'; and stated his support for 'the firm maintenance of established rights, the correction of proved abuses and the redress of real grievances'. Along this line Peel educated his party to accept change, and began to show that a vote for the Conservatives could be a vote for practical reform, not for diehard resistance to change[1]. Reward came at the election of 1841 when, the outstanding statesman of the day and the unquestioned leader of his party, he became Prime Minister with a majority of 76. The electorate saw Peel as a champion of law and order; protectionist farmers thought of him as a barrier against the free trade proposals of the newly-formed Anti-Corn Law League.

3 Peel's reforms 1841–6

His Conservative government was an able one, containing five past or future Prime Ministers besides himself. A strong yet somewhat aloof leader, he drove his cabinet and his party hard. He took pains to win over the young Queen, and did so surprisingly quickly, mainly by cultivating the support of Albert, the German prince whom Victoria had married in 1839. His unyielding treatment of the Chartists earned him the confidence of the upper and middle classes. His policy of moderate and practical reforms – continuing the line of the Tamworth Manifesto – won him widespread public support. Most of the men on the benches behind him in the the Commons were landowners, yet his policies ranged widely, bringing benefits to merchants and manufacturers and to urban working men as well.

At the centre of Peel's work was a financial policy which encouraged **Finance** the growth of trade. This, he believed, was the right way to help raise Britain from the depression which marked much of the later thirties and of what came to be called 'the Hungry Forties'. In the budgets of 1842 and 1845, of which he took personal charge, he moved towards Free Trade, following Huskisson's policy of twenty years before. That of 1842 cut down import duties on manufactured goods to a maximum of 20 per cent of the value of the goods, on semi-manufactured goods to 12 per cent, and on raw materials to 5 per cent. These reductions inevitably meant – at first – a sharp fall in revenue. To balance this Peel reintroduced income tax – a bold step, for this had been a hated wartime measure on whose abolition the Commons back-benchers had insisted in 1816. He set it at 7d in the £ for three years, on all incomes over £150 per annum. In 1843 the old law forbidding the export of machinery was repealed. A second great budget, in 1845, extended

[1]'Conservative' replaced 'Tory' in general use as the name of the party from about 1832 onwards.

income tax for a further three years[1], and removed or reduced many more tariffs. By 1846 timber was the only raw material which paid any considerable duty; while the maximum on all manufactured articles except silks was 10 per cent. Taxation on many imported foodstuffs, among them butter, cheese, meat and sugar was abolished or reduced. The total effect of these measures was great. They stimulated trade and created employment; increased the profits of industry and cut the cost of living for the poor; and, as trade expanded, brought more, not less, revenue to the government.

Along with them went the Bank Charter Act of 1844. This was an attempt by the government to stabilise the currency and prevent the periodic financial crises which caused widespread bankruptcies and damage to business. It had three main terms. First, it divided the Bank of England into two separate departments, one for issuing notes, the other for ordinary banking business. Secondly, it provided that for every £1 note printed by the Bank above £14,000,000 there must be £1 in gold in its vaults. Thirdly, no other note-issuing bank was to increase its issue, and no new note-issuing bank was to be opened. The Act brought greater stability in company business and investment and helped to check the development of financial panics in later years: it also created the situation whereby the Bank of England eventually secured a monopoly of note-issue in England and Wales.

Social reforms The government also carried through a variety of measures to deal with problems thrown up by the social changes of the 1840s. Thus the Mines Act of 1842, instigated by Lord Ashley (later Shaftesbury) prohibited the employment of all women and children underground, and stopped children under ten working in mines at all; while the Factory Act of 1844 fixed a maximum day of twelve hours for women, and of six and a half hours for children between eight and thirteen, in textile mills, and also introduced regulations for fencing machinery. Railways, over 7000 miles of which were in active use by 1852, called for some degree of government regulation, even though there was no national plan for their building. The Railway Passengers Act of 1844 compelled each company to run at least one train per day which carried third class coaches, charged one penny per mile, and stopped at every station. Besides creating this 'parliamentary train' (satirised by Gilbert and Sullivan in *The Mikado*) the Act gave the state the right to buy up every railway built after 1844 – an option never exercised. Peel's government also turned its attention to Ireland. Against much hostility from those many Conservatives who could not forget his about-turn on Catholic Emancipation, he increased the government grant to the colleges at Maynooth which trained Roman Catholic priests, believing that well-educated priests were more rather than less likely to train their flocks to be law-abiding; and set up the Devon Commission in 1843 to investigate the problems of Irish landholding.

[1]It has remained ever since.

4 Foreign affairs

In foreign affairs the policy of the government, conducted by Lord Aberdeen, was less venturesome and more conciliatory than Palmerston's had been under the Whigs. Its greatest constructive achievement was in a sphere not regarded as of much moment in the 1840s, yet of great future importance in British history, that of relations with the United States. Here Aberdeen concluded two notable agreements which between them completed the boundary between Canada and the U.S.A. (see p.8 for Castlereagh's earlier settlement). One, the Webster-Ashburton Treaty (1842) fixed its eastern end, settling the 'Maine Boundary' dispute which had dragged on for sixty years. The second, the Oregon Treaty (1846), defined the boundary from the Rockies to the Pacific Ocean. Resisting the American cry of 'Fifty-Four Forty or Fight', Aberdeen eventually secured a line running along the forty-ninth parallel of latitude, except for Vancouver Island, which went entire to Canada. The establishment of some four thousand miles of peaceful international frontiers may be seen on a long view as one of the most notable events of the nineteenth and twentieth centuries – when contrasted with the countless boundary disputes which have bedevilled European history since 1846.

It was Aberdeen who in 1842 made peace with China after the Opium War (above, pp.62–3). Yet the main concern for contemporaries was relations with France. Aberdeen, pacific by temperament and with an approach wholly different from that of Palmerston, improved these, aided by the visit of Victoria and Albert to France in 1843. But there were difficulties over the French annexation of the Pacific island of Tahiti, and distrust over King Louis Philippe's schemes to marry his children into the Spanish royal family. More alarming, the French navy was ahead of the British in turning over to steam, and Wellington, with some reason, was badgering the government about the state of the defences along the south coast. Peel was a good deal less conciliatory than Aberdeen, and in 1845 the government began a rearmament programme which it was clear could only be aimed at France.

5 The Repeal of the Corn Laws

But the year of 1846 brought to its climax a crisis which destroyed Peel's ministry. This was the controversy over the Repeal of the Corn Laws, an event of nineteenth century history almost as important as the Reform Act of 1832. What was at stake in this crisis? Why did it lead to his fall? What were its chief results?

The Corn Law of 1815, passed by Parliament in the final stages of the struggle with Napoleon, stated that no foreign wheat could be imported into Britain and Ireland until the price of home-grown wheat had reached 80s. per quarter[1]. Its purpose was to safeguard British farmers and landlords against the flood of cheap foreign grain which would pour into the country once the wartime barriers were down. It was understandable that British farmers should demand protection of this kind, and that a parliament most of whose members were landowners should grant it to them. But the obvious purpose of the Corn Law was to keep wheat prices up – and its result to keep the cost of bread, the staple diet of the poor, high. So it was equally understandable that from the start working-class people should be bitterly hostile to the Corn Law, particularly in the hard years of depression and unemployment after Waterloo. There were other critics, too, whose arguments differed from those of the poor. Middle-class manufacturers and merchants, especially those whose business depended on overseas trade, maintained that the Corn Laws were a great handicap to British commerce and prosperity. Foreign countries could not sell us their corn, and therefore could not buy our cotton textiles, machinery, hardware and other manufactures; hence came stagnation in trade, unemployment and poverty.

Peel trying to use the sliding scale to push the price of bread down, while Wellington looks on

[1]Historians commonly write of 'the Corn Laws' of 1815. Strictly, the significant law was that concerned with wheat. Similar regulations were passed affecting barley and oats.

In 1828 Wellington's government modified the Corn Law of 1815 by the introduction of 'the sliding scale'. This replaced the absolute prohibition of imports below 80s. by a variable scale of duties, at prices between 52s. and 73s.: the higher the British price, the lower the tax on foreign corn. This was thought to be fairer all round, but it did not work at all well, for dealers deliberately held corn back so as to send up the price of British corn and thus enable them eventually to get their imports in at a low rate of duty. Meanwhile contemporary economists argued strongly in favour of free trade in general and for the abolition of all such restrictions as customs duties. They claimed that business could prosper only when government interference was at a minimum. In the 1820s the tide began to run powerfully for free trade, influencing the Liberal Tories in Liverpool's government (above, p.26). To many outside the government the Corn Laws were the chief example of a misguided policy of protection, and pressure against them increased as manufacturing industry expanded in such areas as Lancashire, the West Riding and the Black Country. For their part the Protectionists argued that to allow Britain to become dependent on imports of corn would be disastrous in wartime – whereas their opponents maintained that Free Trade would usher in an era of peace between nations. Perhaps more realistically, the Protectionists alleged that the real reason why manufacturers wanted cheap food imports was in order to keep wages down.

In the early 1830s the great political crisis over Parliamentary Reform blotted out other issues. But the depression of the later 1830s turned many minds to economic rather than to political questions – and to the Corn Laws above all. Why should agriculture be privileged to enjoy protection? Why should the aristocratic landowners, whose political power had been undermined if not destroyed by the Reform Act, be able to maintain their great wealth by what was in effect a tax on the bread of everyone in the land? In 1839 the Anti-Corn Law League was founded, with its headquarters in Manchester, the heart of England's greatest exporting industry. Its members were for the most part business men of Radical opinions, and its leading spirit was Richard Cobden (1804–65), a farmer's son from Sussex who had developed a successful calico-printing works in Manchester. An able speaker, Cobden was dedicated to Free Trade, and after his election as M.P. for Stockport in 1841 he did much by the sheer force and range of his arguments to convince opinion in the Commons. In the country at large he was powerfully seconded by John Bright (1811–89), a Quaker millowner from Rochdale, an orator who made effective use of moving biblical imagery.

Cobden was also a skilful organiser who did more than any other man to make the Anti-Corn Law League the most successful of nineteenth-century pressure groups. Its methods of propaganda – which took full advantage of two new developments of the time, railways and the penny

The Anti-Corn Law League

John Bright, left (1811–89) and Richard Cobden, right (1804–65)

post – included meetings and petitions, full-time lecturers as well as speaking tours by Cobden and Bright, Free Trade posters, handbills, newspapers, and magazines (including the foundation in 1843 of *The Economist*), and specially designed Free Trade pottery. For working people the 'Big Loaf' was widely used as the League's symbol. The League paid particular attention to everyone who had the right to vote. It bombarded all electors with bundles of Free Trade tracts. Its agents annually checked the electoral registers to make sure that all its known supporters among those qualified to vote actually had their names on the lists, and to press every possible objection to known Protectionists (once they even objected to Peel's claim to vote at Tamworth). In some constituencies the League created voters by buying up properties and installing Free Trade supporters in them as forty shilling freeholders, still qualified to vote under the Reform Act of 1832. Another aspect of the League's activity was to be found in Manchester: to prevent its meetings there from being broken up by hostile Chartists, it formed an alliance with the local Irish, who, armed with 'good blackthorn sticks', usually emerged victorious from the brawls which occurred.

But it was Parliament that had to be converted, and above all Robert Peel, the manufacturer's son who led the party of the landowners. When Peel took office in 1841 he pledged himself to maintain protection for 'the agricultural interest', the landowners and farmers

PAPA COBDEN TAKING MASTER ROBERT A FREE TRADE WALK.

PAPA COBDEN.—"Come along, MASTER ROBERT, do step out."
MASTER ROBERT.—"That's all very well, but you know I cannot go so fast as you do."

PUNCH'S MONUMENT TO PEEL.

whose representatives filled the benches behind him in the House of Commons. Yet it was plain from the budget of 1842 that he was moving towards Free Trade, and in that same year he modified the sliding scale of the Corn Laws in a direction unfavourable to the farmers. The Budget won him warm approval from the 'commercial interest', the merchants and manufacturers. Cobden and the League kept up the pressure with arguments to which Peel became increasingly sympathetic. It is clear that by 1845 he had changed his mind on the Corn Laws[1]. Yet it was not argument but a natural disaster that provided the occasion for their repeal. In the wet autumn of 1845 the English wheat crop failed and, far more catastrophic, the Irish potato crop was destroyed by blight. As the Irish starved and bread prices rose steeply in England, so opposition to the Corn Laws grew. To save Ireland by importing foreign grain, they would have to go. Once repealed they would never return.

In November 1845 Lord John Russell, who had taken over from Melbourne as Whig leader, announced his conversion to Free Trade.

Meanwhile the Conservatives were bitterly divided. Most of the ministers came to believe with Peel that the Corn Laws must go, whereas most of the rank and file remained staunchly Protectionist. So in December Peel resigned as Prime Minister, only to return to office when Russell found it impossible to form a government. In January 1846 Peel introduced a bill to repeal the Corn Laws, arguing that it would be in the interest of the nation as a whole to abandon them; to retain them would bring 'a desperate conflict between different classes of society.' It was fiercely debated, the Protectionists among the Conservatives seeing Peel as the betrayer of their principles and of their pockets. They found two strangely-contrasted leaders in Lord George Bentinck, a notable racing man who was so moved by Peel's 'treachery' that he sold his stud and devoted himself wholly to politics, and Benjamin Disraeli, a Jewish novelist, sore at Peel's failure to give him office. Grasping this chance of political triumph, the latter accused Peel of 'having caught the Whigs out bathing and walked away with their clothes.' Together they led a pack of Peel's former followers in hounding him. With the votes of the Whigs and of Cobden's supporters Peel eventually got Repeal through in June 1846. Defeated a few hours later on another issue by an alliance of Whigs and Protectionists, he resigned office at once. In his final speech, after a handsome tribute to Cobden as the man whose name ought to be associated with Repeal, he ended with the claim: 'It may be that I shall leave a name sometimes remembered with expressions of good will in the abodes of those whose lot it is to labour and to earn their daily bread by the sweat of their brow, when they shall recruit their exhausted strength with abundant and untaxed food'.

[1]There is a famous story of Peel, after listening to a speech by Cobden in a debate on the Corn Laws in 1845, crumpling his notes in his hand and saying to his front bench neighbour, '*You* must answer this, for *I* cannot'.

PEEL'S CHEAP BREAD SHOP,

OPENED JANUARY 22, 1846.

The Repeal of the Corn Laws was a turning point in British history. For Peel it was at once victory and defeat. He claimed to have put national needs before those of party, doing what Carlyle called 'a strenuous, courageous and manful thing' – but to most Conservatives it was a betrayal of pledges, a repetition of his conduct over the Catholic question in 1829. Although he remained in Parliament, he never again held office, dying unexpectedly in 1850 as a result of a riding accident. For the Conservative party, Repeal meant a disastrous split. Nearly all its leading men backed Peel, forming a small group known as the Peelites, most of whom later joined the Liberal party. The body of the party, though still numerous, did not again possess a majority in the Commons until 1874, when it did so under the leadership of the rebel of 1846, Disraeli.

For the nation as a whole, the effects of Repeal cannot be so straightforwardly assessed. The Act itself left small duties on imported corn for three years, and thereafter a registration duty of 1s. a quarter. Its immediate economic consequences were not entirely what its supporters had prophesied: bread prices did not fall steeply. Nor were British farmers ruined, as opponents had forecast; indeed, even though wheat imports rose considerably, Repeal was followed by thirty years of solid prosperity for British agriculture. Further, British business in general, and not least the exporting industries like textiles, was much more profitable in the thirty years after Repeal than it had been in the thirty years before. The evidence about working-class wages and conditions also indicates a general improvement. It is difficult not to believe that Free Trade and Repeal contributed to this by the stimulus they provided.

One wider comment may be made. The Corn Laws had become a kind of symbol of aristocratic misrule. Many of the supporters of Repeal, especially those in the middle and working classes in the North, saw Repeal as a second mighty blow at the power of the landed aristocracy. The first had been the Reform Act of 1832, which would, it was thought, deprive the landowners of political power by giving the right to vote to the middle class. Now, fourteen years later, the removal of agricultural protection would destroy their economic power. Such beliefs were shared by a great many landowners both in 1832 and in 1846. Neither belief was justified. After 1832, as before, the landed aristocracy continued to provide most of the members of the Cabinet and Parliament and of those who ruled national affairs. So too after 1846, as before, the landowners, greater and lesser, continued to prosper, at least for the next generation, and to dominate the country-side and to draw substantial incomes from it.

5
The first industrial nation

1 Victoria and Albert and the Great Exhibition

Victoria and
Albert

When William IV died in 1837 his successor was a girl of 18, the daughter of his deceased brother the Duke of Kent. (One consequence of this was the breaking of the link created in 1714 between the thrones of England and Hanover, where no woman could reign; William's most unpopular brother, the Duke of Cumberland, became its King.) After the bloated and immoral George IV and the obtuse and comic 'Silly Billy', Victoria brought to the monarchy a new style welcome to most British people. Coming, as Palmerston put it, 'from the nursery to the throne', she showed from the start determination and dignity: the former in shaking off her mother's attempt to continue to rule her life, the latter in dealing with elderly and worldly politicians. Deeply sincere in a simple Evangelical faith, on the first day of her reign she recorded in her *Journal* that 'very few have more real good will and more real desire to do what is fit and right than I have', and an immense sense of duty was to sustain her through her reign of sixty-three years. After her initial romantic dependence on 'dear good Lord Melbourne', she came to recognise that, whatever her personal feelings, she must as sovereign accept as Prime Minister only that politician whose government could secure a majority in the House of Commons, and admitted that she had behaved mistakenly over the Bedchamber Affair (p.52). Yet she was always to show prejudices about politicians. Thus she mistrusted Palmerston both for his reputation as 'Cupid' and for his anti-German foreign policy; fell an easy victim to the flatteries of Disraeli; and thought Gladstone at once ill-mannered and unpatriotic.

In 1839 she married Albert, a young prince from the minor German state of Saxe-Coburg, to whom she bore nine children in eighteen years. Her devotion to him was profound, and his death at the age of 42 in 1861 was a shattering blow. 'Albert the Good', serious-minded and immensely hard-working, himself did much to give the monarchy a new image. He made the Court respectable and efficient, getting rid of waste and scroungers, and insisting upon high moral standards in all appointments. Such activity, conducted by a young foreigner with little sense of humour, did not make him universally popular. Nor did his political role, active yet behind the scenes. He read all the state documents and gave his wife endless advice which she usually followed. He led her to appreciate Peel, yet encouraged her distaste for Palmer-

Queen Victoria and Prince Albert

ston. When the Crimean War began in 1854 there were widespread rumours, which had to be denied in Parliament, that he had been imprisoned in the Tower as a Russian spy. In fact his services to his adopted land were considerable, not the least of them coming just before his death in 1861, when he helped to avoid a war with the United States over the *Trent* affair (below, p.133).

The most famous of the Prince Consort's achievements was the Great Exhibition of 1851. This gave substance to his dream of a vast international display which would celebrate both science and work. The latest products of technology from the entire globe would be on view, and he believed that this spectacle would promote trade, industry, well-being, and peace between the nations. The Exhibition opened in Hyde Park on 1 May 1851, in a huge building of iron and glass swiftly nicknamed the Crystal Palace. Designed by Joseph Paxton, the Duke of Devonshire's head gardener and chief agent, it was 1848 feet long, 408 feet broad, and 66 feet high, tall enough to cover the great elms which grew in the park. The event, to which there had been much opposition, was a great triumph, attracting six million visitors

The Crystal Palace

The Crystal Palace

Inside the Crystal Palace – the Great Exhibition

One of the most popular items at the Great Exhibition – Delarue's patent envelope machine

from Britain and overseas during the 141 days on which it was open. The cost of admission was lowered from one pound to one shilling during that time, and the profits of over 100 per cent were used in building the Victoria and Albert and other museums at South Kensington. The 13,000 exhibits covered the whole range of contemporary industry and craftsmanship: among them were James Nasmyth's steam hammer, twenty-three of Joseph Whitworth's machine tools, Joseph Bramah's patent lock which had not been picked since he made it in 1784 (an American picked it after fifty-one hours on the job at the Exhibition), one machine which turned out 2,700 envelopes an hour and another which produced fifty medals a minute, musical boxes, Turkish carpets and Colt revolvers, fabrics and heavy furniture galore, and the largest porcelain dish in the world. The Great Exhibition was a mighty landmark of British material progress and an expression of the spirit of the age. The great majority of the prize-winners were British – though two notable American entries, the Singer sewing machine and the McCormick reaper, were omens for the future.

2 The coming of the railway

Early railways One of the most popular pieces on view at the Crystal Palace was a giant Great Western Railway express locomotive, the *Lord of the Isles*, designed by Daniel Gooch for the 7ft gauge. It symbolised the arrival of the railway as a universal means of travel (though Victoria and Albert had first travelled by train, from Slough to Paddington, in 1842). In 1839 there were only about 500 miles of railway track open to passenger use in Britain; by 1852, after the 'Railway Mania' of the 1840s, when hundreds of new railway companies promoted bills in Parliament, and scores actually began operations, there were almost 7500 miles. The railway had more far-reaching effects on the people of Britain than any other technological or social change of the nineteenth century. It linked country and town, port and hinterland, raw materials and factory, manufacturer and market, farmer and housewife, London and the provinces, far more quickly, firmly and profitably than any previous means of transport in human history. The people of mid-nineteenth century Britain were the first generation to enjoy its results in full measure, and its coming was a major event in the history of that time.

Daniel Gooch's *Lord of the Isles*

The origins of steam-driven railways go back before 1815, to the tale of William Murdock's model of 1784 appearing like the devil to a vicar in a Cornish lane, and to Richard Trevithick's locomotive hauling its five trucks at five miles an hour on an iron tramway near Merthyr Tydfil in 1804. But the major developments came after that date, and first among them were the two lines engineered by George Stephenson, the Stockton-Darlington of 1825 and the Liverpool-Manchester of 1830. The Stockton-Darlington line gave us the 4 ft. 8½ in. gauge which was to become universal on British lines. Yet the Liverpool-Manchester, the first fully public line, connecting two of the greatest commercial cities of the world, was the more important. The famous Rainhill Trials (1829) were conducted by its directors in order to find the best means of locomotion for the line, and were won by Stephenson's *Rocket* at the then incredible speed of 30 miles per hour, faster than any rate previously sustained by man. They aroused national excitement, and opened British eyes to the immense potential embodied in steam railways.

George Stephenson's *Rocket*

Both these lines were largely financed by local business men. The state played no part in the creation of Britain's railways, beyond requiring parliamentary approval for each proposed line. Development, thus left to private enterprise, was risky and costly. There was plenty of opposition, not least from the owners of canals and the trustees of turnpike roads, as well as from farmers convinced that their crops would catch fire from the sparks from the engines, doctors believing that tunnels would send people crazy, and university authorities sure that their students would be demoralised. Perhaps more important,

The major developments

83

most landowners were ready to charge exorbitant sums for the land the railway companies needed to buy. The 1830s, with the Reform Bill crisis and a spell of industrial depression around 1837, were not an encouraging time for investors. Nevertheless several major lines were started then, most notably the London to Birmingham (begun in 1834 by George Stephenson's son Robert) and the London to Bristol (built 1838–41 with Isambard Brunel as its engineer). But the great boom came in the 1840s, with a network of lines mainly radiating from London. By 1852 they extended to Plymouth, Southampton and Dover; to Yarmouth and to Hull; to Newcastle and Carlisle, Glasgow and Edinburgh; to Liverpool, Holyhead, Gloucester and Cardiff.

Isambard Kingdom Brunel (1806–59)

The consequences of this development, even as soon as the 1850s, were innumerable. Three are worth emphasis here. First, in their day railways were not unfairly called 'the greatest liberty man has taken

Brunel's Royal Albert Bridge (1859)

The Stockport Railway Viaduct (1842)

with nature'. Their cuttings and embankments, tunnels and bridges, wrought massive change in the landscape. Such works of these years as Brunel's Box Tunnel near Bath (1841) and Robert Stephenson's Britannia Bridge across the Menai Straits (1850) may serve as examples. Likewise by such buildings as the London termini like King's Cross (1852), the handsome main station at Newcastle-upon-Tyne (1850), or the viaduct of 1842 which strides across Stockport, they left their mark on townscapes. Secondly, their actual construction, carried out by gangs of 'navvies', successors to those who had earlier built the canals, was an astonishing achievement, done very largely with pick and shovel and wheelbarrow. It provided much-needed employment for many thousands, helping to overcome the industrial depression of the early 1840s. Thirdly, the challenge of railway building brought to the fore some remarkable men. George Stephenson (1781–1848), the miner's boy and self-taught engineering genius from Wylam in Northumberland, 'the father of the improved railway of modern times', was one. His son Robert (1803–59) was another: he designed the famous *Rocket*, engineered the London to Birmingham line, and built the Royal Border Bridge at Berwick-upon-Tweed. A third was the Stephensons' great rival, Isambard Brunel (1806–59), a many-sided genius, architect of Clifton Suspension Bridge and of pioneer steamships like the *Great Britain*. To railways he contributed the G.W.R. from London to Bristol; the wide – and, as he said, safer and more comfortable – 7 ft. gauge, eventually rejected by Parliament in 1846 in favour of Stephenson's 4 ft. 8½ in.; and the forward-looking yet unsuccessful vacuum-powered atmospheric railway in South Devon. A fourth, of world-wide renown, was Thomas Brassey (1805–70), the great contractor who made railways a leading item in Britain's export trade, selling rails and locomotives and installing railways throughout continental Europe, the Americas, India, and Australia.

St Pancras Station (1868)

More generally, railways quickly began to transform the daily life of millions of people. Partly this resulted from the stimulus they gave to industry and trade and so to employment, most notably in the coal mines and the ironworks. They were a vital element in the progress of British industry after about 1850, in making Britain 'the workshop of the world'. Yet also they changed habits and patterns of life in innumerable particular ways. For example, they helped make Rowland Hill's Penny Post a triumphant success; drove many canal-owners into ruin; started running excursions to the seaside[1]; created 'railway towns' like Crewe and Swindon; hastened the growth of suburbs, set new and fearful problems of rush-hour congestion in London and the big cities; and encouraged the establishment of boarding schools for the sons of the well to do. Perhaps the most far-reaching consequence of all is to be found in the comment of the Duke of Wellington (who never liked railways after seeing Huskisson fatally mangled at Rainhill), when he growled that they encouraged 'the lower orders to move about'.

3 The workshop of the world

Great Britain has been called 'the first industrial nation', meaning the first country in the world to develop modern power-driven industry as

Mid-nineteenth century Sheffield – an industrial city whose population quadrupled between 1821 and 1881

[1]And in 1851, most successfully, to the Crystal Palace.

the economic basis of its way of life. By the middle of the nineteenth century the British, using steam as the essential source of power, had taken an industrial revolution much further than any other nation. As the contents of the Crystal Palace demonstrated, Britain far outstripped her nearest competitors. The reasons for this are complicated. Yet certainly they do not include any elaborate scheme of state planning by far-sighted governments. The growth of British industry during the eighteenth and nineteenth centuries took place spontaneously as the consequence of individual decisions by many thousands of men.

James Nasmyth's steam hammer (invented 1839)

Circumstances which played some part in the process included the extraordinary growth of population shown in Tables 1 and 2, a rate of development quite unparalleled in British history, which provided both a reservoir of cheap labour and an expanding market for manufactures; the presence in parts of Britain of good supplies of coal, iron and water; the existence of a tradition of skilled craftsmanship, especially in the textile and metal industries; a liberal system of government, which in various ways favoured individual enterprise; and the world's strongest navy, which opened the high seas to British trade.

Between 1815 and the late 1840s trade and industry suffered much from depressions, as for example in 1815 and 1837, which brought in their wake the closing down of businesses, unemployment and disturbances in the industrial areas. But thenceforward until about the early

1870s times were in general prosperous, with, for most people, real gains in living standards, in food and clothing, housing and transport and leisure. Traditionally the Repeal of the Corn Laws in 1846 is often seen as the turning-point. Certainly Peel's policy of Free Trade, carried forward by later ministries, particularly by Gladstone in the 1850s and 1860s, did much to stimulate overseas trade. Yet there had also been highly important industrial developments in the earlier years, like James Neilson's hot blast (1829), which vastly increased the output of iron; Richard Roberts' self-acting mule (1830), which immensely accelerated the work of textile spinning; and James Nasmyth's steam hammer (1839), which made it possible to forge iron bars and plates far larger and more numerous than ever before. The statistics of trade and industry over the years before 1850 point to a great growth in production, especially in those branches of industry most directly influenced by the use of steam power. Between 1815 and 1852 Britain's output of textiles multiplied six-fold; of coal about three-fold; and of pig-iron about six-fold.

Table 1. Population of the United Kingdom, 1801–51 (in thousands)

	England & Wales	Scotland	Ireland
1801	8,893	1,008	—
1811	10,164	1,806	—
1821	12,000	2,092	6,802
1831	13,897	2,364	7,767
1841	15,914	2,620	8,175
1851	17,928	2,889	6,552

(Note: No satisfactory figures are available for Ireland until 1821)

Table 2. Rate of increase in the United Kingdom population, 1801–51

The figures below show the *percentage* increase in population at *ten-year intervals*: e.g., the figure 18.06 in the column headed 'England & Wales' and opposite the dates 1811–21 was the percentage increase during the ten years from 1811.

	England & Wales	Scotland	Ireland
1801–11	14	12.3	—
1811–21	18.06	15.8	—
1821–31	15.80	13.0	14.9
1831–41	14.27	10.8	5.25
1841–51	12.65	10.2	−19.85

Note particularly:
(a) the peak rate between 1811 and 1821
(b) the high, yet declining, rates in England and Scotland after 1821
(c) the remarkable behaviour of the Irish rates, especially the terrible *minus* figure for 1841–51.

By the mid-century Britain could fairly be called 'the workshop of the world', and during the next twenty-five years her export trade, as Table 3 indicates, went ahead by leaps and bounds. The main staples of this trade were textiles (above all cotton and woollen goods to the United States and India), iron and steel (including, e.g., railway lines, hardware and cutlery), machinery (whose export had been officially but not very effectively forbidden until 1843), and coal. British mills, foundries and mines were sending their produce to every part of the inhabited globe, from the established nations of Europe to newly-developing areas like the American West and New Zealand. The goods were being increasingly carried in British ships, especially after the development of the iron hull and the steamship. Ships and contents were insured at Lloyds of London, and the financial transactions involved carried out by British banks. London was the financial capital of the world. Moreover British investors with money to spare were increasingly investing it overseas – notably, for example, in railways in the U.S.A., India and the Argentine – and their income was added to the credit side of Britain's balance of trade. Meanwhile Britain's technical progress continued, marked by such inventions as Henry Bessemer's converter, which for the first time made bulk supplies of cheap steel possible, and William Perkin's discovery of mauve, the first synthetic dye, both dated 1856.

A casting operation in a mid-nineteenth century foundry

Table 3. Growth of Exports from the United Kingdom, 1840–79

The figures below (in £ millions) show the average annual *value of exports* for each of four periods of ten years.

	All Textiles	Cotton Goods	Iron and Steel	Machinery	Coal	Total of·all Exports
1840–9	38.6	25.0	8.2	0.8	0.9	55.4
1850–9	59.9	35.6	17.9	2.4	2.3	100.1
1860–9	98.5	57.6	24.0	4.6	4.5	159.7
1870–9	118.6	71.5	34.9	7.7	8.8	218.1

4 The countryside and farming

The industrial expansion just outlined was mainly centred upon towns, apart from coal-mining which continued to be a rural industry in areas like County Durham and the Rhondda. Yet Britain in the 1850s still remained very much an agricultural land. In 1841 the first census taken in Victoria's reign showed that over half her British subjects still lived in the countryside. Ten years later the balance had tilted the other way: of the 18 million people in Britain over one half were now town-dwellers. Yet agriculture still gave work to one-quarter of all employed males, and to more people than any other single industry in the land.

By 1850 the great enclosure movement, which had been at its peak fifty years before, was virtually over, and the pattern of hedged fields, the familiar landscape of the midlands and south of England, was established. The political conflict over the Corn Laws had been resolved in 1846 (pp.75–6). British landlords and farmers were no longer protected against imports of foreign corn. In fact, for nearly thirty years after Repeal they – like contemporary factory-owners and merchants – prospered. For this was the 'golden age of agriculture', marked by steady profits, technical improvements, and expansion of farms, their buildings and their equipment. In 1851 Britain was nearly self-sufficient in food production. External circumstances greatly helped British farmers at this time. The new railways widened their markets at home; while the Crimean War (1854–6) and the American Civil War (1861–5) cut off the threat of imports from the world's potentially biggest granaries, Russia and the United States. Moreover prosperity in industry, with steadier employment and rising real wages, brought prosperity to farmers, with people spending more on bread, meat and beer.

Yet within agriculture itself there were notable advances of various kinds from the 1840s onwards. Drainage was revolutionised by the coming of the mole plough and the invention of a new process for the

The Golden age

mass production of perforated pipes, and aided by government loans. Guano, potash and chemical manures, particularly superphosphate of lime, began to be widely applied. Steam threshing machines came into general use, and steam ploughs spread from Scotland. Experiments began with various machines, including reapers, mowers, horse rakes and harrows. These developments, backed in many places, though by no means universally, by enterprising landlords, led to a period of 'high farming' in which the majority of farmers did well, with rising incomes, bigger barns and more comfortable houses.

A steam driven threshing machine, about 1840

A demonstration of steam-ploughing, about 1851

The farm labourer, by contrast, usually had only a small share in this The labourer's lot prosperity, though his conditions of life varied of course from farm to farm, and also from one region to another: in particular he was substantially better off in the north of England, where wages were higher because alternative jobs were available in industry. For most agricultural workers hours were long (from 6 a.m. to 5 p.m. on six days a week, longer at harvest, shorter in winter), the work hard and tedious, and the wages lower than in industry. Child labour was common from about six years old: there were no Factory Acts to save small children from being sent out bird scaring or minding the sheep. Gangs of women and children were employed for little pay in jobs like weeding, stone-picking and muck-spreading; the Gangs Act of 1867 required gangmasters to be licensed, and forbade them to hire children under the age of eight. Rural housing for farm labourers, sometimes romantic from the outside with thatch and roses and usually less squalid than town slums, often enough consisted of overcrowded hovels and garrets, with leaking roofs and broken-down furniture. The system of the tied cottage left the labourer exposed to the threat of the workhouse if he was sacked by his employer. Poverty was general in English villages and the beerhouse commonly provided the farm labourer's main solace for his hard lot.

5 Towns and public health

Towns in Britain, as Table 4 (p.95) shows, grew fast during the first Cholera half of the nineteenth century. This was true of all towns, yet notably so of London and of towns in the newly-developing industrial areas of the north and midlands of England. Inevitably this rapid growth brought with it tremendous social problems on a scale never before known – of health and housing, law and order, education, and local government. The most fundamental and urgent was that of public health, dramatised in 1831 when for the first time an epidemic of Asiatic cholera – a disease mysterious in its origins, unknown to English doctors, killing with terrible swiftness – struck this country. The first death was reported at Sunderland in late October; by the end of June 1832, when the disease began to subside, there had been 22,000 more. This calamity sharply awakened concern about public health and hygiene, and the concern was strengthened by outbreaks of other diseases like typhus fever as well as of cholera (another epidemic of the latter in 1848–9 killed nearly 70,000). Also the evidence of population figures revealed not merely that the population was not increasing as fast in the 1830s as it had done in the first twenty years of the nineteenth century (Table 1, p.89); but also that the death rate was higher in towns than in the countryside – and far higher among the poor than among the well-to-do.

A great series of investigations, the first of their kind, followed in the Edwin Chadwick 1830s and 1840s. These were in great part promoted by Edwin Chadwick (1800–90), a sharp-minded, zealous north countryman, since 1834 the Secretary of the Poor Law Commissioners, the greatest public health reformer in our history. In particular Chadwick himself published (the government having been too timid to do so) a *Report on the Sanitary Conditions of the Labouring Population* (1842) which shook public opinion by its detailed demonstration that overcrowding, filth, bad drainage and inadequate water supplies not only brought disease and an early average age of death among the poor (22 for labourers as against 43 for gentry), but also led inevitably to drunkenness, crime, prostitution and vice. Peel's government was prompted into setting up a commission of enquiry into the *Health of Towns*, which published in 1844 and 1845 two Reports based on enquiries into sanitary conditions in a group of large industrial towns. These produced a horrifying picture of acres of close-packed slum dwellings with few and noisome privies, inadequate sewers, open drains and refuse accumulating in the streets, water available only from standpipes for an hour or two on stated days, pigs and rats roaming the alleys and courts and few or no public sanitary regulations. Many contemporary local investigations, in cities and small towns alike, confirmed the appalling tale of dirt, disease and public neglect – and the close connection between these three. Those of the swiftly-growing industrial centres (such as a famous and

Edwin Chadwick (1800–90)

controversial one by the German socialist Friedrich Engels) drew particular attention to the abominable conditions of working-class housing – the cellar-dwellings of Manchester, the back-to-back houses of Leeds, the jerry-building common in factory towns.

Table 4. Populations of British towns, 1801–51 (in thousands)

	1801	1811	1821	1831	1841	1851
London	1,088	1,259	1,504	1,778	2,073	2,491
Birmingham	71	83	102	144	202	264
Bolton	18	25	32	42	51	61
Bradford	13	16	26	44	67	104
Cardiff	2	2	4	6	10	18
Edinburgh	83	103	138	162	166	194
Exeter	17	19	23	28	31	33
Glasgow	77	101	147	212	287	363
Liverpool	82	104	138	210	299	395
Manchester	75	96	135	194	252	338
Oxford	12	13	16	21	24	28
Stockport	17	21	27	36	50	54

Note particularly:
(a) the huge size of London, with almost one-seventh of the entire population of England and Wales
(b) the great size, and rapid, steady increase, of the next group of cities, Glasgow, Liverpool and Manchester
(c) the contrasting developments of towns similar in size at the beginning of the century: e.g. of Bolton, Stockport and Exeter, or of Oxford and Bradford
(d) that only one of the towns in this table was less than twice the size in 1851 that it had been fifty years before (and then only slightly so), and that most of them were three or more times as great.

All this led to measures of reform in the 1840s and 1850s. At national level there was the first Public Health Act (1848), setting up a central Board of Health to supervise local boards whose task it would be to tackle the nuisances. The Act contained a number of detailed regulations about sanitation: e.g. all new houses were to have privies or water-closets, and no more cellars for living were to be built. But it was not very effective. Local boards were only compulsory where the death rate was more than 23 per 1000. They were furiously attacked by property-owners whose incomes and 'rights' were affected, and many

The First Public Health Act (1848)

achieved little. The central Board had little real power or money to spend, and survived only ten years. Chadwick was dismissed in 1854 (at the time of another cholera epidemic). He was tactless and dictatorial, and *The Times*, glad to see him go, said 'we prefer to take our chance of cholera and the rest than to be bullied into health.' Nevertheless in some great cities including London itself real improvements were started. 'Chadwick's Act' of 1848, like his propaganda for glazed and water-flushed drains, was to bring important results before long (pp.154, 211).

London traffic problems, mid-nineteenth century

6 The working-class movement

When we think of nineteenth-century industry we tend to have in our minds a picture of an early factory, a big barrack-like building of several storeys, placed by the side of a river or canal and filled to the rooftops with whirring and dangerous machinery and hundreds of men, women and children workers. During the century the factory did indeed become the most significant unit of employment – partly because of the problems it created as well as for its obvious advantages for several sorts of work. But we should remind ourselves firmly that factories were by no means universal around 1850, or indeed for many years after that. For most of the century they were largely limited to the textile areas, notably parts of Lancashire, the West Riding of Yorkshire and the Clyde Valley. In other highly important manufacturing districts, like Birmingham and the Black Country with its numerous metal trades or Sheffield with its cutlery, goods were made in small work-shops by independent masters with a handful of workmen. Factory 'operatives' or 'hands', as they were commonly known, were only a minority of the 'labouring poor' or 'industrious classes', as nineteenth century writers described those whom we call 'the working class'. In 1851, despite a big increase during the 1840s in the number of workers in cotton mills (the largest of the factory trades), the entire number of factory workers was only half that of the domestic servants and less than one-third of that of the agricultural labourers. In fact there were three times as many men, women and children at work in the non-mechanised industries as in all the power-driven ones put together (including coal miners as well as factory workers).

Coal miners. Ton Pentre, Rhondda. The price of cutting clean coal was 1s 5d (7p) per ton

Nevertheless the growth of factories during the nineteenth century coincided with the rise of an organised working class movement. For factories – plus the larger collieries and ironworks – threw workers together in great numbers as never before, and so enabled them to organise for united action. And harsh conditions of work led to the rise, especially during the 1830s and 1840s, of widespread demands for reform. We have already noted the Ten Hours Movement and the Factory Acts to which it opened the way (p.47); and seen how discontent with working conditions contributed to the political move-ment for the People's Charter (p.54). Two other forms of working-class self-help, very active around 1850 and of much significance in later years, deserve special mention. One was trade unionism, the other the co-operative movement, associated with Robert Owen on the one hand and the Rochdale Pioneers on the other.

The repeal of the Combination Acts (1824–5) (pp.26–7) made trade unions legal bodies, even though much of their effectiveness was limited by those clauses of the 1825 Act which forbade picketing and intimidation. During the next ten years many unions came into being. Their objectives were either to secure higher wages when trade was good or to fight against reductions when it was bad; or to prevent employers taking on unqualified workers, something happening widely as machinery was introduced, particularly in the textile industry. Most of these early unions consisted of skilled men, and were local affairs. A few, like the Spinners Union of 1829, were national bodies. All were short-lived, in view of employers' opposition and the existence of a large pool of unemployed.

The most famous of them was the Grand National Consolidated Trades Union of Great Britain and Ireland, which rose and fell in 1834–5. The G.N.C.T.U. was in reality mainly a London body, it apparently never had more than 16,000 paid-up members, and it survived only a very short time. It became historically famous partly because of its connection with Robert Owen (1771–1858), the so-called 'Father of English Socialism' and campaigner for social reform. He had run a celebrated cotton mill, using no child labour under the age of ten, at New Lanark on the banks of the Clyde. He had come to believe in co-operative communities, and had established one at New Harmony in the United States. This failed and Owen had come back to Britain in the 1830s, where he saw in trade unions a means of creating a 'new moral world' in which industry would be founded upon co-operative principles and capitalism would vanish. For a brief time he played a leading role in the G.N.C.T.U., trying to gather workers of every trade into its ranks, until both he and the more practical trade unionists grew tired of one another and parted company.

The case of the Tolpuddle Martyrs also became linked with the G.N.C.T.U. Some farm labourers of the Dorset village of Tolpuddle formed a union in 1833 and were admitted to membership at a ceremony where they swore secret oaths on the Bible. Melbourne's government, nervously recalling the Swing Riots of 1830 and suspicious of any unions, made an example of six of them by trying them under the Unlawful Oaths Act of 1797. They were sentenced to seven years transportation to Australia. There was a great public outcry, and after some years all the 'Martyrs' were eventually brought back to England. The affair helped to kill off the G.N.C.T.U., as did the use of 'the document', a statement agreeing never to join a trade union which many employers required their workers to sign on pain of dismissal.

In the early 1840s trade unions were overshadowed by Chartism, yet later in the decade they recovered ground, and by the 1850s there was in existence a group of well-organised trade unions of skilled workers, often called 'New Model Unions'. The typical example of these was the Amalgamated Society of Engineers (the A.S.E.), founded in 1851. It had a relatively high subscription of one shilling a week, and employed a full-time paid secretary. Its rules laid much stress on respectability, saying 'our object is not to do anything either indiscreet or illegal', and emphasised the benevolent side of its work. Its main aim was clearly to maintain the superior status of its members, as craftsmen rather than labourers; and its policy about strikes was usually – though not invariably – cautious. The secretaries of the A.S.E. and of several similar unions of craftsmen and artisans, e.g., the Carpenters and Joiners, the Bricklayers, and the Iron Founders, met together in what came to be known as 'the Junta' to discuss common problems and form a common policy, and this foreshadowed the Trades Union Congress, which first met in 1868.

About the same time as the New Model Unions were establishing themselves, another working-class movement of great influence in later years was taking root – the Co-operative Movement. In 1844 twenty-eight weavers from Rochdale, contributing one pound a head, opened a shop in Toad (T'owd) Lane in that cotton town. Their aim was to sell to their neighbours pure food and groceries at reasonable prices: this was a reaction against the adulterated food (e.g., flour mixed with chalk and sugar with sand) which was widespread. Robert Owen had tried, notably at his Labour Bazaar in the Gray's Inn Road in London, to develop producers' co-operatives, in which the goods made by members of a community were sold at prices based on the work put into them as well as on the cost of raw materials; he had little success. The 'Rochdale Equitable Pioneers', as the enterprising weavers called themselves, ran by contrast a consumers' co-operative. What made it

The Co-operative Movement

The Rochdale Pioneers – the founders of the Co-operative Movement

successful were the twin devices of the dividend on purchases, which could be collected annually, and the shares in which every member could invest. The Toad Lane shop prospered and the idea spread swiftly, especially through the textile areas. Out of it sprang (1863) the North of England Co-operative Wholesale Society, later to become the modern C.W.S., with its chain of shops and its factories, ships and bank, its concern with adult education, and its political link with the Labour Party.

6
Church, state and the individual in mid-nineteenth century Britain

1 Religion

Religion was a central feature of Victorian life, and its influence was probably at its greatest in the 1850s. Most people then accepted the Christian faith without any doubts; a majority were regular church or chapel goers, even though a very large number in London and the other big cities certainly never went inside a place of worship. New sects – including the Methodists, Plymouth Brethren, the Catholic Apostolic Church – won thousands of believers. For many, humble and eminent alike, religion was the dominant force in life, laying foundations both for everyday conduct and major social reforms. Through such outstanding men as Shaftesbury the social reformer and Gladstone the statesman, religious faith inspired some of the most notable of Victorian achievements. On the other hand, Victorian religion can also, from a later point of view, seem narrow in its beliefs and intolerant in its attitudes, not least in the hostility which Christians of different persuasions frequently displayed towards one another. Protestants were ready to denounce Roman Catholics on the slightest provocation; Anglicans and Dissenters quarrelled passionately over education and church rates; while within the Church of England 'High Church' and 'Low' treated one another with a mixture of contempt and abuse.

The Evangelical Movement is the name we give to a religious revival which arose in England in the late eighteenth and early nineteenth centuries. Strongest among the middle and upper classes, it was in part – like the Methodist Movement – a reaction against the slackness of the eighteenth-century Church of England; in part also it was a conscious response to the challenge contained in what seemed to be the evil and atheist ideas of the French Revolution after 1789. Its emphasis lay upon individual faith, upon Bible reading, family prayers and sermons, upon duty and strict moral conduct. Gradually during the first half of the nineteenth century it permeated clergy and laity alike, and transformed the way of life of the ruling class. Politicians were much influenced – not merely such men as William Wilberforce (1759–1833), who underwent conversion at 26 and became the champion of the negro slaves, but also Prime Ministers, like Lord Liverpool and the 14th Earl of Derby, who combined a passion for the turf with the writing of religious tracts for young children. Like the Queen herself, Evangelicals within the Church of England were 'Low Church', hostile to Rome

The Evangelical Movement

and to ritualism in services, yet friendly to dissenters; great fighters, too, for Sunday observance. Yet the Evangelical attitude of mind, austere and active in good causes, also governed the daily conduct of many 'High' Churchmen and of those rare mid-Victorians who rejected Christian beliefs.

In those days the churches drew into their service great numbers of the ablest and most sincere minds, and a good many of these spent their days labouring for the gospel in remote country parishes or, if they were dissenters (nonconformists, as we have come to call them), in the factory towns of the north. The outstanding Evangelical layman, the 7th Earl of Shaftesbury (1801–85), may serve to illustrate the movement at its strongest. A man of brilliant mind and fierce determination, the son of a Dorset landowner, denied love from his parents and disliking school, he found fulfilment of his Christian faith in an immense range of reforms to help the poor and the ill-treated. Known

Lord Shaftesbury (1801–85) reviewing the donkeys at the Annual Meeting of the Golden Lane Costermongers' Mission

as Lord Ashley until he inherited his earldom in 1851, his first prominence came from his leadership in parliament of the factory reform movement after 1833 – in itself achievement enough for many reformers. To it he added a campaign in the 1840s for the ending of child and female labour in the mines; a lifelong effort to civilise the treatment of lunatics; a prolonged struggle on behalf of 'climbing boys', the wretched child chimney sweeps; the establishment of the Ragged Schools and the National Refuges (later called the Shaftesbury Homes) for destitute children; and membership of the 1848 Board of Health. His famous meeting with four hundred thieves to discuss emigration, on behalf of the outcasts of London, is commemorated by the statue of Eros in Piccadilly Circus. Shaftesbury was no radical; he had no time for the Chartists or for Richard Cobden. He believed firmly in 'rank and property as gifts of God, bringing with them serious responsibili-

Lord Shaftesbury visiting the coal mines of the Black Country, 1840–2

ties'. Parliament's task was to make it possible for the working class to 'avail themselves of the opportunities of virtue, of morality and religion'. He revealed also the other sides of Evangelicism: he got postal services and the opening of the Crystal Palace stopped on Sundays, and he was bitterly hostile to ritualism. Often awkward and disagreeable, Shaftesbury was too able a man to be typical; yet he illustrates the immense power and range of Victorian Evangelicism.

We have already seen in the matter of Catholic Emancipation the role religious belief could play in politics. The 1830s provided further examples. They were a testing time for the Church of England. During the Reform crisis of 1830–2, bishops were very unpopular, for some of them were extremely wealthy and many were Tories and voted against the Reform Bill in 1831. That Fifth of November effigies of bishops replaced Guy Fawkes in the bonfires; for example, at Exeter the yeomanry guarded the bishop in his palace while outside the cathedral a howling mob burned his effigy, with a turnip for his head and a mitre on it. After the Act many churchmen expected the Whig government to carry out a sweeping reform of the Church of England, confiscating its endowments, abolishing pluralism (the simultaneous holding of more than one living), and disestablishing it so that it was no longer the official church of the whole nation. For the Whigs had always been sympathetic to dissenters (nonconformists), who traditionally voted for

The Church of England

103

them, and English clergymen feared the worst.

In fact nothing very drastic happened to the revenues or the powers of the Church of England. An Ecclesiastical Commission consisting mainly of bishops was set up to manage its property; bishops' stipends were to some extent levelled out; some sinecure posts were abolished, and more money was made available for poorer clergy. For many Anglican clergymen of the 1830s the main and most irritating problem lay in their relations with dissenters. The latter, stronger in Parliament than at any time since the days of Oliver Cromwell and demanding complete equality with the Church of England, pressed a range of practical grievances. As the law stood, Methodists, Baptists and the other dissenting bodies could have their births legally registered only in the parish church, and in most places had to be buried in the churchyard with the Anglican service. Quakers and Jews excepted (for whom special laws existed), marriage was legal only if conducted in the parish church. University degrees were open only to Anglicans. Most exasperating of all, every inhabitant of a parish, whatever his religion, had to pay rates to maintain the fabric of the parish church. This last requirement led to much bitterness all over the country. Parliament in the 1830s spent long hours debating these issues, which in the minds of many thousands of English people loomed far larger than the major 'Whig reforms'. In 1836 two related Acts changed the law about marriage and registration. They had three main terms. First, registrars of births, marriages and deaths were to be appointed throughout the country, and empowered to conduct civil marriages. Secondly, dissenting chapels could be licensed for marriages, which could be solemnised there in the presence of the registrar. Thirdly, Anglican parsons continued to act as registrars of marriages in their churches, but henceforward had to send copies of the registers to the official registrar. This compromise has remained law ever since. But no solution was found to church rates, the greatest grievance of all, until they were made voluntary in 1868, and the local conflicts, with brawls in church and forced sales of dissenters' goods to extort the rates from them, went on for another thirty years. Nor were dissenters admitted to degrees at Oxford and Cambridge until 1871.

At the same time as these quarrels with dissenters, a sharp conflict arose within the Church of England itself. In 1833 there was published at Oxford the first of a series of *Tracts for the Times*. It was written by John Henry Newman (1801–90), Fellow of Oriel College, Oxford, and Vicar of St. Mary's, the University Church. The aim of the *Tracts* was to awaken the Church of England to the need to fight for its independence in these days of Parliamentary reform, radicalism and threats of state interference. Anglicans should do so by emphasising that the Church of England, though now owing no allegiance to the Pope, was nevertheless still part of a universal Catholic Church. Newman and the other leaders of what came to be known as the Oxford

Cardinal Newman (1801–90)

Movement, John Keble and Edward Pusey, laid much stress also on the revival of the ancient ceremonies of the Church. Newman, a preacher of rare power whose sermons captivated many students, had much influence in Oxford. The movement at first spread fast, particularly among conservative 'High Churchmen', who believed that the Church of England was betraying its traditions and yielding too readily to the state.

But the Tractarians aroused suspicion and hostility among 'Low Churchmen' and also among moderate Anglicans – not because the latter were anxious to defend the state, but because they saw Newman and his friends as traitors to the Anglican Church, romanists in disguise – an appalling state of affairs at a time when perhaps 60 per cent of all Oxford's students took holy orders. A war of pamphlets broke out in Oxford, while clergy throughout the land divided into rival camps. Crisis came with the publication in 1841 of *Tract XC*, which appeared to most Anglicans to approve of the teaching of Roman Catholic doctrines in the Church of England. It was condemned by the university authorities, and Newman had to resign his Oxford posts. Evangelical suspicions seemed fully confirmed as Tractarians in some numbers joined the Roman Catholic Church – above all when Newman himself was converted in 1845. He was later (1864) to defend his conduct in a notable autobiography, his *Apologia Pro Vita Sua,* and eventually (1879) to become a Cardinal. The Church of England inherited from this crisis a legacy of disagreement between 'High Church' and 'Low Church' which from time to time has flared up in local disputes. In the nineteenth century, while a growing number of clergy tended to be 'High Church' or 'Anglo-Catholic' in outlook, most laity, like Queen Victoria herself, remained hostile to such beliefs and to the ritualism which accompanied them.

Roman Catholicism

Hostility to Roman Catholicism itself was deeply-based and widespread in nineteenth century Britain. A very large number of people thought Catholic practices and teachings, such as the Mass and the veneration of the Virgin Mary, sinful as well as absurd. Rumour greatly magnified the number of followers of the Pope in Britain (the reality in 1850 was perhaps 600,000). But the influx of tens of thousands of poverty-stricken Irish into such cities as Glasgow and Liverpool was sending it up fast, and caused much bad feeling. Itinerant Protestant preachers stirred up violence; in 1852 rioters in Stockport sacked two Catholic chapels in an Irish area of the town. In 1845 the increased grant to the Catholic seminary at Maynooth in Ireland provoked a great outcry, its opponents saying 'we are fighting anew the battle of the Reformation'. Five years later came a noisier storm, when in September 1850 Pope Pius IX announced the establishment of thirteen Roman Catholic bishoprics in England, one of them being the Archbishopric of Westminster, whose holder was made a Cardinal, the first in England since the reign of 'Bloody Mary' Tudor. The uproar this created was encouraged by a letter from the Prime Minister, Lord John Russell, describing the 'Papal aggression' as 'insolent and insidious' and talking of Catholic (and High Anglican) practices as 'mummeries of superstition'. The letter was published on 4 November, and the next day millions of English people burned guys of the Pope, the Cardinal of Westminster and Roman priests with great relish. Parliament in 1851 was persuaded to pass an act forbidding the use of any ecclesiastical titles attached to places in England, except by clergy of the state church. The act was never enforced, and was repealed twenty years later.

'Papal aggression' was never a very serious affair in reality. A greater challenge – to all Christians, Catholic or Protestant – was in the making in the 1850s. Around the beginning of the nineteenth century the biblical account, in the book of Genesis, of the making of the world was generally accepted as true. In 1830 Sir Charles Lyell had written *The Principles of Geology,* which argued that the evidence from changes in the earth's crust, whether by violent earthquakes or by the slow wearing away of rocks, suggested that the earth had been created over a far longer period than the Bible indicated. In 1859 Charles Darwin (1809–82), a naturalist whose father had once said to him 'You care for nothing but shooting, dogs and rat-catching, and you will be a disgrace to yourself and all your family', published what was perhaps the most significant book of the nineteenth century, *The Origin of Species*. This short book, based on twenty years' study, put forward a theory of evolution which used the evidence of biology to show that man had not been separately created by God, and thus demolished the literal truth of the biblical record. The controversy which followed went far to destroy the confidence at the heart of Victorian religion.

2 Education

To begin to understand English education at the middle of the nineteenth century we need to forget most of the ideas and practices we now take for granted. For there was at that time no national system of education open to all. The state gave no money for schools before 1833; locally-elected boards to provide schools did not come until 1870. Elementary education did not become compulsory until 1880, or completely free until 1891. Moreover it was almost universally assumed that education for the well-to-do should be entirely different from that provided for the poor. 'Secondary education' meant in fact fee-paying schools for the middle and upper classes, and at its heart was a study of the classics of Greece and Rome. Education for 'the labouring poor', where it existed, involved elementary Bible study and 'the three Rs' (Reading, Writing and 'Rithmetic), and usually stopped at the age of 10 or 11. Attendance was very irregular, and a child's school life was probably three or four years at most.

Schools for the poor were of immensely varying kinds and standards. Anybody could open a school, and all sorts of people did so – among them pious ladies and devoted vicars, cobblers and ex-seamen, factory owners and coal miners, Chartists, cripples and poor widows. The Whig M.P. and historian Macaulay, in a speech of 1847, was not exaggerating the worst type of school when he spoke of 'the wretched education of a common day school ..... a room crusted with filth, without light, without air, with a heap of fuel in one corner and a brood of chickens in another; the only machinery of instruction a dog-eared spelling book and a broken slate; the masters the refuse of all other callings, discarded footmen, ruined pedlars, men who cannot work a sum in the rule of three, men who cannot write a common letter without blunders, men who do not know whether the earth is a sphere or a cube, men who do not know whether Jerusalem is in Asia or America'. At the opposite extreme was the school run from 1842 by Richard Dawes, a Cambridge don who had become Rector of the poverty-stricken village of King's Somborne in Hampshire. His purpose in teaching was to make children 'think and reason about the objects around them' and 'to bring their minds to bear on the everyday work of life'. So he taught science by observation and experiment in the countryside (his pupils worked out the velocity of the wind by watching the shadows cast by clouds over the meadows); grammar was related to daily life and crafts, history to local remains, geography to globe, magnetic compass, and local relief models. The School had a well-patronised lending library. Fees were charged according to the parent's ability to pay. The number of pupils rose from 38 in 1842 to 219 in 1850, when Dawes moved on to be Dean of Hereford.

The monitorial system in action

The societies and the monitorial system

In quality most schools fell between these extremes. Sunday Schools, started in the 1780s, still provided all the teaching thousands of children got. There were many 'dames' schools', often little more than child-minding places while mothers worked in the mills. A few factory owners built schools, like Robert Owen at New Lanark or the Strutts at Belper in Derbyshire. The most important change in elementary education in these years came through two religious societies specially founded to provide schools for the poor. These were the National Society for Promoting the Education of the Poor in the Principles of the Established Church, an Anglican body set up in 1811, and the undenominational British and Foreign Society of 1814. Each made use, with slight variations, of the same plan of teaching and class organisation, the monitorial system. Indeed, the two societies backed rival 'inventors' of the system: the British and Foreign took it over from the Quaker Joseph Lancaster, who had used it in London since 1798, while the National Society supported Dr. Andrew Bell, a clergyman who had tried it out in Madras about the same time. It was peculiarly appropriate to the dawning factory age. One teacher taught older boys called 'monitors' who in turn taught groups of younger boys, all in one great room. The teaching was mechanical, and children spent most of their time learning meanings and spellings by rote; the noise was tremendous; an elaborate pattern of rewards and punishments ranged from medals and merit tickets to suspension in a basket and confinement in a dark closet. Nevertheless the system was cheap and catered for large numbers of children, and was widely used until about 1850.

Thoughtful people were finding many reasons for concern about the education of the poor. One obvious one was the very large numbers of children: even in 1851, when their proportion was falling off, the United Kingdom contained 7,300,000 children under 14 years old (35 per cent of the total population). Yet the main motives came from other sources, and religion was probably the most powerful. The Evangelical Revival stressed the need to enable the poor, notably by instruction in the Bible, to resist the atheistic doctrines set free by the French Revolution. In the years of disturbance after Waterloo, this attitude merged easily with the belief that education was socially desirable. It encouraged habits of piety, industry and obedience among 'the lower orders'; though there were many who took an opposite view, that all education was dangerous, for it might open the minds of the poor to radical ideas. Right on into the 1840s indeed it was widely argued that good schooling was essential in order to maintain law and order. Macaulay, for example, in the speech already quoted, laid the blame for the Luddites and the Swing Riots, the Reform Bill riots in Nottingham and Bristol, and the Chartist outbreak at Newport, on 'the gross ignorance of the common people', and proclaimed it the duty of the government to 'take care that the common people shall not be grossly ignorant'.

By then the state had taken some hesitant steps to intervene in education. Stimulated no doubt by the Great Reform Act, the Whig government had in 1833 made the first government grant to schools, a sum of not more than £20,000, to be divided between the two religious societies (not equally: the National Society, which had far more schools, got the lion's share). It was to be spent only on buildings, and money was to be given only where local voluntary contributions raised an equal amount. Six years later Melbourne (who had little belief in education; he once said to the Queen 'I do not know why there is all this fuss about education. None of the Paget family can read or write, and they do very well') allowed his government to set up in 1839 a committee of the Privy Council to supervise education. The government took over from the two societies the distribution of the grant, and inspectors ('Her Majesty's Inspectors', universally known as 'HMIs') were appointed to see that it was properly spent. In these two events of the 1830s lay the start of state intervention in English education. In 1839 the grant went up to £30,000, and by 1850 it was £125,000.

From the start HMIs were active in trying to improve standards of teaching as well as of school buildings. A pupil teacher system was launched, whereby bright older pupils became apprentices to head teachers. Yet the main responsibility for founding and running schools

State Education

H.M. Inspectors

109

remained with private individuals and organisations, most notably with the churches, who did much in various ways (e.g. by opening teacher training colleges) – but also quarrelled vigorously with each other about what should be taught. Most Englishmen at this time did not want the state to take over the task of schooling their children, and some were violently hostile, like the Somerset vicar who wrote to the local HMI saying 'I love you very much; but if you ever come here again to inspect, I lock the door of the school and tell the boys to put you in the pond.'

Yet many were growing convinced that in education as in matters like health voluntary effort could no longer cope. In 1858 the government appointed the Newcastle Commission to report what should be done for 'the extension of sound and cheap elementary education to all classes of the people.' Its principal result was the adoption in 1862 of a Revised Code of Education, including a new system of paying grants known as 'Payment by Results'. Henceforward two-thirds of a school's grant was to depend on the performance of its children at the annual examination conducted by the visiting HMI. Robert Lowe, the minister responsible, said of the new system 'If it is not cheap it shall be efficient; if it is not efficient it shall be cheap.' Certainly it saved money during the thirty years it lasted; certainly a higher proportion of English children learned at least the elements of the three Rs than before. But many contemporaries, including leading HMIs like Matthew Arnold, thought that it encouraged many teachers to do little more than the elementary mechanical work needed to get as many children as possible through the examination.

Secondary Education

The story of secondary education, of schools for the sons and daughters of the middle and upper classes, was very different. Here it was not just a matter of creating schools where there were none, but also of reviving those that had fallen into decay. In the early nineteenth century most of the old-established English and Welsh grammar schools, since the fifteenth and sixteenth centuries the traditional schools for the town middle classes, had fallen into a parlous state of decay. With few pupils or none at all, headmasters drawing their stipends but doing no teaching to earn them, and endowments embezzled or converted to other uses by town councils, their long history seemed to be reaching its end. The age of reform of the 1830s, however, brought recovery to them as it did to town councils. Often new boards of trustees were set up to govern them. The growing wealth of middle class Victorians, notably of merchants and professional men, gave them financial security by paying their fees. By mid-century many were firmly re-established. At the same time demand for education was great enough to lead to the opening of numerous private schools, profit-making or philanthropic. Some certainly were dreadful establishments, like the fictional Dotheboys Hall of Dickens' *Nicholas Nickleby*, with its headmaster Whackford Squeers and his instruction

'W-i-n-d-e-r, winder, go and clean it'. Others, like the real schools Hazelwood and Bruce Castle run by Rowland Hill (the future pioneer of postal reform) and his family, set high standards and experimented in teaching methods. Taken together such places taught at least as many children as the grammar schools.

For the Public Schools, the boarding schools patronised by the rich, the first half of the nineteenth century was a period of great progress. At its start most had been in poor shape, a condition illustrated by such episodes as the mutinies at several of them, e.g. at Winchester, where in 1818 troops had to be called in. But by its end they were flourishing as never before: full of boys, transformed in academic and moral standards, in foreigners' eyes the supreme feature of English education, producing the great majority of those who attained high rank in church and state. The leading figure in this change was Thomas Arnold (1795–1842), the headmaster who between 1828 and 1842 made Rugby School the outstanding school in the country, the one on which many new ones were modelled in the 1840s and 1850s. The success of Arnold, an immensely energetic and sincere though rather unorthodox Christ-

The Public Schools

Dr Arnold of Rugby (1795–1842)

ian, rested upon personal qualities like the force of his sermons, his power as a teacher of the Classics and History, and his appeal to his Sixth Form boys. One of these, Thomas Hughes, in his novel *Tom Brown's Schooldays* (1857), drew a remarkable portrait of Arnold as a teacher and a source of 'faith in and loyalty to Christ'. Arnold's influence was inevitably exaggerated, by others as well as by Hughes. There were other eminent headmasters during the nineteenth century, some of them Arnold's former colleagues and pupils. Such elements in the Public School system as the separate 'houses' and the prefects existed before him elsewhere than Rugby. And he was not very interested in the organised games which became a central feature of Public School life in the 1860s. Nevertheless his legacy to English life was extraordinarily deep and lasting.

The most notable change of all in English secondary schooling in these years remains to be mentioned – the beginnings of good quality secondary education for girls. Almost without exception such girls' secondary education as existed between 1800 and 1850 was bad – limited to 'accomplishments' like embroidery, dancing, and 'deportment'; rarely making any serious attempt at developing the mind; notably snobbish and commonly expensive. Change began in the 1840s, starting with the foundation of Queen's College in London for the training of teachers. In the 1850s two of its former students became headmistresses: Dorothea Beale of Cheltenham Ladies' College (1858), and Frances Mary Buss in 1850 of a private school in Camden Town which later (1871) became the North London Collegiate School. Both were determined that girls should have as full an opportunity of a good academic education as their brothers, and both were energetic and formidable personalities who dedicated long lives to their schools and to the education of girls. Miss Buss as the head of a day school which drew

Miss Frances Buss (1827–94)   Miss Dorothea Beale (1831–1906)

its girls from a wide social range had immense long-term influence on the pattern of girls' education in England. She deliberately used the system of public examinations (the Oxford and the Cambridge 'Locals', the direct ancestors of GCE, were founded in 1857–8) to demonstrate that girls were as intelligent as boys, a truth not very palatable to many Victorians; and she played a prominent part in founding the Girls' Public Day School Trust (1872). By the year of her death, 1894, there was in vigorous existence a group of girls' grammar schools of high academic standards.

In 1815 there were only two universities in England, Oxford and **Universities** Cambridge. They were open only to Anglicans. The range of their studies was virtually limited to Classics and Mathematics. Little knowledge was required for a degree, and examinations were something of a farce. The teaching was dull and slack. Fellowships at colleges were often limited to 'founders' kin' or to particular regions of the country. Many students spent much of their time in field sports, gambling and drinking. Thus the need for reform was plain, and in some ways it had already made a modest beginning. In particular, the Evangelical Revival was encouraging higher standards of personal conduct and a concern for social problems. By the middle of the century, change had come in two different ways – one, the effective reform of the two older universities, the other the foundation of new ones.

At Oxford and Cambridge improvement came partly from within, in the form of more effective examinations, increased devotion to learning at some colleges, and better lecturing by some professors; partly from outside, in Acts of Parliament (1854 for Oxford and 1856 for Cambridge) which led in particular to the opening up of college fellowships to real competition (among other things, by abolishing the rule that practically all fellows had to be in holy orders), and to an efficient system of government for the two universities. In effect, this meant that the resources – in cash and brains – of the two ancient universities might now be mobilised to play a far more effective role in English education and life.

The development of new universities was a sign of dissatisfaction with the old ones. University College, London, which had no religious test for admission and so was nicknamed 'the godless institution in Gower Street', was opened in 1828; King's College, London, followed in 1829 as an Anglican reply. In 1836 the University of London was formed, at first merely as a degree-granting institution. In 1833 the University of Durham opened its doors to 'nineteen young gentlemen'. The year of the Great Exhibition (1851) brought another kind of pointer to the future – the foundation of Owens College in Manchester out of a legacy of £93,000 from a radical nonconformist merchant. This, the first such institution in a great industrial city and the first to lay particular emphasis on science in its studies, was the nucleus of the later University of Manchester.

3 Government and people

By the middle years of the nineteenth century it was clear that British life was changing fast. New-built farmhouses, smoking factory chimneys, the railways and their ceaseless traffic, the iron-hulled steamers with their funnels; the new public buildings of the great northern cities, like St. George's Hall in Liverpool and the Free Trade Hall in Manchester; London's endless outward surge of bricks and mortar to Hammersmith, St. John's Wood and Kentish Town, Limehouse and Deptford, Brixton and Clapham – here were the visible marks of growth and change. They were signs of a nation becoming richer in wealth as well as bigger in population: richer than any country had ever been in human history, and easily the richest nation of the day, with an average income per head in 1860 about fifty per cent greater than that of France and well over twice that of Germany. Yet every thoughtful Englishman also realised that this change had brought with it huge social disorders of the kinds noticed earlier in this book – poverty and unemployment and industrial depression, with dire problems of health and housing, law and order and education. None of these was new, yet size and technical progress had given them new shape and greater scale.

Laissez-faire **and industrialism** What part was government, central and local, to play in solving these problems? To us in the second half of the twentieth century this appears a meaningless question, for we take it for granted that

Leeds Town Hall (1858)

114

governments exist in great part for this purpose. But most Englishmen about 1851 thought and felt quite differently. In economic matters the doctrine of *laissez-faire* (p.18) was strong. The less state regulation of these, the better. Free Trade and the Repeal of the Corn laws (1846) provide a supreme example. Others included the ending of laws prohibiting the emigration of skilled workers (1825) and the export of machinery (1843), and the repeal in 1849 of the Navigation Acts which had confined the long-haul carrying trade to British shipping. More generally, the early Victorians had a confident belief in individual liberty and independence. In the words of Samuel Smiles' best-seller *Self Help* (first published in 1859, it sold 250,000 copies by 1900), 'The spirit of self-help is the root of all genuine growth in the individual. National progress is the sum of individual energy and uprightness, as

Samuel Smiles (1812–1904)

national decay is of individual idleness, selfishness and vice.' It seemed to follow that state aid to the poor, like excessive private charity, was demoralising, making them unfit for the competition of life. The keys to success lay in hard work, thrift, and initiative. Freedom itself would be threatened by state help: as one champion of voluntary schools put it in 1856, 'the more people are taught to depend upon the government, the feebler becomes their love of liberty.'

Yet by the time these words were spoken the state had in fact taken on a wide range of responsibilities. Especially since the Reform Act of 1832 government was interfering considerably in the lives of individual people. No doubt the most important reason for this – in such matters as police, education, and the poor law – was fear of the lower classes, notably in the days of the Chartists. Well-organised campaigns by pressure groups also brought government action.

The most successful of these were Daniel O'Connell's Catholic Association, the Anti-Slavery Movement and the Anti-Corn Law League. Much seems to have happened as a result of urgent need to deal with particular problems, like that of the children opening and closing doors in the darkness of the pits or the threat of smallpox epidemics. Some of the various reforms no doubt owed something to the ideas of the legal reformer Jeremy Bentham (1748–1832), who wished to apply to each institution the test 'what use is it?', and whose followers were therefore called Utilitarians. The most notable of them in practice was Edwin Chadwick, whose part in Poor Law and Public Health Reform we have seen (pp.48–50, 93–6).

The coming of Government action

The Whigs in the 1830s and Peel's Conservatives in the 1840s greatly extended government interference in the life and work of citizens. Between them they imposed regulations upon working hours and conditions in textile factories and mines, upon the building and running of railways, and upon the conduct of banks; set up new patterns of poor relief and of local government; extended police forces outside London and reorganised prisons; created a new system of registration of births, marriages and deaths, abolished tithes, and reshuffled the finances of the Church of England. Laws of the later 1840s dealt with police in towns and with public health. During the 1850s the laws passed were perhaps less important, but the matters they dealt with ranged ever wider. They included the adulteration of food, the treatment of servants and apprentices, industrial schools, the organisation of the universities of Oxford and Cambridge, limited liability in business, divorce, the qualifications of doctors, the removal of nuisances, common lodging houses, reformatories and compulsory vaccination. Such laws were attempts to keep up with the demands for a fast-growing community. Clearly not all these laws protected the poor or weak or interfered with individual rights or property, but a good many of them did one or both of these things.

Civil Servants

Certainly all of them required people to enforce them, to see that their details were carried out. Here were the seeds of one of the most important practical developments of the nineteenth century – the rise of an efficient civil service and at local level of local government service. At national level this meant the gradual creation of a body of full-time permanent officials. Some were at Whitehall as the government's offices near the Houses of Parliament came to be known. Others were at work throughout the country, like the Factory Inspectors first appointed in 1833, Chadwick's assistants in the Poor Law, and the School HMIs from 1839 onwards. Whereas in the 1820s the total staff of the Home Office was seventeen, by mid-century there was a well-established civil service. The Northcote-Trevelyan Report of 1853 recommended the selection of civil servants by competitive examination, instead of by the previous method of patronage which had only too often 'provided the higher aristocracy with a sort of foundling hospital for their waifs and strays, their sons legitimate and illegitimate.' In 1855 the Civil Service Commission was set up to reorganise the methods of entry. The disasters of the Crimean War and the incompetence they revealed in the War Office stimulated reform; so did Charles Dickens' novel *Little Dorrit* (1857), with its satirical account of the Circumlocution Office and its family of Officials, the Tite-Barnacles.

At local level, as the councils which developed after the Municipal Reform Act (1835) began to provide services, so they began to appoint officials. Many of the laws passed were 'permissive': local authorities were not compelled to apply them but could do so if they wished. The need was most urgent in the great industrial cities, and in matters of police and health. The first Medical Officer of Health was appointed in Liverpool, in 1847. During the 1850s pressure from the central government increased, compelling local authorities to take action. Thus in 1856 the Nuisances Removal Act made them appoint sanitary inspectors, while the County and Borough Police Act obliged every county or borough to set up a police force. Here were the modest beginnings of a system soon to be seen as essential to a civilised British community.

7
The age of Palmerston 1846-65

1 Party divisions and ministries

Whigs, Peelites
and Radicals vs.
Tories In the thirty years following Waterloo there had been three important
issues on which Whigs and Tories sharply divided – Catholic Emancipation in 1829, the Reform Act in 1832, and the Repeal of the Corn
Laws in 1846. On each issue the Tories had had to give way, and twice,
in 1829 and 1846, the party itself had been seriously split. In the twenty
years after 1846, however, there was no urgent demand for major
controversial changes. There were still extremes of great poverty and
great wealth, but the middle class and the skilled working class were
prospering, and the latter, though they had no vote, gave up political
movements like Chartism and turned to economic self-help. The
unskilled working class, desperately poor, with no vote and now no
natural leaders, had to rely on reformers like Shaftesbury and Fielden
to plead their cause. In politics it was a time of confused party divisions.
On the one side there were the aristocratic Whigs led by Russell and the
ex-Tory Palmerston, and to them were somewhat unwillingly allied,
after Peel's death in 1850, the Peelites under Aberdeen and Gladstone
as well as middle-class Radicals such as Cobden and Bright. In the
middle there was a group of about fifty Irish M.P.s, as yet politically
powerless. On the other side there was the Conservative rump which
had unsuccessfully defended the Corn Laws. Led by Derby, Bentinck
and Disraeli, they had, by 1852, accepted Free Trade, and, by 1865,
were even prepared to extend the franchise. For much of the period the
big questions of the day were in foreign policy rather than in domestic.
The nearness of the parties to each other, indeed the whole spirit of this
twenty years, was epitomised in the person of Palmerston. In an age
when all the main politicians seemed to dislike working with each
other, when party discipline was loose, and when the ideas of Liberalism and Conservatism were still being worked out, Palmerston was
indispensable. It was he who brought together men of such differing
views as Russell, Gladstone and Bright in the first Liberal cabinet of
1859. Yet he was so opposed to further parliamentary reform that
Derby offered him a cabinet post in a Conservative government. Once
he had gone, parties and principles polarised, and once again large
issues were bitterly fought over by two clearly opposed sides.

Between 1846 and 1865 there were six administrations, several of
which had no real working majority. Russell's Whig ministry lasted

Lord John Russell, later Earl Russell (1798–1878)

from 1846 to 1852. When, to Queen Victoria's delight, he dismissed Palmerston from the post of Foreign Secretary, Palmerston led a vote of censure on the government within weeks and brought it down. He wrote to his brother 'I have had my tit for tat with John Russell and I turned him out on Friday last'. Derby formed a Conservative protectionist government with 310 seats against 270 Whigs, 40 Peelites and 40 Irish, but Disraeli's budget was so successfully attacked by Gladstone that this government was out in nine months. In December 1852 Aberdeen formed a Coalition ministry of Whigs and Peelites which included Palmerston as Home Secretary and Gladstone as Chancellor of the Exchequer. Prince Albert reported, no doubt cheerfully, when the new Home Secretary took his seals of office, 'Lord Palmerston looked excessively ill and had to walk with two sticks from the gout'. If he and Victoria thought that their old enemy was no longer a serious candidate for the post of Prime Minister, they were to be disappointed. Aberdeen's government blundered into the Crimean War and, once in, mismanaged its conduct. In September 1855 Aberdeen resigned. The Queen sent first for Derby, then for the seventy-five year old Lord

Lansdowne, then for Russell, but none of them could form a government. The choice of Palmerston became inevitable. Public opinion demanded a successful end to the war and saw Palmerston as the only man who could provide it. He had already made his reputation through his foreign policy. The middle class approved of his expansion of overseas markets and of his protection of British interests; the working class approved of his encouragement of liberal movements abroad. He was immensely popular with almost everyone except the Court and his colleagues, and so, for the remaining ten years of his life, the 'Whiskered Wonder', as some of his supporters called him, was willingly accepted as Prime Minister, even though he was known to be the main hindrance to further parliamentary reform. Had there been a working-class electorate in his lifetime it would almost certainly have voted him in with a huge majority. As it was, when he decided to go to the country in 1857, a general election gave him the biggest majority a party leader had won since 1832, with 85 more seats than all his opponents. An ill-advised attempt to pass the Conspiracy to Murder bill in 1858 ending his first ministry, but the Conservatives under Derby were again unable to hold office for more than a few months. In 1859 he began his second ministry, this time with Russell as Foreign Secretary and Gladstone at the Exchequer, and he remained in power until 1865. He won the general election of that year but died at the age of 81 before he could take office. His last delirious words were 'That's Article 98; now go on to the next'.

2 Domestic reforms: Gladstone at the Exchequer

When Free Trade ceased to be the main domestic issue after 1852, the most far-reaching reforms at home were those carried out by Gladstone as Chancellor of the Exchequer. Gladstone was born in 1809, the son of a wealthy Liverpool merchant, and he became a landowner with large estates at Hawarden in North Wales. He began his political career in 1832 as Tory member for the rotten borough of Newark and served his apprenticeship at the Board of Trade in Peel's ministry of 1841–6. He admired Peel both as a man and as a financier, and approved of his policy of making the country 'cheap for living' and of using his budgets to stimulate trade and industry. He went further than Peel. He felt that all individuals should be given the greatest possible freedom and encouragement to help themselves, and that it was the government's task to create opportunities for this self-help. In his view, there were three major obstacles to be avoided – war and the preparations for war, which were not only costly but morally wrong; wastage of public money by government departments; and the stifling of trade and industry by tariffs. His watchword was to be Peace, Retrenchment and Tariff Reform.

As Chancellor from 1852–55 and again from 1859–65, he produced a series of fiscal reforms which he himself in later life considered his greatest achievement. To raise revenue he kept duties on a small range of widely used goods such as tea, beer and tobacco. To reduce the cost of living he cut direct and indirect taxation in the hope that money 'should fructify in the pockets of the people.' By 1860 the total number of articles carrying any significant tax was down to sixteen and the duties on tea, sugar and dairy produce had been steadily lowered. By including, for the first time, all financial measures in one budget in 1861 he forced the House of Lords to accept the repeal of the paper duties and so made possible a popular press. The Commercial Treaty with France in 1860, which Cobden negotiated for Gladstone, was typical of the whole policy. Britain dropped the duties on French manufactured goods and reduced those on French wine and brandy; in return, France reduced duties on a wide range of British goods including coal, steel, tools and machinery. 'At a small loss in revenue' said Gladstone 'we have gained a great extension of trade.' Free Trade was now virtually complete, and remained so until 1932.

Gladstone also hoped to lower income tax from the 1853 level of sevenpence in the pound and to do away with it by 1860. The Crimean and China Wars and the two million pounds which Palmerston insisted was spent on fortifying the south coast made this impossible, but at least it was down to fourpence by 1865. Meanwhile he attacked government extravagance with the same enthusiasm as he chopped down trees on the Hawarden estate. He was prepared, he said, 'to save candle ends and cheeseparings in the cause of the country.' Like Ireland from 1868 and the Bulgarians in 1877, economy became a cause that he fought for like a crusade. His hope that this example would encourage thrift among the poor was shown by his creation in 1861 of the Post Office Savings Bank, the forerunner of modern National Savings. Any Chancellor who steadily reduces taxation becomes a popular politician, and Gladstone's reputation was high at the very time when Palmerston's was fading. Palmerston himself was unhappy about the future, saying, 'Gladstone will soon have it all his own way, and whenever he gets my place, we shall have strange doings.'

Other important reforms at this time were passed through Parliament largely through the influence of Ashley, later Lord Shaftesbury, and John Fielden. First Fielden, in 1847, secured the passage of the Ten Hours Act which reduced the working day for women and children in mills to ten hours. Employers soon got round the spirit of the Act by working women in relays so that mills could be kept open longer and the men's day would be longer. Shaftesbury, who had been fighting for factory reform for over twenty years, persuaded Parliament to stop the relay system in the Acts of 1850 and 1853, though the maximum working day was now fixed at ten and a half hours. Shaftesbury, as well as being a great humanitarian, had the advantage of being related to

Palmerston by marriage. He gained the latter's help in 1861 in setting up a Children's Employment Commission which exposed the terrible conditions in such industries as the potteries, where children of six worked fifteen hours a day, and the match industry where women workers developed 'phossy jaw' from contact with the chemicals. As a result, Factory Acts of 1864 and 1867 attempted to give some protection to those who were being so cruelly exploited. Many other Acts during the period continued the gradual process of reform; for example, the abolition in 1853 of part-payment of wages by 'truck' bought from 'tommy shops' (hence, 'tommy rot'), and the ending of transportation as a punishment. As a period of legislation it was not as spectacular as the 1870s, but at least it kept the politicians in some touch with everyday life.

3 Palmerston as Foreign Secretary, 1846–51

The Spanish MarriagesPalmerston's return to the Foreign Office in 1846, against the known wishes of the Court, began with a minor diplomatic defeat in the strange affair of the Spanish Marriages. In a fresh attempt to bring together the French and Spanish thrones, Louis Philippe and Guizot had arranged husbands for the sixteen year old Queen Isabella of Spain and her fourteen year old sister, the Infanta Luisa. Isabella was to marry a sexually impotent cousin while Luisa was to marry Louis Philippe's youngest son. Aberdeen had been negotiating with the French to postpone the second marriage, but, when Palmerston began to interfere, Guizot took the chance to get his revenge for the French defeat over Mehemet Ali. The marriages took place and, though there was to be no long-term benefit for Louis Philippe, there was much anti-French feeling in Britain. Palmerston realized that he had underestimated Guizot, and played down the affair.

1848–9 RevolutionsWhen, in 1848, liberal movements against despotic rulers broke out all over Europe, Palmerston took each case on its merits. His general view was that British interests needed a peaceful Europe, and that the rulers could not expect peace until they were prepared to grant constitutions on the British model. With revolutions aimed at this limited goal he was prepared to sympathize. If they involved the downfall of the Austrian Empire, which he saw as a bulwark against Russia, or if they invited French interference, or if their demands were as radical as those of the Chartists in Britain, then he was against them. In the troubles of 1848–9 he enjoyed his role as 'judicious bottle-holder', distributing encouragement, advice and criticism in a way that irritated foreign rulers and Victoria. The right wing continental press produced a rhyme which, translated, said, 'If the Devil had a son, his name is surely Palmerston'. He had, in fact, a far greater reputation as a leader of liberalism that he deserved, but it was a reputation he cultivated and whose value he understood. He never seemed to entertain the idea that justice and British interests, could, in any way, be contradictory.

His flexible policy thus enabled him to recognize the republican government of Lamartine in France, as soon as it was seen to be not too revolutionary; to encourage the liberals in Sicily by sending them arms to fight the tyrant King 'Bomba'; to send blunt warnings to Spain to grant reforms; and to try to persuade Austria to let the Italians in Lombardy join Piedmont-Sardinia. At the same time, he gave no support at all to the German, Polish or Hungarian rebels when it mattered, and he made no formal protest when Russian troops were brought in to put down the Hungarian rising. But once the revolutions were over he continued to build up his reputation as a man of the people. When Russia and Austria wished to extradite refugees from Turkey, he encouraged the Turks to resist by sending British gunboats to the Dardanelles to act, as he put it, 'like a bottle of salts to the nose of a frightened lady.' In 1850 the Austrian general Haynau, notorious for his recent floggings of Hungarian women, visited Barclay's Brewery in Southwark incognito. He was recognised by his 'far-flung mustachios' and set on by the draymen. Palmerston was delighted and wrote privately to the Home Secretary that 'they should have tossed him in a blanket, rolled him in the kennel and sent him home in a cab.' The Queen, of course, was furious and pressed him to make an official apology. Palmerston sent his regrets to Vienna but added that Haynau should never have come to England and that, if charges were brought, the defence would make the most of his atrocities. Not for the first time, he failed to show the despatch to the Queen, as she was entitled to expect. He was made to replace it with an unqualified apology and he promised not to offend again. Then, in 1851, when Kossuth, the defeated Hungarian leader, visited England, thousands came to cheer him. The *Morning Post* announced that he was to call on Palmerston; the Queen forbade the visit, and Palmerston told Russell that he would not be dictated to as to whom he received in his own house. The cabinet pressed him and he gave way, but two days later he publicly thanked a Radical deputation for approving his help to refugees. He was increasingly going his own way, in defiance both of the Crown and of his colleagues. He was also beginning to earn another nickname – the 'People's Darling'.

No single incident in his foreign policy so impressed the British **Don Pacifico** public as his handling of the Don Pacifico affair. The Chevalier Pacifico, as he called himself, was a Spanish Jew born in Gibraltar and so British by birth; having spent his early life in Portugal, he became also a naturalized Portuguese. In 1839 he was Portuguese consul in Athens but was later dismissed for forgery. In 1847 his house was burnt down by an anti-Jewish crowd which included the son of the Greek Minister of War; for three hours, the police stood by and watched. Pacifico asked the British Ambassador to take up his case. His claims were preposterous – £5,000 for the property and £27,000 for the loss of documents to be used in a lawsuit against the Portuguese Government. Palmerston decided to back him as a British subject and added £500 to the claim; the Greeks refused to pay or to prosecute, and for two years there the matter lay. In 1850 British warships were in the area to protect the refugees in Turkey, and Palmerston decided to operate the same gunboat diplomacy as he had used in China. The fleet arrived off the Piraeus, the port of Athens, and the Greek government was handed a demand for £33,000, to include interest, payable within twenty-four hours. When the money was not paid, the screw was slowly tightened as Greek shipping was either seized or blockaded. Austria, Russia and France all protested. Palmerston first agreed with a French plan for settlement, and then went back on the agreement with fresh demands on Greece. The uproar spread to Parliament at home, and Russell gave Palmerston the chance to defend himself on a vote of confidence. Against his critics, who included Gladstone, Cobden and Peel, whose last appearance it was, he made the speech of a lifetime, four and a half hours long, with a telling appeal to national pride, 'As the Roman in days of old held himself free from indignity when he could say *Civis Romanus sum,* so also a British subject in whatever land he may be shall feel confident that the watchful eye and the strong arm of England will protect him against injustice and wrong'. The debate lasted four days but the vote of confidence was won. There was tremendous support for Palmerston throughout the country, and many M.P.s who voted against him expected to lose their seats. As for Don Pacifico, he finally accepted £150 for his lost documents. It seemed that Palmerston had lost the battle but won the war.

Dismissal 1851   Then suddenly, as Prince Albert put it, 'he thrust his neck into the noose'. In France, Louis Napoleon, nephew of Napoleon I and President of the French Republic which had overthrown Louis Philippe, seized power in December 1851 as dictator. Russell and the Queen were agreed that Britain should remain strictly neutral. Palmerston not only assured the French Ambassador of his support for Louis Napoleon; he sent the despatch without showing it either to the Queen or to Russell. Less than a year earlier he had undertaken not to offend in this way again, and Russell now made this promise public. For once Palmerston could expect no support. He had misjudged what reaction there would be in Britain to Napoleon's *coup d'état.* Russell dismissed him.

4 The Crimean War 1854–6

Ever since the days of the Holy Alliance, distrust and dislike of Russia had been growing in Britain. British liberals condemned Tsardom and its attitude to reform, while British politicians feared Russian expansion in the Levant and even in India. The Crimean War was an expression of this hostility. It was also a stage in the Eastern Question, that recurrent problem facing British politicians throughout the nineteenth century. With the steady decline of the Turkish Empire and the expansion of Russia to the south west, the question for Britain was what action or attitude to take at each fresh crisis. Only once was there open war between the two countries, and even that once might well have been avoided.

Causes

In 1844 the Tsar Nicholas I had had talks in England with Aberdeen, then Foreign Secretary, and he became convinced that Britain and Russia understood and would respect each other's position in the Eastern Mediterranean. With Palmerston as Foreign Secretary, and Russia particularly unpopular over her treatment of the Poles and Hungarians, Nicholas waited. Then, in 1853, he suggested to the British Ambassador at St. Petersburg that the Powers should partition European Turkey. Russell, who if anything was even more anti-Russian than Palmerston, drafted the stiff reply that 'neither Britain, nor France, nor probably Austria would be content to see Constantinople permanently in the hands of Russia'. With no other complications, that might have been that.

Unfortunately, a separate quarrel had developed between France and Russia. The Holy Places in Palestine had, by agreement with the Turks, long been guarded by both Greek Orthodox priests, whom the Tsar claimed to protect, and Roman Catholic priests. The latter were beginning to lose influence, and one of Napoleon III's first actions on becoming Emperor in 1852 was to intervene on their behalf. He wished for the support of French catholics at home. He was also hostile to Russia and to Nicholas; Russia was the scene of his uncle's disastrous retreat in 1812, and Nicholas had disputed his title by addressing him as *cher ami* instead of *cher frère*. The Tsar objected to French interference and, in 1853, sent Prince Menshikov to Constantinople with a curt demand apparently for Russian powers inside Turkey. When this was refused, Nicholas threatened to send troops to occupy the Danubian provinces of Moldavia and Wallachia, in what is now Romania.

Britain had no wish to be involved in the matter of 'a few Grik Prists' as the wife of the Russian Ambassador once called them, but the Russian attempt to bully Turkey alerted all the Powers. Had Palmerston or Metternich been still in office, they might have restrained both the Tsar and Napoleon, but Metternich was in exile in Brighton, and Palmerston, though in the cabinet, was there only as Home Secretary. His advice to Aberdeen was 'to make a clatter' and the Tsar would withdraw, but, when a British fleet was sent to the area, Nicholas invaded Moldavia, though he did not declare war. At this stage, in July 1853, the Austrian Government tried to mediate and, with the Ambassadors of Russia, France and Britain, drew up the Vienna Note suggesting a compromise; Russia and France agreed and, again, that might have been that. Even at this late stage, it was very doubtful whether either Russia or France really wanted war, and a firm lead from Britain, backed by Austria and Prussia, might have prevented it.

Aberdeen's cabinet, however, was fatally divided. The doves were led by Aberdeen who was in much the same position as Neville Chamberlain in 1938–9. He said he had 'a terrible repugnance for war in all its forms'; he had convinced himself that Nicholas would listen to reason, and his policy was one of appeasement. In the cabinet he was supported by Gladstone, and in the country by Cobden, Bright, and the Peace Society. Aberdeen's attitude encouraged Nicholas not to withdraw. The hawks were led by Russell and Palmerston, and they had behind them most of the press, except *The Times*, and a public spoiling for a Russian war. Tennyson's poem 'Maud' voiced middle-class demands to end 'a peace that was full of wrongs and shame', and to 'wreak God's just wrath on a giant liar'. Behind the scenes was the strongly pro-Turkish Lord Stratford de Redcliffe, British Ambassador in Constantinople. Critics of Britain's entry into the war saw him as actively plotting our involvement; even Clarendon, the Foreign Secretary, said of him, 'The titular Sultan is for peace, but the real Sultan thinks now or never is the time for putting an end to Russia'. Whatever Stratford's influence, the Turks took his presence as confirmation of British support and were encouraged to resist; they rejected the Vienna Note and, in October 1853, declared war on Russia. In December, they sent their fleet into the Black Sea where, with the loss of 4,000 Turkish sailors, it was promptly destroyed by the Russians at the battle of Sinope. When the news reached Britain it ended the cold war, and the Anglo-French fleet took up position outside the Russian Black Sea base of Sebastopol. On 25 February 1854, Aberdeen told the Queen he was 'all for patching up' the situation, but within forty-eight hours an ultimatum was sent by Britain and France for Russia to withdraw from the Danube provinces within a month. On 28 March they joined Turkey as co-belligerents.

Conduct of War   The British government had drifted into war, and they were to mismanage it with monumental incompetence. The original plan was to drive the Russians from the provinces, but, by the time the Allied troops landed at Varna, in what is now Bulgaria, the Russians had handed the territory over to a neutral Austria and had withdrawn. The war could have ended almost before it began, but the Allies, seeing the alternatives as either advance or retreat, decided to adopt Palmerston's plan of landing in the Crimea and capturing Sebastopol, in the hope that this would end Russian power in the Black Sea. Palmerston, the generals and the public all looked forward to a quick and easy victory. What they got was a bitter two year struggle which cost some 25,000 British lives and £70 million. While it was in progress, so much went wrong that four Parliamentary Commissions of Enquiry separately investigated. Since Waterloo, the British Army had, through both economies and laxity, become ill-equipped and under-manned; in 1852 the total artillery for the whole army consisted of forty field pieces. When the troops were embarked for the Crimea, lack of shipping meant that most of the tents, bedding, cooking and hospital equipment and pack animals were left behind; twenty-one wagons held the supplies for thirty thousand men; no winter clothing was issued. Within seven weeks 6,000 men were dead and 8,000 suffering from wounds or cholera in filthy, overcrowded conditions. Half the dead had been lost in September 1854 in the first battle, the crossing of the river Alma, described by Victoria in terms familiar to a much later generation: 'Never in so short a time has so strong a battery, so well defended, been so bravely and gallantly taken'. Sebastopol lay open, but Raglan and St. Arnaud, the Allied commanders, delayed a vital three weeks during which Todleben greatly strengthened its defences, and the moment of opportunity had gone. In October, the Russians attacked at Balaclava, where, through incompetent leadership, the British Heavy and Light Brigades and the French *Chasseurs d'Afrique* made history but lost the battle. In a thick November fog, the allied infantry, perhaps mercifully out of touch with its officers, beat off another bloody counter-attack at Inkerman. Fighting then halted for the bitter Crimean winter, as both sides settled in to fight this common enemy.

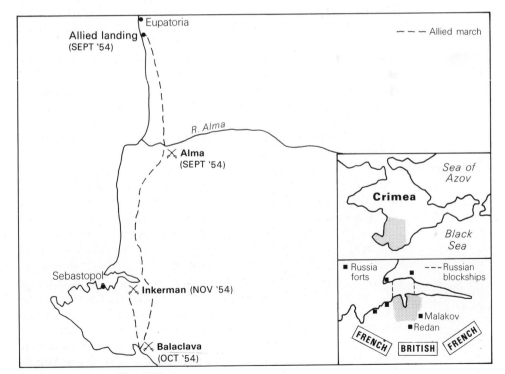

Fig. 2   The Crimean War, 1854–6

At home, public opinion was changing from enthusiasm to anger and frustration. *The Times* had sent out an Irishman, W. H. Russell, as the first journalist ever to report as a war correspondent, and his furious attacks on hospital conditions at the military base at Scutari, together with news of the blunders at Balaclava, produced two quick reactions. Florence Nightingale received permission to take a group of forty nurses to Scutari and, from November, carried on her long struggle against prejudice and red-tape. Then, in January 1855, the government lost a vote of confidence on its conduct of the war and Aberdeen resigned. The Queen tried desperately to avoid having Palmerston as Prime Minister but, in the existing mood of the country, he was the inevitable choice. The hopes that he would bring a new spirit into the conduct of the war were not entirely fulfilled. If anything, the men he put in charge were worse than those he replaced: the most able officer, Colin Campbell, was ignored. Then, in March, Nicholas died and was succeeded by the more liberal Alexander II, prepared to abolish serfdom and to consider peace. The allies were joined by 15,000 troops from Piedmont, itself hoping for French support in its fight against Austria. The French had a new and more skilful commander in Pellisier and, in September, Sebastopol at last fell; the British failed to take the Redan, the southern defence, but the French captured the Malakov, the even stronger eastern fortress. Tactically, the war was over, though negotiations and sporadic fighting dragged on until Napoleon III threatened either to withdraw or to widen the war to help the Poles and

British troops in the Crimea (officers and men of the 8th Hussars)

Hungarians. It seemed a fitting end to the whole proceedings that it came from an ultimatum from neutral Austria. Only when she threatened to join in did Alexander agree to accept terms and so the Treaty of Paris was signed in March 1856.

Treaty of Paris

The Treaty had three main terms. No naval bases or warships were to be allowed in the Black Sea which was to be open to international trade. Moldavia and Wallachia were made self-governing, though still nominally part of Turkey, and were guaranteed by the Powers. The Sultan, not for the first or last time, promised better treatment for his Christian subjects. In addition, the Powers agreed to abolish privateering and not to seize the cargoes of neutral ships in wartime. The peace was more popular in Britain than the treaty, but fear of Russia receded until the mid-1870s. Palmerston did not expect the Black Sea clause to last ten years and it was broken by Russia in 1870. The Balkans still looked to Russia as their protector while Napoleon III had increased his reputation and his ambitions. The Turkish Empire continued to decline. At the same time, Russia had suffered a substantial defeat, and the powerful influence which she had exercised in Europe before 1854 was not seen again until 1945.

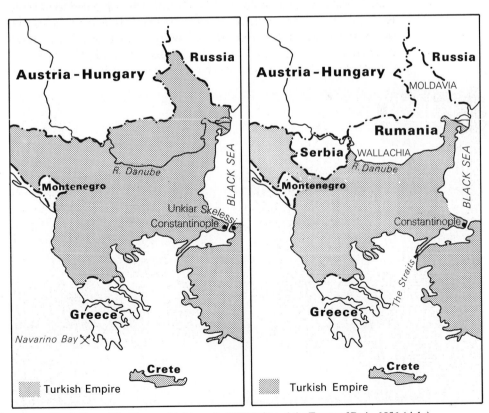

Fig. 3 The Balkans: The Treaty of Adrianople, 1829 (left) and the Treaty of Paris, 1856 (right)

5 Palmerston and foreign affairs 1856–65

Second and Third China Wars

It is not surprising that Palmerston, as Prime Minister from 1856, dominated foreign policy even more than when he was Foreign Secretary. Although his government played little part in putting down the Indian Mutiny (pp.282–5), he was soon back on familiar ground putting the Chinese in their place. In 1856 the 'Arrow', a small vessel known as a 'lorcha', was seized by the authorities because of its piracy in the Canton river and its crew of twelve Chinese were imprisoned. Since the 'Arrow' had been registered in Hong Kong as a British ship some two years before, the British consul demanded an apology and the release of the prisoners, and did not withdraw even when he later discovered that the registration was out of date. The Chinese offered to hand over the seamen but not to apologise, and British gunboats thereupon bombarded Canton. This action produced many local clashes but no reaction from Peking, while, at home, there was another major attempt to censure Palmerston's foreign policy; for although the consul, seventy-eight days distant from London, had acted largely on his own initiative, the Cabinet had now approved his actions. The Conservatives supported the vote of censure mainly as a matter of party politics, but it was Cobden, Gladstone and Russell who led the opposition to their former colleague. The vote of censure was lost in the

Chinese envoys on board a British warship

Lords but carried in the Commons, and Palmerston decided to call a general election. For the first time a British Prime Minister made a personal appeal to the country as well as to his own constituents. The middle classes were solidly behind him, the election of 1857 gave him a thumping majority, and the old policy towards China continued. Lord Elgin was sent out to extract compensation, and the capture of Canton had the desired effect of forcing the Chinese Emperor to take action. By the time the Second China War (1858–59) began, Palmerston was out of office (the Conspiracy to Murder bill, below). But the war was continued by the Conservatives, the same men who had taken so moral a tone the year before; by the Treaty of Tientsin, the Emperor agreed not only to receive a British minister but also to legalize the opium trade. While the British delegation was on its way to Peking to ratify the treaty, it was fired on and, at about the same time, a French missionary was murdered in Shanghai. With Palmerston now back in power, Napoleon III suggested a joint Anglo-French expedition, and in 1860 this force attacked Peking, the French looting and the British burning down the magnificent Summer Palace. The Treaty of Peking ended this Third China War, confirmed the previous treaty, and opened Tientsin and other ports to foreign trade. It was not until 1906 that there were sufficient stirrings of an international conscience to ban the iniquitous trade in opium.

The only break in Palmerston's last ten years of office came as a result of his wish to improve Anglo-French relations when, just as in 1851, he seriously underestimated public hostility to Napoleon III. In January 1858 a bomb was thrown at the Emperor and the Empress Eugénie as they drove to the Opéra in Paris; it missed them but killed several of the crowd. The assassin was an Italian named Orsini, and when the French police discovered that he had links with Italian refugees in London and that the bomb had been made in Birmingham, Napoleon asked the British government to take steps against foreign terrorists. Palmerston considered this a reasonable request, and introduced into the Commons a Conspiracy to Murder bill to make it a criminal offence for aliens to plot in Britain to commit murder abroad. Once again, the Radicals and Peelites would not support him and, with the Conservatives, brought his ministry down. For once his public deserted him, and on the day after his defeat he was hooted by the people as he rode in the park; but his recovery was almost as quick as his fall, and in June 1859 he was back in office.

In this final spell, he faced formidable problems over Italy, the United States and Schleswig-Holstein. In Italy, Palmerston had been glad to see in 1849 the granting of a constitution in Piedmont-Sardinia, and he would have welcomed a united kingdom in northern Italy under its king Victor Emmanuel. A large part of northern Italy, however, was, as Lombardy and Venetia, still under Austrian rule, and when Napoleon III joined with Piedmont and defeated the Austrians at

131

Solferino in 1859, Palmerston and Russell, now Foreign Secretary, had some difficult decisions to make. They wanted Italy free but not freed by France. As Canning's policy had been to try to prevent Russia acting unilaterally in Turkey, so Palmerston wished at all costs to prevent France acting unilaterally in Italy, since a Franco-Italian *bloc* would upset the balance of power. When Napoleon annexed Nice and Savoy as his reward almost everyone in Britain, from the Queen to Gladstone, supported Palmerston's pro-Italian, anti-French policy, though Gladstone, as Chancellor of the Exchequer, grudged every penny spent on the preparations for war. In 1860 Garibaldi and his thousand Redshirts invaded Sicily in an attempt to conquer the Kingdom of Naples for Victor Emmanuel. Palmerston was suspicious of Garibaldi, both because he was so popular among British Radicals and because the expedition was thought to be French-inspired; but when the French themselves suggested that a combined Anglo-French fleet should patrol the Straits of Messina to prevent Garibaldi crossing to the mainland, he agreed. At the last moment, Russell, always more in favour than Palmerston of direct help to Sardinia, won over the Cabinet and the British decision to stop Garibaldi was reversed. Napoleon III did not wish to intervene alone, and so Garibaldi was able to conquer Naples and hand it over to Piedmont. Russell made public the British attitude to Italian unity – 'The Italians themselves are the best judge of their own interests'. Once more Britain was seen as the champion of liberalism against the old order and, for accepting the decision not to act against Garibaldi, Palmerston was hailed as one of the architects of a united Italy.

American Civil War   Whereas Palmerston had had a united public opinion to back his Italian policy, he found that, in trying to decide Britain's attitude towards the American Civil War (1861–5), he had behind him a sharply divided nation. Most of the well-to-do in Britain, among them many employers in the textile industry, approved of the desire of the South to secede. From the Southern states came some four-fifths of the raw material for the Lancashire cotton mills, involving the livelihood of about half a million workers, and there was strong pressure by the employers, though not by the workers, to break the tight Northern blockade. Most of the working class opposed the South on the grounds that the South supported slavery; they accepted the blockade even though by 1863 many thousands of them were out of work because of the growing 'cotton famine', and, in that year, a great rally of trade unionists met in London to express solidarity with the North. The basic problem for the British government was whether to recognize the South, and Palmerston's policy tended to change with the fortunes of war. At the start, when General Lee and the South were doing well, Russell and Gladstone were all for recognition. Gladstone said, 'Jefferson Davis and other leaders of the South have made a nation'. Palmerston was pro-Southern but far more cautious; supported by the

Conservative opposition and by the pro-North Radicals, he delayed recognition and gradually the South was forced into surrender. Understandably the North was, during the war, quick to take offence, and two disputes, involving two ships, the *Trent* and the *Alabama*, led to considerable bad feeling.

The *Trent*

Two Southern envoys, Mason and Slidell, were on their way to Britain in 1861 in the British Mail Steamer *Trent* when Federalist sailors from the *San Jacinto* boarded her and took off the envoys in mid-ocean. Southern sympathizers in Britain were up in arms at the news, and Palmerston agreed that Russell should send a despatch to Washington demanding an apology and the release of the envoys. Three thousand extra troops were ordered to embark for Canada. Such a policy had worked well with Greece and again with China but to attempt it here was an error of judgement. When Russell's strongly worded despatch was shown to the Queen, who herself described the Federalists as 'ruffians', Prince Albert, already dying from typhoid, decided to try to avert an almost certain war. His suggested amendments changed an ultimatum into a loophole through which the North could retreat with honour; Lincoln, in his turn, accepted the olive branch and war was avoided. The second ship, the *Alabama*, was a cruiser built at Birkenhead in 1862 and allowed to put to sea in spite of Northern protests that she had been commissioned by the South; the British government, after much delay, had ordered her to be detained but the ship had sailed two days before the papers arrived. For two years she did extensive damage to Northern shipping before being sunk off Cherbourg, and the North

The *Alabama*

The *Alabama*

claimed full compensation. Palmerston and Russell denied that Britain was in any way responsible and refused both the claim and the proposal that it should be put to arbitration, and it was not until Gladstone was Prime Minister that the matter was finally settled (p.150). But it was significant that, after the decisive battle of Gettysburg in 1863, Palmerston took a different line over more ships being built for the South at Birkenhead. This time he made sure that they did not sail.

Schleswig and Holstein
In 1863 the Poles again rebelled against Russia and there was pressure from public opinion in Britain and from Napoleon III to help them. Palmerston took the realistic view that the only way he could help was by going to war, and this he was not prepared to do. Then, at the very end of his career came his biggest diplomatic defeat. Bismarck, the new Prussian Chancellor, had persuaded Austria to join in an attack on the two small Duchies of Schleswig and Holstein, then part of Denmark. As with Poland, there was support in Britain for the underdog, though many leading figures in the government, like Gladstone, Granville, Cobden and Bright, were firmly against involvement. Palmerston and Russell, the 'two dreadful old men' as Victoria now called them, decided to support Denmark even though there were no British interests at stake and even though they had no intention of seeking French help. Russell threatened to send the fleet to Copenhagen while Palmerston told the Commons that those who attempted to overthrow Denmark would find 'that it would not be Denmark alone with which they would have to contend.' The result was that, while Bismarck was not deterred, the Danes were encouraged to resist. In 1865 the Duchies were seized and Denmark invaded. The Danes agreed to an armistice, but, after a second offer of help from Russell, decided to fight on. The House of Commons expected a declaration of war and, with Russell in charge, this might have come; but Palmerston, under strong pressure from the Queen, and realizing, as he must have done from the start, that an army of 200,000 could not be defeated by a few gunboats, announced that Britain would not intervene. In spite of losing face, he survived another vote of censure and then won another general election. Two days before his eighty-first birthday he died.

There is no doubt that he had had a full life. He had been cited in a divorce case when he was seventy-nine, had run up the stairs at the House of Commons when he was eighty, and enjoyed mutton chops and port for breakfast the week before he died. In his time he had been called Lord Cupid and Lord Pumicestone; he had been a natural charmer or deliberately offensive as the occasion required, an international bully and the centre of London society. With his death an era ended. For most of his last ministry he had been fighting a rearguard action against reform at home, and had sensed the break-up of the old Concert of Europe he had used so skilfully. The next ten years saw the rise of the German Empire, the defeat of Austria and France, and a dramatic decline in British influence, and even interest, in foreign affairs. Palmerstonian policies and methods were no longer workable and came to be condemned. Bright's advice to Salisbury, the Foreign Secretary in 1886, was, 'Do the exact opposite of what he did. His administration at the Foreign Office was one long crime'. No doubt, at the end, he had lost his touch and no doubt, after an exceptionally long record of service to his country, one certain legacy he left was that of a Britain internationally distrusted and disliked. This would not have disturbed him unduly. He once put as his two main objectives the abolition of the slave trade and the defence of the country, and for both of these he worked tirelessly. Victoria's epitaph on him was as apt as any: 'He had many valuable qualities, though many bad ones, and we had, God knows, terrible trouble with him about foreign affairs'.

8

The establishment of the Liberal party 1866-74

1 The Second Reform Act, 1867

Demand for reform

In spite of the apparent failure of the Chartist movement there was, by 1849, a growing acceptance in Britain that the Reform Act of 1832 would have to be extended. Revolutionary Chartism, of the type that demanded one-man-one-vote, and equal electoral districts, had been defeated and discredited, but the underlying movement for parliamentary reform grew every year stronger and more respectable. In each big town and within the larger trade unions there was an increasing demand for the working man to be given the vote by peaceful and constitutional means. Economic and cultural standards were rising in the towns, if not in the rural areas; the Free Trade budgets, the working men's clubs and mechanics' institutes, the whole climate of self-help all helped to feed the demand, and attempts to block it would be much more dangerous than any counter-Chartist measures had been. While Palmerston was alive Parliamentary opposition was too strong for even limited changes to be accepted, but even before his death it was clear that electoral reform was imminent. So it was that the Parliament which had been elected to give Palmerston a third term of office found itself, within two years, passing the Second Reform Act.

Russell's and Gladstone's Bill 1866

The struggle for the Act dominated the parliamentary scene and involved six prominent figures – Russell, a Whig, Gladstone, a Liberal, Lowe, a Palmerstonian Liberal, Bright, a Radical, and two Conservatives, Derby and Disraeli. Russell, although Prime Minister in place of Palmerston, was now seventy-three, an earl, and in the House of Lords. His 1832 Act had gained middle-class support for the Whigs and he had tried, by unsuccessful bills in 1849, 1852 and 1854, to increase Whig strength among a wider electorate. He saw as the crowning of his life's work the bill which he now brought in with Gladstone in 1866. Gladstone was leader of the government in the Commons and was determined to become leader of the Liberal party. He was much more in touch with working-class aspirations than Russell; in 1862 he had provided relief work on his Hawarden estate for mill-workers made unemployed by the 'cotton famine'; and in 1865, rejected by Oxford University, he was returned as candidate for the industrial South Lancashire constituency. In 1864 he had startled everyone by saying, in a typical Gladstonian sentence, that 'every man who is not presumably incapacitated by some consideration of personal unfitness or of political danger is morally entitled to come within the pale of the constitution'. It did not mean that he had been converted to the idea of one-man-one-vote, but he was prepared to see the vote as a privilege to be earned by self-improvement, a process in which many thousands of responsible working men were at that time involved. The bill that he and Russell brought in, in March 1866, proposed to lower the property qualification from the 1832 figures of £10 a year rental in the boroughs and £50 in the counties to £7 and £14 respectively. Within these carefully calculated limits some 400,000 voters would be added to the electorate reckoned at 800,000 in 1832. In this way the vote would be extended to the working class without giving them a majority in the new electorate.

Although Gladstone hoped that this moderate bill would be supported by the whole party, it was still too democratic for a group of about forty Palmerstonian Liberals led by the 'waspish albino', Robert Lowe. He and his sympathizers, whom Bright called the 'Adullamites'[1], argued that good government was entirely possible under the existing franchise, and Lowe himself caused much bitterness by attacking the working class as unfit to have the vote. In June thirty-five Adullamites voted with the Conservative opposition on an amendment, and, after a week's hesitation, Russell resigned. The Earl of Derby accepted the Queen's invitation to form a ministry and the Conservatives took over with Disraeli leading in the Commons. Public interest in the reform question was now intense: 1866 was proving to be a year of crises. The leading London banking house of Overend and Gurney failed; there was heavy unemployment in the cotton and shipbuilding industries, and there was a bad harvest. At the end of June a large crowd marched from Trafalgar Square to Gladstone's London house shouting 'Gladstone and Liberty'. A month later, when the authorities closed the gates of Hyde Park against a reform demonstration, the mob tore down nearly a mile of railings, and the army had to be called out. Gladstone decided on an Italian holiday to escape the pressures, and it was Bright who, at this critical stage, organized Radical, Nonconformist and working-class interests together behind what was to be a new, Gladstone-led Liberal party. He concentrated on support outside Parliament, on the northern Reform Union, founded in 1861 and very much on the lines of the old Anti Corn Law League, and on the Reform League, set up in 1865 with many ex-chartists among its members. With their help, he built up Gladstone's reputation as the hope of the working classes. At monster meetings in the midlands and the north the motto on the banners was simple – 'Household Suffrage'. All this activity gave Derby and Disraeli food for thought, and when Parliament reassembled in 1867 it was clear that some action on reform could no longer be delayed.

It was Derby and not Disraeli who first decided that the Conservatives should introduce their own bill. The party had not won an election

[1]After the companions of King David in the Cave of Adullam (*I Samuel*, *XXII*, vv. 1–2).

Reform demonstration in Hyde Park, 1866

on the existing franchise since 1841, and clearly some things were less worth 'conserving' than others; change was coming anyway, and the Conservatives might well be the gainers from it. Disraeli was at first cautious. He was, for all his novels, less interested in reform than in his own position in the party. He had already failed with a reform bill in 1859; designed to allow a number of 'fancy franchises' as Bright called them, but not to lower the borough qualification, it had proved too liberal for the Conservatives and too conservative for the Radicals. This time, to succeed, there would have to be a more sweeping reform with much depending on how it was piloted through the Commons. The vital thing was to stay in power. Thus, for Disraeli, the tactics of getting a bill accepted came to be more important than what the bill contained.

Derby's and Disraeli's Act, 1867

The Conservative bill, in its first form, had been hastily cobbled together over a week-end and only agreed to an hour before Disraeli presented it in the Commons in February 1867. During the debate, three cabinet members resigned at what they felt was a betrayal of Tory principles, but the bill got so hostile a reception from the opposition that Disraeli and his leader replaced it in March with a more radical measure. This would have based the franchise in the boroughs on personal payment of rates, thereby excluding all those who, like most modern council tenants, paid their rates with their rent. There was to be no great redistribution of seats, but 'fancy franchises' were kept; university graduates, professional men, and those who paid income tax or had at least £50 savings were to have a second vote. As the bill went through its various stages Gladstone attacked it in detail, with Disraeli conceding or resisting as he read the mood of the House, and carefully keeping his party together, until all the 'fancy franchises' had disappeared and the inevitable concession of household suffrage had been granted. Disraeli claimed later that the whole sequence of events had been premeditated, but this was not so. Nevertheless, he had shown great parliamentary skill and powers of improvisation. He had run rings round Gladstone and produced, like a conjuror, a radical Reform Act to which Gladstone had contributed virtually nothing but for which the Conservatives could take most of the credit. It also ensured that, when Derby resigned in 1868, Disraeli became the new leader of the party.

The bill passed the Commons in August 1867. Little remained of the original proposals except the important £12 county franchise, aimed at safeguarding many Conservative majorities. The vote in the boroughs now went to all male house-holders and £10 lodgers. 45 new seats were created by taking one M.P. from each borough with fewer than 10,000 inhabitants; 25 went to the counties, 15 to the towns, a third member each to Liverpool, Manchester, Birmingham and Leeds, and one to London University. Where Gladstone's bill would have added 400,000 new voters, the 1867 Act added almost a million, giving a total electorate of nearly two and a half million, a third of the adult male population. A working-class majority among the electorate was now a fact. Finally, the Act laid down that the new franchise should apply to municipal as well as to parliamentary elections, and Acts of 1868 extended this to Scotland and Ireland.

Derby and Disraeli had not planned such a sweeping Act, perhaps the most important political change in Victoria's reign; but they were happy to have 'dished the Whigs' as Derby cheerfully remarked. He also recalled Macaulay's description of the 1832 Act as a 'leap in the dark' and applied it to the present Act: Carlyle called it 'shooting Niagara'. Certainly many saw the act as another final settlement and not as the next stage towards universal suffrage; many who supported it were soon to oppose the move for a secret ballot; and neither Gladstone nor Disraeli could foresee how its changes would influence the policies of their two parties. By February 1868 both Russell and Derby had retired, and Disraeli had had his first glimpse of power from the 'top of the greasy pole'. The main issue in the next general election was the disestablishment of the Irish Church and, although not all the new electors were yet registered, it was the Liberals who were in with a majority of over a hundred. The next bill for the extension of the franchise would not be introduced for another seventeen years.

In the meantime, the Second Reform Act began to affect the working

Results of the Act of 1867

of the political parties. Bigger constituencies and electorates called for more efficient party organization. In the new three-seat constituencies, for example, electors could only vote for two candidates. The Birmingham Liberal Association soon found that, by organizing its supporters, it could increase its chances of capturing all three seats, and the Birmingham 'caucus', or party machine, became the pattern for other areas. In 1867 the National Union of Conservative and Constitutional Associations was set up, followed in 1877 by the National Federation of Liberal Associations. Another significant development was the widening of the gap between the interests of Lords and Commons; the more democratic the one became, the more aristocratic the other appeared. The working-class voter, though he was in the majority, still voted

F U N.—April 6, 1867.

POLITICAL MILLINERY.

Miss G.:—"YOU SHA'N'T DRESS YOUR DOLL LIKE THAT!"
Miss D.:—"YOU'RE NOT TO DICTATE TO ME, MISS!"
B. in the background:—"AH, I THOUGHT IT WOULD COME TO THIS, THEY BEGAN SO AMICABLY!"

Gladstone and Disraeli fight over the Reform Bill, 1867

either Liberal or Conservative; but the party leaders had now to pay more attention to his needs. As for the two leaders, their personal rivalry, sharpened by the Reform Bill debates, demanded a greater commitment to the party leader than ever before. During the 1867 debates small boys had invented a riddle, 'Why is Gladstone like a telescope?' The answer was, 'Because Disraeli draws him out, looks through him, and shuts him up'. The bitterness that Gladstone felt for his tormentor was not the least legacy of the Second Reform Act.

2 W. E. Gladstone

William Ewart Gladstone was fifty-nine when in 1868 he took office as Prime Minister for the first time. At the height of his powers, a man of superb intellect and abundant physical energy, he was the leader of a newly-born Liberal party which had just won a general election by the largest margin since 1832. He was an outstanding parliamentarian, already a member of the Commons for 35 years, and an orator with an

William Ewart Gladstone (1809–1898)

astonishing mastery of detail. His Cabinet covered all Liberal opinions including old-fashioned Whig aristocrats, ex-Peelites like Gladstone himself, and the celebrated John Bright, veteran of the Anti-Corn Law League and hero of the recent campaign for parliamentary reform. Gladstone's political beliefs had changed a good deal since Macaulay had described him in 1833 as 'the rising hope of the stern unbending Tories'. He had learned much about Free Trade and economic matters from Peel, whose political disciple he always considered himself. In some ways he remained cautious and conservative like Peel, never a radical seeking change for its own sake. Yet his support of parliamentary reform and his views on Italy showed how liberal in outlook he had become by 1868. A profoundly religious man, he was above all to show himself the crusader in politics, often to the embarrassment of many members of his own party. Ireland, whose challenge he took up at once in his first ministry, was to illustrate this through his long later career.

3 Ireland

The background The Irish Question is a complex problem which has faced the English for over 800 years. Its underlying cause was the desire of the conquered Irish to regain their freedom. Over the centuries, time had added to the political problem religious, social and economic grievances, all of them fuelled by frustration, violence and misunderstanding. Since 1801 Great Britain and Ireland had legally become one United Kingdom, yet whereas one partner was a rapidly growing industrial society, the other remained retarded and underdeveloped. A French traveller in rural Ireland in 1839 described a typical mud hut, with a pig running loose inside, no furniture, and a single bed of straw for the whole family. A German visitor in 1842 thought there was more wretchedness and begging in Ireland than in any other part of Europe. The average wage of an Irish labourer was then fivepence a day compared with 1s 6d in England.

In 1845–6 this depressed society was struck by the failure in two successive years of its staple crop – the potato. The British government agreed to give as much relief money as was raised by private charity, to open workhouses, and to bring yellow maize from India to make broth (known to the Irish as 'Peel's brimstone'), measures which proved quite inadequate to deal with a major disaster. The workhouses were besieged. Starving thousands turned to cabbage leaves and turnip tops. In the remoter areas the dead lay in the open. The exact number who died was never known, and there are certainly no statistics to measure the suffering of the Irish people or the extent to which Anglo-Irish relations were further embittered. Estimates of the deaths vary between 300,000 and 800,000 and many of the two million or so who emigrated to America died on the voyage. The census of 1841 showed that there were about eight million Irish compared to about sixteen million in England, Scotland and Wales – a startling contrast to the present day figures of about four million and fifty-nine million respectively. The Irish who remained after the Great Famine were no longer content with Daniel O'Connell as their leader, a man so moderate that he had forbidden his followers to join the Chartists. They turned increasingly to existing secret societies such as the Whiteboys and the Ribbonmen, and to the Young Ireland movement led by extremists such as John Mitchel and the M.P. William Smith O'Brien. They staged a rising in Munster in 1848, the Year of Revolutions, but it was soon crushed and its leaders transported.

Irish emigrants on Cork Quay

When Gladstone took office in 1869, the anti-landlord, anti-Protestant agitation of the secret societies had been reinforced by a new anti-British organization called the Fenians, the nineteenth-century version of Sinn Fein and the I.R.A. Founded in the United States as the Irish Republican Brotherhood, the Fenians aimed to destroy British rule in Ireland. By 1865 they had begun to operate on this side of the Atlantic. A policeman was killed in Manchester in 1867 during an attempt by five Irishmen to rescue Fenian prisoners from a police van; they themselves were captured, and three of them, the 'Manchester Martyrs' as they came to be called, were hanged. Another rescue attempt resulted in the dynamiting of seventy feet of the wall of Clerkenwell Prison in London, crushing innocent bystanders. At this stage, the Fenians had little real hold over the Irish people, and this, perhaps, encouraged Gladstone to believe that the Irish might be satisfied with something less than independence. 'My mission is to pacify Ireland', was his first remark on hearing that he was to become Prime Minister. They were revealing words as well as the most quoted of his whole career. He saw Ireland, as he had seen economy and tariff reform, as a cause for which he could fight as God's agent, a crusading attitude which grew into an obsession. In 1845 he had written, 'Ireland! Ireland! That cloud in the West! That coming storm! Ireland forces upon us those great social and great religious questions. God grant that we may have the courage to look them in the face!' Now the moment had come, but, since his policy was one of pacification, he ignored the vital question of independence, and this was bound, in time, to force itself upon his attention.

Disestablishment of the Irish Church. He had already, in opposition in 1867, begun to deal with an obvious religious grievance. Irish Catholics outnumbered Protestants by about nine to one, yet by law they were obliged to pay tithes to the established Anglican Church in Ireland which was Protestant. Gladstone made his attack on this state Church the main issue of the 1868 election. He proposed that it should cease to exist; that its property and endowments, worth over £16 million, should be confiscated; and that the money so raised should be used to start a new, voluntary, self-supporting Protestant Church of Ireland as well as to help Irish higher education, agriculture and fisheries, and the poor. The Lords were not happy with the bill, and neither was the Queen whose second son Alfred had only recently been wounded by a Fenian bullet. Gladstone however pushed ahead with tremendous vigour and debating skill, and Victoria worked behind the scenes to avert a head-on clash between Lords and Commons, and the Disestablishment of the Irish Church Act became law in 1869. It removed one clear injustice but by no means solved the religious problem. The mutual distrust between the Catholic majority in Ireland and the Protestant majority in the rest of Britain continued to poison Anglo-Irish relations, while the rift deepened between Protestant Ulster and the rest of Ireland.

Gladstone tackled next, and with equal determination, the problem of agrarian discontent, working at little else for the next three months. The great mass of the Irish population had, for generations, depended on the land for a livelihood which was never far from starvation level. Even after the Great Famine there was still too little land for too many people. By the 1870s some tenant-farmers in the east of Ireland were prospering, but the typical Irish working man was an agricultural labourer exploited by an absentee English landlord on land originally confiscated from the Irish. His low wages had to be supplemented by cultivating a plot of land for which he paid rent. If his crop failed or if prices were low, he fell into arrears, and this entitled the landlord legally to evict him. He thus had no security of tenure and evictions were commonplace, for there was no shortage of new tenants. If he improved the plot and was later evicted, the improvements became the property of the landlord. In Ulster the custom was to compensate the outgoing tenant for improvements, but there was strong opposition to this system spreading elsewhere. Palmerston, a more considerate landlord than most, had been firmly against compensation. 'Tenant's right is landlord's wrong' was his view.

A Leinster cottage in the early nineteenth century

First Land Act

Nevertheless, when Gladstone decided to bring in a bill to protect Irish tenants from unfair treatment his main proposal was to extend Ulster 'Tenant Right' to the whole of Ireland; landlords would be required to compensate tenants for 'unfair' eviction and for improvements. In its original form, drafted with Gladstone's own quill pen, it laid down that no landlord should charge an excessive rent, and courts were empowered to revise such rents and to decide rates of compensation. British landlords did not like the bill and the Lords altered 'excessive' to 'exorbitant'. In this form the bill became the First Land Act (1870). As an attempt to protect tenants the Act proved inadequate. Eviction was still allowed for non-payment of rent, and, since no court could be found to say that a rent, however high, was 'exorbitant', landlords were still able to force tenants out by frequent increases in rent. For all Gladstone's good intentions, the Act was not what the Irish tenants wanted. Eviction was their constant fear for it meant starvation, beggary or emigration. What they needed was security against eviction, not compensation when evicted. Certainly they wanted fair rents, and the free sale of what they had contributed to improve their holdings, but, most of all, they wanted fixity of tenure. These were the 'Three Fs' now being claimed by the Irish Tenant Right Party, and the 1870 Land Act did not grant them. Its failure was completed when a general agricultural depression came in the later 1870s. This hit the better-off tenants of the east even harder than the subsistence farmers of the west. Few tenants could now pay even moderate rents, and in 1879, for example, over 1,000 families containing nearly 6,000 people were evicted.

Education of Catholics

In 1873 Gladstone turned to a third aim in his policy of pacification – higher education for Irish Catholics. He thought that the provision of an Irish University open to both Catholics and Protestants would remove another grievance. The existing Queen's Colleges at Cork and Belfast, and Trinity College, Dublin, were all Protestant institutions to which few Catholics would send their sons. Gladstone introduced the Irish Universities Bill to amalgamate them with the Catholic college of Maynooth into a single University open to men of either religion. The Irish Catholic bishops were bitterly hostile; forty-three Liberals voted against the bill, and it was defeated by three votes.

Gladstone had earlier suggested that the Royal Family should be more closely associated with Irish affairs. He felt that this might not only be well received in Ireland but would also encourage the Queen to end the retirement into which she had gone after Albert's death. He proposed that she, or the Prince of Wales, should acquire an official Irish residence to use as they used Balmoral in Scotland, and that the Prince should even take up a new part-time post of Viceroy of Ireland. The first idea had already been suggested by Disraeli, and turned down. Edward was nearly thirty years old; yet his mother wrote, 'Any encouragement of his constant love of running about and not keeping at home or near the Queen is to be deprecated'. Both of Gladstone's ideas were rejected by Victoria, who had at least visited Ireland (which was more than he had yet done). On that occasion, in 1861, the Irish crowds had demonstrated against the Prince Consort, six months before he died. It was an experience she was not likely to forget or forgive.

Gladstone left office in 1874 with the Irish Question unsolved. There was still religious bigotry on both sides, still widespread agrarian discontent, and soon there was to be a dramatic resurgence of political demands. All the same, a start had been made towards finding a solution, and a British politician had at last made a gesture of goodwill. Only someone with Gladstone's sense of mission could have achieved even this small beginning.

4 Reform at home

Gladstone's first ministry was one of the great reforming governments of the nineteenth century. The new situation created by the death of Palmerston and by the Second Reform Act released a pent-up flood.

The general aims of the Liberal reforms between 1868 and 1874 were to open the way to greater freedom and wider opportunities for the individual (e.g. by changes in education), and to make government more efficient (e.g. by measures dealing with the army, the civil service and the law courts). For Gladstone paid little direct attention to social reform in the shape of measures attacking problems like slums. He threw much of his own energy into his response to the challenge of Ireland. Although he took a full share, for example, in the tough parliamentary battles over Forster's Education Act and Cardwell's Army Reforms, most of the credit for these and other measures must go to the ministers concerned.

Education was the subject of three acts. The Endowed Schools Act (1869), by redistributing local charitable funds, reinvigorated many grammar schools. The Universities Tests Act (1871) opened fellowships at Oxford and Cambridge colleges to non-Anglicans; Gladstone, a devout High Churchman personally disapproved but eventually yielded. But the most important, and by far the most controversial, measure was the Education Act of 1870. There was general agreement about the urgent need to provide many more schools for the children of the poor, especially in the big cities where the Liberals were strong. England was lagging behind other nations in educating its people. In the wars of the 1860s victory had gone to the nations which provided schools: the Prussians had crushed the Austrians, the American North had overcome the illiterate South in the Civil War. At home the new voters after the Second Reform Act required schooling: as Robert Lowe put it, 'it will be absolutely necessary to compel our new masters to learn their letters'. But, as always in nineteenth century education, controversy broke out over the role of religion. Rival pressure groups were founded. The National Education League of October 1869, with headquarters in Birmingham, wanted a system of free, universal and compulsory education, which was to be secular, i.e. to offer no religious teaching at all. But the National Education Union of November 1869 insisted on denominational teaching.

The government set out, in the words of W. E. Forster, the minister in charge of the bill, to 'fill up the gaps' in the existing supply of schools, and so 'to bring elementary education within the reach of every English home ..... and of the children who have no homes'. The voluntary societies were given a year (later reduced to six months) to put up proposals for new schools. After that, where provision was insufficient, local school boards were to be elected by the rate-payers, with power to build and run schools and spend a rate up to 3d in the £ for the purpose. They could, if they wished, make education between the ages of 5 and 13 compulsory in their areas. So there was born the 'Dual System' of elementary education, with its two kinds of school – the voluntary schools provided by the religious societies, and the board schools provided by the elected representatives of the people. Both could charge fees, both got government grants; but only the board schools could have money from the rates. There were heated debates in Parliament on the religious question. Nonconformists were violently antagonistic to any use of money from the rates to support the denominational schools – in particular, to promote the teaching of the Anglican catechism to their children. Eventually the government found a compromise in the Cowper-Temple clause of the Act, which decreed that religious teaching in board schools must be undenominational, in effect 'simple Bible teaching'. Forster's Act created for the first time a national pattern of elementary education in England and Wales, one that has lasted until the present day. It was probably the greatest single achievement of Gladstone's first ministry.

A second group of reforms improved the efficiency of government. In 1870 entry to the civil service became wholly competitive, through entrance examination – except for the Foreign Office. In 1871 the Local Government Board was established, creating a government department which supervised most activities of local councils and of the Poor Law; connected with this was a Public Health Act of 1872 which compelled all local sanitary authorities to appoint a Medical Officer of Health. In 1873 the Judicature Act reorganised the main law courts, setting up a Supreme Court of Justice on lines which lasted until 1970. Yet to **Army reform** contemporaries, the most important changes here were those that concerned the Army. Some steps had already been taken to remedy the muddle and incompetence which the Crimean War had thrown into sad relief. But the German triumphs in the Franco-Prussian War of 1870 indicated that much remained to be done to bring British military strength up-to-date, and Edward Cardwell, Secretary for War, carried through a variety of changes. To make the army more attractive as a career he cut the term of enlistment with the colours from twelve years to six, requiring the second six years to be spent instead in a newly-created reserve. A system of 'linked battalions' provided that in each regiment one battalion was to stay at home while the other served abroad, and this ensured that the young boys who formed the vast majority of recruits were trained before going overseas. During his term of office Cardwell increased the number of battalions by 25, and multiplied the number of available reserves tenfold. Enthusiasm was stimulated by giving regiments local names and headquarters. Peace-time flogging was abolished. The infantry was re-equipped with the breech-loading Martini-Henry rifle. The one detail of Cardwell's reforms which aroused serious opposition was his abolition of the purchase of commissions in the cavalry and infantry, thus making it possible to base promotion on merit and seniority. The opposition came from the House of Lords, some of whose members profited from the investment involved in the system of purchases, and which threw out the bill. So Gladstone put through the abolition by royal warrant, triumphing over what he called 'class interest in its favourite and most formidable stronghold'. Cardwell's reforms were in some ways of great value. They made the small British army a very effective force for its main task during the last thirty years of the nineteenth century, that of defeating non-European peoples and holding down an overseas empire.

Other reforms of the ministry included the Ballot Act of 1872, which at last granted the old radical and Chartist demand for the secret ballot, and safeguarded the new working-class voters against pressure from their employers; and a Licensing Act of the same year which tried to regulate the sale of alcoholic drink. Neither of these was much to Gladstone's taste. There were also two acts dealing with trade unions, **Trade Unions** to which events of the 1860s had drawn politicians' attention. These events included the Sheffield Outrages, murderous acts of violence against non-unionists in the cutlery trades; a judges' decision in the case of *Hornby v Close*, 1867, involving the Bradford branch of the Boilermakers' Society, which ruled that trade union funds could not be protected by law, as they were illegal associations; and the first meeting (1868) of the Trades Union Congress. A Royal Commission investigated the whole position of trade unions, and reported favourably on most of their activities. Gladstone was not unsympathetic to most of their demands, and was well aware of the importance of working-class votes to the Liberals. But he did not want to give trade unions a privileged position, and he particularly disliked the threat of violence involved in picketing and the pressure that an organised union of workmen could put on individuals. So while the Trade Union Act of 1871 gave legal recognition to trade unions and their funds, the Criminal Law Amendment Act of the same year outlawed picketing. The Liberals seemed to trade unionists to have given with one hand and taken away with the other.

5 Foreign policy

Palmerston's conduct of foreign policy had been pugnacious and meddlesome. Gladstone's was neither. He was in no sense a pacifist, as his energetic support of Cardwell's Army reforms showed. But he saw no point in gestures and statements which could not be backed by action, as in the Schleswig-Holstein affair. He did, however, believe in applying moral principles to international affairs. States should behave in accordance with a sense of international order and justice – a view which did not earn him much sympathy from the great master of European statecraft at the time, Bismarck, who liked talking of him as 'Professor' Gladstone. Gladstone's principles were put to the test in three episodes between 1868 and 1874.

The first, and much the most serious, of these was the great crisis of **Franco-** the Franco-Prussian War of 1870. That July Bismarck jockeyed France **Prussian War** into declaring war on Prussia – a war that was catastrophic to France.

By September the Emperor, Napoleon III, was a prisoner in German hands, and France had become a republic. In January 1871 Paris, besieged for four months and on the verge of starvation, surrendered to the German army. Ten days earlier the German Empire, with William of Prussia as its Kaiser and Bismarck as his Chancellor, had been proclaimed in the Hall of Mirrors of Louis XIV's palace at Versailles. These events – a turning-point in human history, setting Europe on a road which was to lead to the First World War by 1914 – agitated and alarmed Gladstone and British public opinion. Their meaning could scarcely be grasped. But certainly the fate of Belgium was at stake – and with it the long-established British policy that the entire Channel coastline facing England should not be ruled by one power. Gladstone acted promptly, declaring Britain neutral and getting both France and Germany to sign a treaty reaffirming the neutrality of Belgium established in 1839. British opinion, mistrusting Napoleon's designs on Belgium, was at first anti-French. It later swung against the Prussians, as tales of suffering came out of Paris during the siege. Gladstone himself wanted to mobilise the Concert of Europe to protest against Prussia's annexation of Alsace-Lorraine, 'this transfer of human beings like chattels', but the Cabinet would not agree.

'Black Sea clauses'

The second problem for Britain's foreign policy at this time was a by-product of the Franco-Prussian War. Russia in the Treaty of Paris (1856) at the end of the Crimean War had been required to withdraw her naval vessels from the Black Sea and to demolish her fortresses on its shores. In 1870 her foreign minister Prince Gorchakov took advantage of the misfortunes of France to denounce these 'Black Sea clauses'. Gladstone was outraged by this contempt for international faith, and protested that treaties should not be changed by the action of one signatory alone. An international conference met in 1871 to discuss the matter. Although the Russians accepted Gladstone's principle about treaties (and in fact acted on it in 1878 – p.159) she kept her warships in the Black Sea. In England it looked as though Russia had got away with her breach of faith, and Gladstone's reputation fell.

The U.S.A.

It fell further in 1872 over a dispute involving the United States. As we have seen (p.133), during the American Civil War Palmerston's government had allowed the *Alabama*, a commerce-raider built at Birkenhead for the Confederate States (the South), to put to sea, where it had caused considerable losses to Northern (Federal) shipping. The government of the United States after the war claimed compensation for these and other losses, alleging that they were contrary to international law. Gladstone as Prime Minister referred these 'Alabama Claims' to an international court of arbitration, and when in 1872 this court awarded £3,250,000 damages to the Americans, he paid up at once. This was in accord with the principles which governed his policy in international affairs, and a triumph for the idea of arbitration. (The cheque when cancelled was framed and hung in the Foreign Office as a memento of Anglo-American accord). But it was unpopular in England, not least with some members of his own Cabinet, because it seemed yet another example of his neglect of British prestige abroad.

By this time the Liberal government, like the Whigs forty years earlier, seemed to be running out of reforms. It was now that Disraeli called them 'a range of exhausted volcanoes'. Defeated in the Commons in 1873 over the Irish Universities Bill, Gladstone hung on to office until 1874, when he appealed to the country in a general election. He chose as the main plank of his platform the abolition of income tax (then standing at 2d in the £), and was firmly defeated by the Conservatives. The alleged weakness of his foreign policy was only one element in the defeat. The great reforms themselves had made him many enemies – nonconformists over education, trade unionists over picketing, the upper class over civil service reform and army purchase. For contradictory reasons, both temperance advocates and brewers and publicans (and no doubt many of their customers) disliked the licensing laws[1]. (Gladstone himself said that he had been 'borne down in a torrent of gin and beer', but this seems a gross overstatement, not unrelated to the fact that a distiller named Booth pushed him into second place at Greenwich, then a two-member constituency.) His concessions to Ireland lost him votes in England; while in Ireland itself the Ballot Act lost seats for the Liberals because Irish tenants could now vote for Home Rule without their landlords' knowledge, and sent 59 Home Rulers to Westminster. Finally, Gladstone himself, for all his splendid gifts, was not a good party leader. He was too often aloof, preoccupied with his own crusades, and bothering little about backbenchers at Westminster. Early in 1875 he resigned the leadership of the Liberals.

[1] The year 1876 produced the highest figure recorded in British history for annual consumption of beer per head of the population – 34.4 gallons.

9
Disraeli in power 1874-80

1 Benjamin Disraeli

The Conservative victory in the election of 1874 was a handsome one. They took 350 seats; the Liberals got 245, the Irish Home Rulers 57. The country had grown 'tired of being improved' by Gladstonian reforms. For the Conservatives, the influence of aristocratic landowners was still strong. Undoubtedly the Conservative party organisation was far more efficient than that of the Liberals. Yet the Conservatives' victory – their first since Peel's triumph in 1841 – was a tribute to the skill and tenacity of their leader, the most extraordinary of Britain's nineteenth-century prime ministers.

Benjamin Disraeli (1804–81) was a Jewish adventurer who by a blend of genius and luck had become leader of the political party which above all represented 'the gentlemen of England', the landed aristocracy. In his earlier years he had been notable for extravagant dress, financial escapades, and the writing of romantic political novels (especially *Coningsby* in 1844 and *Sybil* in 1845). But he had also displayed a fierce political ambition which took him into Parliament in 1837 as M.P. for Maidstone, confident that he would one day become Prime Minister. As we have seen (p.75), he became a national figure when he joined the attack on Peel in the battle over the Corn Laws in 1845–6. Nearly all the leading Conservatives followed Peel into the wilderness. For the next twenty years the Earl of Derby's leadership kept the party alive. Disraeli was the only Conservative of real talent in the Commons. Out of office except in the brief Derby-Disraeli ministries (1852, 1858–9 and 1866–8), he showed his brilliance as debater and parliamentary tactician in the conflict with Gladstone over the Second Reform Act. He was the inevitable successor when Derby retired from the premiership in 1868. In his own words, he had 'reached the top of the greasy pole' – though only for a few months. Now in 1874 he had real power at last.

Although Bentinck and his brothers had in 1847 put up the money to buy Hughenden Manor in Buckinghamshire for Disraeli and thus give him the social prestige of a country gentleman, the Conservatives were most unwilling to accept him as their leader. He was so very obviously a careerist. Salisbury (leader after Disraeli's death) described him in 1868 as 'an adventurer without principles or honesty'. His 'foreign' manner, his ornate language, and his sharp wit all aroused doubts and hostility.

Benjamin Disraeli, Lord Beaconsfield (1804–81)

Though nominally an Anglican, he was flippant about religion, as in the notorious comment in the great controversy over Darwin's ideas: 'Is man an ape or an angel? My Lord, I am on the side of the angels.' Politically he seemed utterly untrustworthy. He had deserted Peel and taken up Protection; yet within a few years he dropped Protection and led the party to follow Free Trade and the other policies of Peel. Many, like Salisbury, thought his conduct over parliamentary reform an outrageous betrayal of Tory principles. Moreover, 'Dizzy' was in some ways 'un-Victorian'. A cynical man of the world, he hated moral humbug, and had little faith in progress. All this made him suspect to the earnest and high-minded men who were so numerous and powerful in Victorian politics. Nevertheless he became indispensable to the party, first as Derby's henchman and eventually as leader.

2 Domestic reforms

Power came very late to Disraeli. By 1874 he was 70; his health was not good; he was a lonely widower since his wife's death in 1872. Nor did he enter office with a ready-made programme of reform. Yet this government put through Parliament what Lord Blake has described as

Social Reforms 'the biggest instalment of social reform passed by any one government in the nineteenth century'. While in opposition he had spoken of the need to improve the living conditions of the people, in particular in matters of health and housing, and he denounced the Liberals who criticized this as a 'policy of sewage'. Yet the social measures which the Conservatives passed were moderate ones, dealing with immediate practical problems. There was no deliberate policy to extend the authority of the central government or to strike a blow against 'laissez-faire', nor did the laws threaten the power of the landed gentry. Most of the credit for the bulk of this legislation must go to the Home Secretary, Richard Cross, rather than to Disraeli himself; Disraeli was not interested in the details.

The year 1875 brought a group of reforms. The great Public Health Act laid down a code of public health, covering an enormous range (e.g. sewerage and infectious diseases, infirmaries and slaughterhouses, cleaning and paving highways, impure food). It stated clearly and fully the duties of local councils in dealing with all nuisances to health. The Artisans' Dwellings Act (sometimes called Cross's Housing Act) gave local authorities wider powers to demolish slums and to replace them by homes for the working classes. Other measures of the same year checked the sale of adulterated and impure food and drugs; safeguarded the funds (and therefore the members) of building societies; and

Trade Unions restricted the enclosure of commons like Epping Forest. Finally there were two acts dealing with trade unions. The Conspiracy and Protection of Property Act repealed Gladstone's Criminal Law Amendment Act of 1871, and legalised peaceful picketing, thus making the strike a far more valuable weapon. The Employers' and Workmen's Act made both employers and workmen liable for damages for breach of contract – hitherto the latter had been open to a criminal charge. These last two acts were understandably very popular with trade unionists – and Disraeli believed that they would 'gain and retain for the Conservatives the lasting affection of the working classes.'

The following years produced further measures. Thus in 1876 the Rivers Pollution Act attempted to prevent the fouling of rivers by effluent from industry; the Merchant Shipping Act – passed only after a scene in the Commons during which Samuel Plimsoll, M.P. for Derby, 'the seamen's friend' who for years had demanded reform to prevent overloaded and overinsured ships being sent to sea, shook his fist at Disraeli – required the painting of a loadline on all British merchant ships; and Sandon's Education Act moved towards compulsory education by requiring local authorities to appoint school attendance officers. Last among major reforms came the Factory Act of 1878, which brought together a detailed code of regulations for factories consolidating the long succession of laws introduced since 1833.

It is easy to exaggerate the effect of all this legislation. Some of it was pioneering, all of it was limited in scope. Much was merely permissive, i.e. local authorities could apply it only if they wished. So, for example, only a few places set about slum clearance – and then mainly for making wider streets rather than building 'council houses'. One was Birmingham, under its vigorous mayor (1873–6) Joseph Chamberlain. Nevertheless, Disraeli's social reforms provided a significant pointer to the future. The role of government, of Conservative government at least as much as of Liberal government, in the life of British people was changing. As Disraeli himself said, 'the time had arrived when social not political improvement is the object which they ought to pursue.'

A quite different aspect of Disraeli's domestic policy is to be found in his relations with the Queen. Victoria, who thought Gladstone 'a very dangerous and unsatisfactory Premier', welcomed Disraeli's return to office. In 1868, when he had first kissed hands, she had found him 'vy. peculiar, but vy. clever and sensible and vy. conciliatory.' She added later, 'He is full of poetry, romance & chivalry. When he knelt down to kiss my hand wh. he took in both his – he said "In loving loyalty & faith." ' Now he went out of his way to flatter 'the Faery', as he called her, by a blend of elaborate courtesy, calculated informality, and entertaining letters; laying it on, as he himself said, 'with a trowel'. He was very successful, and no doubt enjoyed the comedy. It had its disadvantages, however. The crown was still sufficiently important for its wearer to be able to exert pressure on ministers over policy in certain matters, and two Acts of these years reveal that Victoria did this. Both brought criticism upon Disraeli, and not only from Gladstone. The Public Worship Act (1874) was described by Disraeli as an attempt to bring to book Anglican clergymen who used ritualist practices, and was warmly backed by the Queen. It caused much protest from many quarters, and was very ineffective. Two years later there was a storm over the Royal Titles Act of 1876, which declared the Queen Empress of India (p.163). She was very angry at the opposition voiced both by Gladstone and the Liberal party and by many people in London 'society'.

Politicians and statesmen may be measured by what they do not do as well as by what they achieve. Disraeli's second ministry offers a highly important example of this. It harked back to the events of thirty years before, when Disraeli the rebel against Peel had backed Protection against Free Trade and in the interests of farmers and landowners had opposed the Repeal of the Corn Laws (1846). In the years after Repeal was passed, farmers and landowners had prospered as never before, in the era of 'high farming'. Prices had been steady, profits great; new farm buildings had been put up, thousands more acres ploughed, drainage and other improvements widely introduced. Disraeli himself had dropped Protection as a party policy early in the 1850s. Then in the mid-1870s came disaster for British agriculture. With the opening of the vast cornlands of the prairies, American wheat flooded in at prices well below those which the British farmer had to charge if he were to make a living. Depression hit the countryside. Within six years the area under wheat in Britain fell by 25 per cent; hundreds of farmers went bankrupt, thousands of labourers left the countryside for the towns or to emigrate. Understandably, Conservative landowners and the farmers appealed to Disraeli to reintroduce Protection, to bring back the Corn Laws. He declined, saying frankly it was 'a hopeless question'; for to do so would have resulted in a rise in the price of bread and lost the votes of the town-dwellers, now so dominant in the population. It was a sharp irony for the man who had denounced Peel thirty years before.

Ireland

His decision confirmed the supremacy of trade and industry over agriculture in Britain, where the town-dwellers at least benefited from the policy. But in Ireland (a land which Disraeli never visited), where the great majority of people depended on agriculture for their living and town-dwellers were relatively few, the results of the depression were catastrophic. So the last years of Disraeli's ministry were marked there by the rise of a much more militant movement for Home Rule, and by the foundations in 1879 of the Land League, whose ultimate aim was to get rid of English landlords from Ireland. In the countryside rick-burning, cattle-maiming and murder spread: agrarian crimes multiplied tenfold in four years. Meanwhile the demands of Ireland were brought home in a novel way to the Commons at Westminster. From 1877 a new young Irish M.P., Charles Stewart Parnell, and a small group of colleagues developed techniques of parliamentary obstruction in order to wreck the work of the Commons. No answer to this problem was found before the end of Disraeli's ministry in 1880.

3 The Eastern Question and the Congress of Berlin

The conduct of foreign affairs was, for Disraeli, a new and eagerly-awaited experience. The Conservatives had had little chance in the previous thirty years to formulate an active foreign policy. Because they had been in almost continuous opposition to Palmerston, they had generally condemned Palmerstonian aims and methods; if they had any policy of their own, they tended to be 'Little Englanders', opposed to interference abroad. Privately, however, Disraeli admired Palmerston. He himself was no linguist, had not travelled extensively, and was, in many ways, un-English, but he followed Palmerston in that he was intensely pro-English and determined to leave his mark on foreign policy. He felt, as a character in one of his novels said, that 'real politics means foreign affairs.' Now he had plenty of opportunity to become involved. For most of this ministry he was saddled with an extremely ineffective Foreign Secretary in Derby, son of his former leader, and he was also faced with a new and complicated stage of the Eastern Question. Illness and a bitter confrontation with Gladstone added to his problems.

Gladstone also had opposed Palmerston's foreign policy, and had voted with Disraeli on such issues as the Don Pacifico affair. When he became Liberal Prime Minister he took as anti-Palmerstonian a line as he possibly could, going back to the Tory traditions of Peel and Aberdeen, when policy was based on non-intervention and morality. The British public, encouraged by Disraeli, thought this a weak policy, damaging to British prestige. It is not surprising, therefore, that when the Conservatives came to power in 1874 much of the Palmerstonian tradition came back into favour. The support of liberalism abroad was played down; but the ideas first, that Britain must be involved in matters affecting the general security of Europe, and second that the Crimean System, as it was called, was the best answer to the Eastern Question, were both firmly accepted. The Crimean System, which Palmerston had sought to set up by the Treaty of Paris (1856), was based on the hope that the Turkish Empire, if it behaved properly towards its Christian subjects, could be supported, along with Poland and Hungary, by the Western Powers against an expanding and autocratic Russia. This policy was now to be severely tested, and Disraeli's decision to back it was to bring Britain to the brink of war.

By 1875, not only was the Sultan bankrupt, but the European part of his ramshackle Empire was split by nationalist revolts in the Balkans. First to rebel were the Serb peasants of Bosnia and Herzegovina. Austria was afraid that Russia would follow the same policy as in 1853–4, move in to protect fellow Christians and Slavs, and so threaten the southern part of the Austro-Hungarian Empire. To remove the cause of friction, the Austrian Foreign Minister Andrassy sent a Note to the Sultan demanding reforms in the rebellious provinces, and asked the other powers for their support. Austria, Prussia and Russia were already joined in the League of the Three Emperors, a resurrection of the old Holy Alliance. Disraeli had no intention of playing a supporting role. He reluctantly agreed to the Andrassy Note but, when this was rejected by the Sultan, and replaced by the more threatening Berlin Note, Disraeli withdrew. He had little sympathy for the Balkan nationalists, and he did not want to see Turkey weakened; above all, he wished to impress on the other European powers that no settlement should be reached without British approval. To show that they were no longer dealing with a 'weak' Gladstonian policy, he ordered warships to Besika Bay, where Palmerston had sent the fleet in 1849 and 1853; the intent was plain – to discourage Russia from invading Turkey. 'Something like the old days of our authority have returned' he said. But any hopes which he might have had of organizing a new Concert of Europe to renew the Crimean System were dashed when the nationalist rebellions spread, first to Serbia and Montenegro, and then to Bulgaria, on the other side of the Balkan peninsula. The Turks treated all the risings with undeniable brutality. In Bulgaria alone, over 12,000 men, women and children were massacred in May 1876 by Circassian irregulars known as 'bashi-bazouks'. There had been, and were to be, even greater atrocities; and Disraeli's efforts to play down reports of Turkish ferocity – which he called 'coffee house babble' – might possibly have succeeded had not a new element in foreign policy appeared, a strong, opposition public opinion, outside Parliament, capable of challenging government policy. The leader, though not the creator, of this public opinion was Gladstone.

Since 1875 Disraeli's old enemy had officially given up the leadership of the Liberal party. He still attended the Commons, occasionally wearing a light coloured suit to show that he was in semi-retirement, and giving his attention to interpretations of Homer and to attacks on the Papacy, subjects which privately he found more interesting than politics. He was, at that moment, not looking for 'a Call from Above', as he described a number of his political decisions; he was, in fact, in the middle of a painful bout of lumbago. There was, however, a growing demand in the country that religious and moral principles should actively influence government action, particularly in its international relations. Leading figures in this movement had been Cobden, Bright, and Gladstone himself, and everyone now looked to Gladstone to voice the sudden surge of moral indignation triggered off by the news from Bulgaria. During the Parliamentary recess when many M.P.s were shooting grouse on the moors, Gladstone wrote a passionate attack on the Conservative policy of supporting Turkey. Called *The Bulgarian Horrors and the Question of the East*, this pamphlet sold 200,000 copies in three weeks of September 1876, and proved to be one of the most influential pieces of British political writing in the nineteenth century. It was not meant to be pro-Russian, and it had no constructive proposals for a solution to the problem, except to demand that the Turks should clear out of the Balkans bag and baggage. Opinion in Britain became very sharply divided, and, when Parliament reassembled, the debates were exceptionally bitter. Disraeli called the pamphlet 'the work of an unprincipled maniac' and described Gladstone as worse than any Bulgarian atrocity. But he knew now that the 'coffee house babble' gibe had been an error of judgement. He had just been created Earl of Beaconsfield, and the first despatch boxes to the Queen bearing the new title had contained confirmation of the reports. Meanwhile, a meeting of the powers had been called at Constantinople to try to settle the whole question of Christian subjects in the Turkish Empire; when

The Bulgarian Horrors

reforms were again refused by the Sultan, Russia declared war on Turkey in April 1877.

Disraeli was now walking a tightrope. He had never seriously believed that Russia would declare war. His cabinet was divided, with Derby in particular counselling caution, while others echoed the Queen's cry that, if she were a man, she would 'give those Russians such a beating'. He was under constant attack from Gladstone and the Radicals. Then, abruptly, the tide turned against Gladstone. The stubborn defence by the Turks of their fortress of Plevna produced, in London at least, a great wave of pro-Turk feeling. The Turks ceased to be butchers and became heroes, and music-halls nightly rang to the strains of

'We don't want to fight, but, by Jingo, if we do,

We've got the ships, we've got the men, we've got the money too.'
with the defiant Palmerstonian ending – 'The Russians shall not have Constantinople!' For weeks Disraeli had been accused by some of being too warlike, by others of procrastination. He was adept at dealing with critics. When a lady at a banquet he was attending loudly demanded what he was waiting for, he replied 'At the moment, Madam, for peas and potatoes'. Now he acted. In January 1878 he ordered the Mediterranean fleet through the Dardanelles to Constantinople and asked Parliament for £6 million towards the cost of a possible war. At this critical point, the Russians, having captured Adrianople, did not feel strong enough to continue to the Turkish capital and, in March, the two sides signed peace terms.

These terms, the Treaty of San Stefano, were designed to ensure **Treaty of San Stefano** Russian domination of the Balkans. A new 'Big Bulgaria' was to be created to include not only the modern Bulgaria but parts of present day Jugoslavia and Greece. It would have extended from the Danube to the Aegean and from Albania to the Black Sea. As a Russian satellite, it could have given Russia an outlet to the Mediterranean, blocked Austro-Hungarian ambitions in Bosnia, and finally demolished the Crimean System. Another conference was therefore called by the powers to revise San Stefano and, when Russia refused to comply, Disraeli called up the reserves and secretly ordered Indian troops to Malta ready for an invasion of Cyprus. Derby, who had been most unhappy as Foreign Secretary ever since the news from Bulgaria, resigned and was replaced by Salisbury. Russia decided to climb down and to attend a congress to meet at Berlin where Bismarck, who saw no advantage to Prussia from a general war, agreed to preside as 'honest broker'. Many secret negotiations took place before the Congress with **Congress of Berlin** Disraeli and Salisbury representing Britain, and the result was the Treaty of Berlin 1878. 'Big Bulgaria' was divided into three; the largest part, mainly Macedonia, went back to Turkey, while the remainder became Eastern Roumelia, under a Christian governor, and a new small Bulgaria, which went no further south than the Balkan Mountains.

Austria was allowed to occupy both Bosnia and Herzegovina, and Britain received Cyprus. With the signing of the treaty, an international crisis had been averted, and Disraeli and Salisbury came home in triumph, claiming that they brought back 'Peace with Honour'.

Although Bismarck heaped praise on Disraeli for his part in the Congress, remarking 'Der alte Jude, das ist der Mann', it was Salisbury who had done the donkey work. Disraeli was ill when he went to Berlin and worse when he returned, though throughout the proceedings his

A BLAZE OF TRIUMPH!

Disraeli successfully negotiating the tightrope between peace and war at the Congress of Berlin, 1878

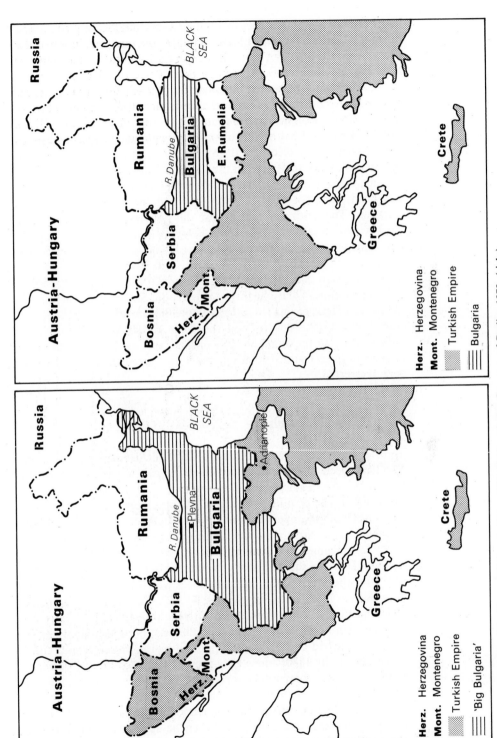

Fig. 4 The Balkans: The Treaty of San Stefano, 1878 (left) and the Congress of Berlin, 1878 (right)

had been the dominant personality. Back in London he had turned down a dukedom but, with Salisbury, had accepted the Order of the Garter – 'Peace with Honours' as one cynic said. Undoubtedly war had been avoided, and the European peace which followed lasted almost as long as that which separated the Congress of Vienna from the Crimean War. Disraeli's reputation was enhanced, though it was only because the bluff into which he had been forced had succeeded. In the words of A. J. P. Taylor, he had won 'a bloodless victory with a music-hall song, a navy of museum pieces, and no land forces at all except the 7,000 Indian troops sent to Malta'. In the long run, however, Salisbury's later comment that 'Britain had backed the wrong horse' was correct, and it was Gladstone, not Disraeli, who had had the clearer view of the situation. The truth was that Britain did not have to choose between Turkey and Russia, but between a decaying Turkish Empire and the new, independent, Christian states of the Balkans. The Treaty of Berlin was no solution to the Eastern Question, and, in some ways, was more unsettling than San Stefano. 'Big Bulgaria' need not have been a Russian satellite. The check by Austria to Serbian nationalism in Bosnia and Herzegovina led directly to the Balkan Wars of 1912–3, and contributed to the outbreak of the First World War in 1914 (pp. 263–4). But, for the moment, 'Beaconsfieldism', as Gladstone called it, seemed to have justified itself; at the very least, British prestige had been reasserted.

4 Disraeli and imperialism

In 1878 Lord Carnarvon, Disraeli's Colonial Secretary, commented 'We have been of late much perplexed by a new word Imperialism which has crept in among us'. The imperialism which existed in Britain in Disraeli's time is difficult to define. What is clear is that it was quite different from the imperialism of Joseph Chamberlain, a decade later. Disraeli's imperialism was, like his support of the Crimean System, a legacy from Palmerston. It never involved the deliberate search for new colonies. It is true that India was transferred to the Crown in 1858, but only after the Mutiny; the only territories which Palmerston acquired were Aden (1839) and Hong Kong (1842). Palmerston's 'imperial' policy meant the jealous protection of trade routes and trading posts, the extension overseas of commercial interests, not political power. In this policy he had been strongly supported by the British middle class. But when, in the 1870s, the steady growth in the wealth and power of Britain's foreign competitors threatened our supremacy, the middle class demanded something more than rearguard action. They found it in Disraeli when he refused to be excluded from discussions by other European powers; and even more when he appeared to be strengthening the ties between Britain and her overseas possessions. The word imperialism came to cover the idea of Britain as an imperial country whose colonies gave her an added strength to play her proper part in world affairs. In many ways it was an attitude of mind rather than a policy.

Disraeli's own connection with imperialism in this sense was more cautious than would appear from his speeches. Certainly, when speaking at the Crystal Palace in 1872, he had put forward Social Reform and Imperialism as parts of a new Conservative policy, but this was partly as a routine attack on the Liberal record, and partly to try to bind the new working class electorate to the Crown and to the Conservative party in a common pride in the 'Empire of Britain'. Equally certainly he was fascinated by India and he was particularly concerned to protect the Indian connection; it was this which involved him in most of the actions which might be called his imperial policy.

In 1873 Victoria, noting that the King of Prussia had elevated himself **Royal Titles Act** to the rank of Emperor, had failed to convince her Liberal ministers that she should be given the title of Empress of India. Disraeli was more co-operative; he wished to please the Queen, and he was nervous about Russian threats to India through Persia and Afghanistan. He had to push hard to get the Royal Titles Bill through the Commons, and its final passage in 1876 was due to considerable pressure from the Queen herself. When the Prince of Wales, largely on his own initiative, visited India in 1875–6, Disraeli again pushed hard to get the Commons' approval for public funds to foot the bill for the visit which, in the end, was a great success. Disraeli's efforts were seen by some as mere flattery, by others as a positive attempt to strengthen imperial ties, but in neither effort was the original idea his.

He took a much more leading role when he bought from the **Suez Canal** bankrupt Khedive of Egypt his shares in the Suez Canal Company. **Shares** Disraeli's motive in buying them was to prevent them from falling into French hands, since this would give France financial control of Britain's most important trade route to India. The way he did it captured the public imagination. The Khedive held 177,000 shares out of a total of 400,000, and, although they were mortgaged for twenty years, the price demanded was £4 million. Parliament was not sitting at the time when it became known that the Khedive was already negotiating with two French companies, so Disraeli arranged an immediate loan from a private banker, Baron Rothschild. According to Disraeli's agent, the Baron asked only two questions – 'When?' and, after eating a grape and spitting out the pips, 'What is your security?' It was typical of Disraeli that he made the Queen feel that it had all been done for her. 'It is just settled; you have it, Madam' he wrote. The purchase of the shares was a profitable investment for Britain and it helped to safeguard Indian trade. At the same time, as Gladstone was quick to point out, it increased the risk of Britain and France fighting for power in Egypt should the Egyptian government break down.

The purchase of the Suez Canal shares, 1875

Disraeli was aware of this, but it was no part of his plan in buying the shares that financial control should lead to political control.

Transvaal In two other areas, the Transvaal and Afghanistan, Disraeli became involved in dealing with problems which, rightly or wrongly, were felt to endanger British links with India. The weakness of the Boer Republic of the Transvaal was proving a temptation to the neighbour-ing, warlike Zulus. A successful Zulu invasion of the Transvaal might lead to a similar invasion of Cape Colony, and the Cape was almost as important as Suez as a trade route. The Amir of Afghanistan had **Afghanistan** accepted, though unwillingly, a Russian military mission in the capital Kabul, and it was felt in London that the Afghans were becoming too friendly with the Russians and had to be discouraged. Because of delays in communication the men on the spot, Frere in the Transvaal and Lytton in India, were able to go their own way in 1879, and both involved Britain in heroic but costly, ill-planned and unnecessary wars. A small British force was wiped out by the Zulus at Isandhlwana in January 1879, and the British Resident in Kabul was murdered with all his staff. Both wars were eventually won, but they were victories for Gladstone rather than for Disraeli (pp.173 and 286).

Gladstone's With a general election not far off, Gladstone in 1879 set off on the **Midlothian** **campaigns** first of several remarkable Midlothian campaigns. This two weeks railway tour of Scotland was something quite new in politics. It was aimed partly at introducing Gladstone to the electors of Midlothian – a seat held by Viscount Dalkeith, and regarded as a safe Tory stronghold – and partly as a crusade against the Conservatives' handling of foreign affairs. The young Earl of Rosebery, the leading Liberal landowner in the area, arranged the details, hiring halls in towns and villages, and a special American-type Pullman coach from which Gladstone made 'impromptu' speeches. Public interest was enormous. People came from as far away as Shetland, and paid as much as £10, to hear him speak. They listened quietly even on cold November railway platforms, not to promises of material gain if they voted Liberal but to impassioned appeals for justice for weaker nations. He did not use the word Imperialism but aimed all his attacks at 'Beaconsfieldism', his general term of abuse for all Disraeli's policies. He spoke of the invasion of Afghanistan as 'a crime against God', of the naked Zulus defending their homes against British guns, of the Queen's assumption of the title of Empress as 'theatrical bombast', of Cyprus as a 'valueless encumbrance', and of the disgraceful British support for the brutal Turks. *The Times* dismissed the campaign as 'a ten-days waterspout, dealing with all human affairs', while Disraeli made little effort to counteract what he called 'this drenching wearisome rhetoric'. He was frail in health, unemployment was rising, four wet summers had given four bad harvests in succession. His most effective colleagues were either ill or debarred from electioneering because they were peers. He made a snap decision for an election in April 1880 and was defeated. A year later he died.

10
Gladstone's second ministry 1880-5

1 Cabinet and Commons

Although Gladstone had retired from the leadership of the Liberals in 1875 his Midlothian campaigns had not only won him that seat in the 1880 election; they had stamped him in the minds of the electorate as the natural leader of the victorious Liberals. He himself saw in the result 'the great hand of God so evidently displayed' and the opportunity to conduct another crusade, this time against 'Beaconsfieldism'. He made clear to his colleagues that he expected, and the country expected, that he should return as Prime Minister. For the Queen, the prospect of having to work with Gladstone instead of Disraeli was a double blow. She sent for Lord Granville and Lord Hartington as possible alternatives but they tactfully declined: convinced that Gladstone was the leader demanded by the national interest, they consoled her by saying that he was unlikely to be able to cope with the strain of office for long. When she accepted the inevitable and sent for Gladstone she noted that he looked 'very ill' – a comment she frequently made whatever his state of health. She was also astonished to hear that he intended to combine for himself the posts of Prime Minister and Chancellor of the Exchequer. For a man of seventy, even one with Gladstone's physical endurance, it seemed an intolerable burden, and indeed it proved to be the first wrong move in a ministry of disasters.

A 'Ministry of disasters'

On the three other occasions when Gladstone became Prime Minister his aims were largely constructive. This time, they seemed mainly destructive, to rid the country of the evil legacy of 'Beaconsfieldism' as quickly as possible and then to retire for good. In his election campaigns his most bitter speeches had been against the imperial aggressive side of Disraeli's foreign policy which he called 'Jingoism'. Yet, when he opened his attack, it was against the economic measures which had produced a Conservative deficit of £8 million. In 1867 he had made the mistake of becoming so involved with the details of the Second Reform Bill that he failed to see that Disraeli was walking off with the prize. This time he chose to concentrate on financial details when a whole range of political problems needed his full attention. Foreign affairs, demands for wider social reforms, divisions within his own party, and, above all, Ireland, were questions where delaying an answer only added to the difficulties.

From the start, Gladstone found the 1880 House of Commons

unusually difficult to handle. His cabinet consisted mainly of Whig aristocrats with only two ministers to represent the growing Radical element. John Bright, now seventy, took the relatively unimportant post of Chancellor of the Duchy of Lancaster, and Joseph Chamberlain, the former Lord Mayor of Birmingham, became President of the Board of Trade. Gladstone and Chamberlain never trusted each other. Chamberlain felt that more men of radical opinions should have been given cabinet rank; that Gladstone did not sufficiently appreciate his work in creating the National Liberal Federation, which had won sixty of the sixty-seven seats it had recently contested; and that Gladstone lacked enthusiasm for two of his own main beliefs – that at home the government should pay more attention to social problems, and that abroad it should take a much stronger line against the despotic Tsar. On the other side of the House, the new leader of the Opposition was the amiable Sir Stafford Northcote, who showed far too much deference towards Gladstone to please some Tories. A small group emerged, headed by Lord Randolph Churchill, calling themselves the Fourth Party, who began a series of brilliant, personal and irresponsible attacks on Gladstone, taking every advantage of the fact that the Prime Minister could be relied upon to treat even their wildest accusations politely and at length. Egged on by Disraeli until his death in 1881, they claimed to be continuing a policy of Tory Democracy. Yet, though they used phrases like 'Trust the People', they had little to offer except opposition to anything that had Gladstone's support. To add to Gladstone's difficulties, the Queen made it clear that she wished to have as little to do with him as possible. Moreover, in the House of Commons generally there was an atmosphere of tension and bitterness. This was largely due to the Irish debates and to the snipings of the Fourth Party, though some at least was a legacy of Gladstone's Midlothian campaigns where he had attacked Tory policy in such strong terms. Much time was wasted over the Bradlaugh case, when Charles Bradlaugh, who had been returned as Radical M.P. for Northampton, asked to be allowed to take his oath of allegiance by affirmation on the ground that he was an atheist. Gladstone strongly disapproved of Bradlaugh's opinions but, characteristically, defended his rights; whereupon the Fourth Party took delight in accusing Gladstone of supporting atheism. Like Wilkes before him, Bradlaugh was shuttled between the electors and the Commons, and did not finally take his seat until 1886.

2 Ireland–Parnell and the Land League

It was the Irish problem, however, which dominated this Parliament. When Gladstone took office in 1880 he was quite unprepared for what he later called 'the crisis which rushed upon us like a flood'. He realized that the 1870 Land Act needed amending but the famous 'mission to pacify Ireland' was not in the forefront of his mind. Since he had last been in office, however, Irish demands had grown in scope and urgency. The Irish were not interested in the destruction of 'Beaconsfieldism' or in budget deficits, and, moreover, they now had a formidable leader in Charles Stewart Parnell. Parnell was a Protestant, born in 1846 to an Anglo-Irish father and an American mother, and educated in England. He had estates in County Wicklow, but little interest in Irish history or culture, and little in common with most of the Irish he represented except a deep hatred of the English. What mattered was that he was a born leader, ruthless, arrogant and incorruptible. He entered Parliament in 1875, and by 1877 he was convinced that 'we shall never gain anything from England unless we tread on her toes'. It was a time when falling agricultural prices made it peculiarly difficult for tenants to pay their rents. The 1870 Land Act, with its failure to define a fair rent, aggravated the problem so that evictions increased, and this in turn led to attacks on landlords and their agents.

Two associations had been formed by the Irish to press for changes. First, the Home Rule League, formed by Isaac Butt in 1870, aimed not at complete separation but at devolution, an Irish Parliament within the United Kingdom. A militant member, Joseph Biggar, began the tactic of obstructing debates at Westminster, keeping within the rules of procedure yet making sure that if English M.P.s would not give time to Irish affairs they would not be given time for English affairs. In 1878 the leadership of the Home Rule group was taken over by Parnell.

Irish Land League

Secondly, the Irish Land League was started in 1879 by Michael Davitt in an attempt to improve the conditions of the Irish peasants, conditions in which – as the Viceroy of Ireland himself wrote to Gladstone – 'you and I would not keep pigs'. Davitt's family had been evicted when he was five years old and had emigrated to Lancashire; he had lost an arm in a factory accident, and had spent seven years in Dartmoor for his Fenian activities. Now he was an M.P. His short term aim was to reduce rents; but the long term aim was, by fair means or foul, to transfer the ownership of Irish land from the landlords to the tenants. Parnell became the first President of the Land League, and was thus able to unite the efforts of the Irish M.P.s at Westminster with those of the Irish tenants. In his first ministry Gladstone had hoped to solve the Irish problem by disestablishing the Church and by satisfying the tenants. Now he was to be made to realize that the Irish wanted not merely the end of tenantry but the end of government by the British.

The first step that Gladstone took was to introduce a bill in 1880 to protect tenants who had fallen behind with their rents. It was passed by the Commons but thrown out by the Lords. Parnell saw the failure of such a moderate bill as proof that an all-out attack was required. He advised members of the Land League to pay nothing at all if they considered their rents unfair, and when the landlords reacted to this by

The Land League agitation in Ireland. A sheriff's sale of cattle to pay rent

widespread eviction (there were 10,500 in 1880 compared with 2,200 in 1877) he began the tactic of 'boycotting'. Landlords, their agents, and anyone who bid for a farm from which a neighbour had been evicted were to be shunned 'like a leper of old'. The first of the 'lepers' was Captain Boycott, agent for Lord Erne. Though Parnell was careful to be seen not to approve of violence, attacks by night on landlords' cattle, ricks and houses increased rapidly, many of them attributed to a mythical 'Captain Moonlight', one of the more popular of the old secret society names. An attempt to prosecute the Land League failed, and, against Gladstone's better judgement, a Coercion Act was introduced suspending Habeas Corpus in Ireland. Parnell's reply was to use the Commons as a battleground. He sharpened the weapons of obstruction and filibustering, organizing teams of speakers and endless amendments; on one occasion, the motion 'That the Speaker do now leave the chair' was debated for forty-one hours on end. New rules of debate, such as the closure, had to be brought in, even though they restricted the freedom of speech so jealously guarded by M.P.s, and most of the Irish members were suspended while the Coercion Bill was passed.

Meanwhile a commission had been working on the defects of the **Second Irish Land Act** 1870 Land Act. Gladstone accepted its findings and, virtually by himself and without consulting Parnell, drew up proposals which became the Second Land Act of 1881. It took fifty-eight sittings for the Act to be passed and Gladstone had to fight for it clause by clause. The

Act extended the Ulster system of tenant rights to the rest of Ireland. It gave tenants greater security of tenure and the right to sell their interest in their holdings, and it set up tribunals to fix fair rents for a period of fifteen years. In a word, the Irish tenants now had their 'Three F.s' (Fixity of tenure, Fair rent and Free sale), and the agrarian problem began to disappear from Anglo-Irish politics. The Act was a setback for the landlords, many of whom, as Whig peers, had supported the Liberals, but it was grudgingly accepted as the only alternative to the breakdown of law and order in Ireland. Parnell declared that the Act did not go far enough, but was quick to appreciate that his methods seemed to produce results. Since the Act did nothing for some 100,000 tenants who, because they were behind with their rents, were still liable to eviction, Parnell now urged Land League members to boycott the tribunals; and when he was arrested in October 1881 and put in

'No Rent' campaign

Kilmainham Goal, Dublin, the League declared a rent strike. The government's reply was to declare the League illegal and to imprison its other leaders. At once there was an increase of violence in Ireland encouraged by a rash of newly formed secret societies. It was to become a familar pattern for Britain's modern wars of colonial liberation. To imprison nationalist leaders like Parnell and, in the twentieth century, Gandhi, Kenyatta and Nkomo, usually meant the removal of restraint and the cutting of channels of communication, a lesson which successive governments found it hard to learn.

Parliamentary obstruction and Parnell's opposition to the Second Land Act jolted Gladstone into a reappraisal of his Irish policy. He accepted that he had to work with Parnell – and began to think seriously of Home Rule as a solution. For his part, Parnell saw the secret societies as a threat to his leadership; also, he chafed at the separation from his mistress, Mrs Kitty O'Shea, the wife of one of the Irish Nationalist M.P.s. He therefore agreed to a pact with Gladstone, the so-called Kilmainham Treaty, negotiated by Joseph Chamberlain with Mrs O'Shea's husband as go-between. Parnell was to call off the 'No Rent' campaign on the understanding that the government would bring in a bill to extend the 1881 Act to tenants in arrears. Parnell and two others were released in May 1882, a triumph for the man who was now widely called 'the uncrowned King of Ireland'. Forster resigned as Chief Secretary in protest at Parnell's release, and was replaced by Lord Frederick Cavendish, husband of Gladstone's niece. Within twenty-

Phoenix Park murders

four hours of reaching Ireland, Cavendish was murdered in Phoenix Park, Dublin, by a secret society called the Invincibles. Murdered with him was the Under Secretary, T. H. Burke; at the time it was believed that Cavendish had been killed by accident, defending his colleague, yet there is police evidence that the deaths of both men were planned. The murders were a disaster for both Parnell and Gladstone. They confirmed the general British opinion that all Irishmen were violent and irresponsible; and they made the task of convincing public and

Phoenix Park, 1882. A contemporary impression

politicians of the need for Home Rule that much more difficult. Another Coercion Act was introduced, this time so severe that it was called 'Martial Law in a Wig', though Gladstone, at the same time, kept his part of the Kilmainham Treaty, and saw through Parliament an Arrears Act cancelling all rent arrears on land worth less than £30 a year. The landowners were furious, but the number of reported agrarian crimes dropped from 4,439 in 1881 to 870 in 1883. Parnell, sobered by the violence of Phoenix Park, began to plan ahead, hoping that the results in the next general election would be close enough for his own party to hold the balance.

3 Foreign affairs

Gladstone's troubles in his second ministry continued when he turned to foreign affairs. Here his policy, conceived as an attack on 'Beaconsfieldism', brought him as many headaches and even more unpopularity than his Irish activities. His first action seemed as jingoistic as any action of Disraeli's. The Treaty of Berlin in 1878 had given parts of the Turkish Empire to Montenegro and Greece; when the Turks delayed handing them over, Gladstone threatened naval action and tried, unsuccessfully, to invoke the Concert of Europe by seeking support from the other powers. Fortunately for him, Turkey gave way and the

Gladstone threatening the Turks in 1880

territories were handed over. Next, Gladstone planned to return Cyprus to Greece but was persuaded by Granville, his Foreign Secretary, that this would prove much too unpopular. He then reversed Disraeli's forward policy in Afghanistan by withdrawing the garrison from Kandahar, and negotiating with the Russians to agree on a frontier. It was not that he was for peace at any price. In 1885, when the Russians sent an army across the River Oxus and attacked the Afghans at Penjdeh, Gladstone at once made it clear in Parliament that Britain would not tolerate this aggression and was prepared to fight. The Russians retreated and border talks were resumed.

South Africa During the Midlothian campaigns Gladstone had strongly opposed Disraeli's annexation of the Transvaal, and this was, not surprisingly, taken by the Boers as a pre-election pledge to grant them early independence (p.165). The election of 1880 over, however, Gladstone was busy on the nation's income tax and similar financial problems. He and his cabinet were also cautious about giving the Boers too much too soon, for fear of offending the British in South Africa; accordingly, the Boers were told that they would have to wait until a scheme of South African Federation had been approved. The Boers were not prepared to wait. They had a determined leader in Paul Kruger and no fear of further trouble from the Zulus. They rebelled, and defeated a British force under Sir George Colley at Majuba Hill in 1881. Less than a hundred British soldiers, including Colley, were killed, but the defeat produced great waves of the very jingoism that Gladstone had hoped to purge from the British public. He could have bowed to the storm and continued the war, but he stuck to his principles and his pledge. The Convention of Pretoria 1881, confirmed three years later in London, gave independence to the Transvaal subject to control of foreign policy and the suzerainty of the Crown. The Boers gained the same impressions as the Irish, that a show of force brought quick results, while the British public were confirmed in their impression that Disraeli stood for the greatness of the British Empire, and Gladstone for its humiliation.

In 1882 trouble arose in Egypt. A nationalist rising, led by army officers under Colonel Arabi, resulted in riots in Alexandria, with the killing of fifty foreigners and injuries to the British consul. Arabi, who in his way was doing for the Egyptians what Parnell was doing for the Irish or what Garibaldi had done for the Italians, mounted guns on the fortifications of Alexandria to prevent interference by the British navy, and declared that he would repudiate Egypt's debt to foreign bondholders. Gladstone thought Arabi a would-be dictator who could threaten the safety of the main trade route to India. He looked again to the Concert of Europe to combine against Arabi, but even the French were unwilling to help and withdrew their fleet. Somewhat reluctantly, therefore, Gladstone authorized the bombardment of Alexandria and the seizure of the Canal. In August 1882 an army under Sir Garnet Wolseley defeated Arabi in 'the moonlit battle' of Tel-el-Kebir, and occupied Cairo. John Bright felt all this to be worse than anything Disraeli had done, and resigned from the cabinet. Gladstone had now to establish a settled pro-British government in Egypt, so that the British occupation could end; and by 1885 he had managed to get an international Board of Control representing six powers to oversee Egyptian affairs, with Egypt still nominally part of the Turkish Empire. Practical control of the country lay in the hands of the British Agent, Sir Evelyn Baring, later Lord Cromer. Though Gladstone never had the slightest intention of acquiring Egypt, he was overtaken by events. The whole Egyptian episode was unpopular in England, while other powers felt cheated. France had always seen Egypt as her special sphere of influence and was particularly bitter; Turkey looked for new friends; Germany took advantage of Britain's lack of allies by annexing territories in Africa and New Guinea.

Yet the most important immediate result of the occupation of Egypt

Egypt

The Sudan

was that it involved Gladstone in the further problem of the Sudan. The Sudanese were governed by the Egyptians, and Arabi's rising encouraged a Sudanese religious leader called the Mahdi (the 'Expected One'), to try to free his country. In November 1883 his forces destroyed an Egyptian army commanded by a British officer, Colonel Hicks. Gladstone, who had described Arabi as 'one of the greatest villains alive', nevertheless decided that the Mahdi 'was struggling to be free' and should not be punished. He agreed that British troops should help the Egyptian garrisons to withdraw from the Sudan, and he made the fatal mistake of approving the choice of General Charles Gordon to advise on the withdrawal. 'Chinese' Gordon, whom Gladstone had never met, was a military eccentric, given to going into action with a cane and a Bible. He held British, French and Turkish decorations from the Crimean War, had helped to capture Pekin in 1860, and fought in over thirty battles for the Chinese against local rebels. He knew the Sudan

The death of Gordon 1885

and had served two campaigns there fighting the slave trade. Now at the age of fifty-one, he had no intention of acting merely as an advisor on withdrawals. He went with the intention of smashing the Mahdi, in defiance of Gladstone's declared policy, hoping that once operations began the government would have to support him. He arrived in Khartoum in February 1884 and demanded reinforcements. In March he was besieged and it was not until August that Gladstone agreed that a relief force should be sent. An army of 10,000 completed a 1,600 mile march along the Nile and reached Khartoum on the 28th January 1885, two days after Gordon and his men had been speared to death. Queen and country were appalled at the news. For about three weeks crowds flocked to Westminster in the hope of personally booing the Prime Minister, and those who had fondly called him Grand Old Man now reversed the initials and denounced him as Murderer Of Gordon. Under this pressure, Gladstone announced that this time the Mahdi should be punished; but within two months the decision was changed and the Sudan left to go its own way.

4 The Third Reform Act 1884

In the midst of all these troubles Gladstone found time to carry out a pledge made by the Liberals in 1877 to make the voting qualifications in the county constituencies the same as those made by the 1867 Act in the boroughs. The Bill he proposed in 1884 was rejected by the House of Lords where Salisbury and the permanent Conservative majority still had the power of absolute veto. They argued that the new proposals would not only increase the total electorate by about two million voters; they would also produce too many large county constituencies and too many small boroughs. At the moment, the Tories controlled the counties, and they were afraid that the new rural voters would all vote Liberal. Gladstone's radical followers were up in arms at the Lords' attitude: Chamberlain talked of 'the Peers versus the People', and John Morley demanded 'mend them or end them'. The Queen worked hard behind the scenes and, after private talks between Gladstone and Salisbury, a compromise was reached; the Reform Bill would go through the Lords followed immediately by a Redistribution Bill. Thus, in 1884, the Third Reform Act gave the vote in the counties to all male householders and created a total electorate of about five million. In 1885 the Redistribution Act disfranchised all boroughs with less than 15,000 inhabitants; boroughs with fewer than 50,000 inhabitants were now to return one member only, not two or three as before. Single-member constituencies became the rule in the first general election held after the changes. It was the Whigs who were hardest hit since many had previously only squeezed in as running partners to Radicals in two-member constituencies. The new rural voters in Ireland enabled

RAISING THE "FIERY CROSS."

MIDLOTHIAN, AUGUST. 1884.

Gladstone promises his constituents a speedy passage of the Reform Bill

Nationalist M.P.s to win almost every election that they fought. Elections themselves had come under stricter control when the Corrupt Practices Act of 1883 fixed election expenses in proportion to the number of voters.

Gladstone's second ministry ended in June 1885 when the government was unexpectedly defeated on the budget. The cabinet had recently split over proposals for local self-government in Ireland[1], and Chamberlain had resigned. Defeat, in a way, was a relief to Gladstone. He had given up the attempt to be his own Chancellor of the Exchequer in 1882 when, overworked and disillusioned, he realized that the burning questions of the day would not be answered by cuts in income tax. Now he had the chance to retire, and with an earldom. He turned down the Queen's offer gracefully and went on holiday to Norway; and it was there that he decided to fight for the cause of Home Rule and to lead the Liberals in the next election.

[1]Between mid-April and mid-May nine ministers had threatened to resign. After one dispute, Gladstone said to a friend, 'A very fair cabinet today – only three resignations.'

11
The age of Salisbury and Chamberlain

1 Ireland

Gladstone's resignation in June 1885 came at an awkward time for the Opposition leader, Lord Salisbury. Because the new electoral registers were not ready there could be no general election for several months. Salisbury realized that, if he took over as Prime Minister of a minority 'caretaker' government before an election, he would be dependent on the support of the Irish Nationalists; to gain that support the Conservatives would have to change their Irish policy. Salisbury decided to take office. At once the new ministry ended coercion and, by the Ashbourne Act (1885), voted £5 million to be loaned to Irish tenants who wished to buy their own land. Parnell was delighted not by the Act but by this proof of the power of Irish support. It seemed to him just possible that either party might now be persuaded to go that vital step further and adopt Home Rule.

Gladstone's
conversion to
Home Rule

Parnell made every effort at this stage to get Gladstone to commit himself publicly to Home Rule, but the Liberal leader remained at Hawarden, where he cut down more trees while deciding on his best course of action. Gladstone now saw the Irish as he had seen the Italians, the Bulgarians and the Zulus – a people struggling to regain their just freedom. In this view he was ahead of most of his countrymen who supported nationalism abroad so long as it was not within the British Empire. Gladstone's mission was no longer to pacify but to set free. What he was undecided about was the way Home Rule was to be achieved. He disliked the two main parties being manipulated by Parnell, and he wanted to see an all-party settlement of the Irish Question. If he himself introduced a Home Rule Bill it would almost certainly not be passed by the Conservative House of Lords. He also suspected that a number of his most influential colleagues, from Whigs like Hartington to Radicals like Chamberlain and Bright, would not support a Liberal bill; and he had no wish to split his party as Peel had split the Tories in 1846. The best plan seemed to be to keep quiet about his own conversion and to hope that the Conservatives would pass Home Rule with Liberal and Irish support. Both Parnell and Chamberlain were thus kept unaware of Gladstone's conversion, and this was to have a most important effect on the forthcoming election. With no sign from the Liberal leader, Parnell decided to ally with the Conservatives and issued a last minute manifesto to all Irish voters to oppose Liberal candidates.

As a result, the election in November 1885 produced what was virtually a dead-heat. The total of Liberal seats won was just not enough to defeat a combination of Conservatives and Parnellites. At the same time, the Conservative-Irish alliance could not continue for it had no overall majority, and Salisbury's cabinet was against further Irish concessions, particularly Home Rule. Before the House of Commons met, Salisbury firmly rejected a private offer made by Gladstone of Liberal support for a Conservative initiative. Any last hope which Gladstone had of this manoeuvre vanished when his son, Herbert, himself a Liberal M.P. and a Home Ruler, gave a press conference in London in December 1885. He worshipped his father; considered him to be the only politician capable of getting a Home Rule Bill through Parliament; and decided to rally the party by making public his own opinion that his father was now converted to Home Rule. The result of the 'Hawarden kite', as it was called, was that Gladstone now had no option but to prepare himself and his party to carry through a Home Rule Bill.

The 'Hawarden Kite'

The new Parliament opened in January 1886 with a Speech from the Throne confirming that the Conservatives intended to preserve the Act of Union. One week later Salisbury's government was defeated on a minor issue by a combined Liberal and Irish vote, though ominously for Gladstone, 18 Liberals voted with the government. The Queen sent for Gladstone with the utmost reluctance – 'a half-crazy and in many ways ridiculous old man', she now privately called him. The cabinet he formed marked an important stage in the history of the Liberal party. Before 1868, the date of Gladstone's first ministry, Liberal policy had been shaped by the great Whig families; even after 1868 it had been greatly influenced by them. Now, with the refusal of Hartington and the Duke of Argyll to serve in Gladstone's third ministry, most of the Whigs drifted away, later to join the Conservative party as Unionists. Chamberlain also resigned from the cabinet once he had seen the text of the proposed Home Rule Bill. The nucleus of the party, however, stuck by Gladstone and prepared for what was to become one of the fiercest debates in parliamentary history.

The First Home Rule Bill took Gladstone three months to draft. He introduced it in April 1886 amid scenes of the greatest excitement in a speech of three and a half hours. For a man of seventy-six it was a remarkable feat – the result of an iron constitution, a determination to complete a mission, and a wife who cherished him with loving care. It was said that, rather than disturb him while he was sleeping, she would tie knots in his nightshirt to remind her of things to tell him in the morning. The bill proposed not to repeal the Act of Union of 1800 but to set up in Dublin an Irish Parliament of two Houses with control over all matters except peace and war, defence, foreign policy, customs and excise; Irish members were no longer to sit at Westminster. There was one vital omission – the protection of the Protestant minority in the

First Home Rule Bill

North. In introducing the bill, Gladstone made his views clear – 'I cannot allow it to be said that a Protestant minority in Ulster, or elsewhere, is to rule the question at large for Ireland.' They were words which sounded the alarm bells in Ulster and worried the British electorate, itself mainly Church of England or Nonconformist. The Conservatives were quick to take advantage. Randolph Churchill wrote to a friend, 'I decided that if the G.O.M. went for Home Rule the Orange card would be the one to play. Please God it may turn out the ace of trumps, and not the two'. He produced a telling slogan, 'Ulster will fight and Ulster will be right'. A monster petition was sent by Ulster women to the Queen at Windsor. The debate raged on and in early June 1886, on a vote taken in the Commons on the Second Reading, the bill was thrown out by 343 to 313. In the Opposition lobby were 93 rebel Unionists led by Chamberlain, Bright and Hartington.

Gladstone refused to accept defeat and decided to go to the country on the single issue of Home Rule. In the election campaign, Churchill's address to his constituents contained another catching phrase. It described Home Rule as 'the ambition of an old man in a hurry', and as election propaganda it helped to defeat Gladstone at the polls. The rebel Unionists opposed official Liberal candidates and, together with the Conservatives, they gained a majority of 118 over Liberals and Irish combined. Gladstone had underestimated the concern in Britain over the future of Protestant Ulster. His own passionate pleas for Home Rule had raised Catholic hopes and Protestant fears in both countries to fever pitch in a situation which called out for a calm approach. He had made no effort at a deal with Chamberlain and the other rebels for it was not in his nature to do so. Nor had he any real answer to the claim that 'Home Rule meant Rome Rule' or to the cold certainty that the Lords would reject any form of Home Rule bill. Gladstone's determination to press on not merely lost the Liberals the 1886 election; with the exception of one brief interlude, it kept them in opposition for nearly twenty years.

Salisbury's cabinet contained no Liberal Unionists. Its Irish policy was based partly on the idea of 'killing Home Rule by kindness' and partly on Salisbury's view that the Irish needed 'twenty years of resolute government'. 'Kindness' in this context meant financial help to tenants; the Ashbourne Act (1885) had been an example. In 1887 there was an Act to suspend evictions where genuine hardship could be proved, while Balfour's Land Purchase Act (1890) set up a central office to deal with all land questions in Ireland; 100 per cent mortgages were now available. It was the 'resolute government', however, which attracted more attention. The new Secretary for Ireland was A. J. Balfour, Salisbury's nephew and a man whose languid exterior hid a surprising toughness. His first task was to deal with the 'Plan of Campaign', a new Irish tactic, not approved by Parnell, by which

Balfour's Irish policy

tenants who thought their rent was too high paid what they considered a just rent into a campaign fund. Balfour's reply was to declare the Plan illegal and to arrest its organizers, O'Brien and Dillon. He was given wider powers by the Crimes Act of 1887, itself only passed by the introduction of a time limit on debates called the 'guillotine'. Breaches of law and order in Ireland could now be dealt with without a jury and, as violence increased, the prisons overflowed; most of the Irish M.P.s were locked up as common criminals. Police and tribunals had even wider powers than under the first Coercion Act. The man whose appointment the Irish had at first derided was now reviled as 'Bloody Balfour'.

Anti-British feeling grew even higher when at an eviction at Mitchelstown in 1887 two men were shot dead by the police. In England anti-Irish feeling was fanned by a series of articles in *The Times* under the heading 'Parnellism and Crime'. Facsimiles of letters alleged to have been written by Parnell were included in an effort to prove that he and his colleagues at least condoned the Phoenix Park murders, and that they approved murder and arson as weapons to gain Home Rule. Parnell at first ignored the charges, but eventually sued for libel. Salisbury's government appointed an independent committee of enquiry into *The Times'* accusations. It established, after an exhaustive investigation, that the letters were forged by a journalist, Richard Pigott who, once he had confessed, fled the country and shot himself. Parnell's stock rose, Liberal candidates were returned in by-elections, and there was increasing criticism of Balfour's policy of coercion. The whole affair cost *The Times* £200,000, of which £5,000 went to Parnell as libel damages.

'Parnellism and Crime'

As fast as the clouds cleared for the cause of Home Rule, however, they closed in again with the scandal of the divorce of Kitty O'Shea. Captain O'Shea, a man of few principles, had tolerated the affair between his wife and Parnell in the hope both of political advancement and of sharing in a legacy from Kitty's aunt. When the aunt died and the legacy failed to materialize, he set out to ruin his wife's lover by naming Parnell as co-respondent in a divorce suit; the case was undefended and the divorce came through in 1890. Parnell's refusal to defend showed as much his arrogance as his love for Kitty, and his apparent indifference to public opinion lost him much support, particularly among Catholics and Nonconformists. The fact that Parnell had lost much of his influence was a further blow to Gladstone's hopes of still getting a Home Rule bill through the Commons, yet he did not hesitate to make public his view that for Parnell to continue as leader of the Irish party would be a disaster for Ireland – a statement which many Irish felt was a stab in the back. Forty-four of the seventy Irish Nationalist M.P.s broke away and formed a separate group under Justin McCarthy. Parnell married Kitty, a fresh affront to Catholic opinion, but his health was already impaired; in June 1891, at the age of

Fall of Parnell

Charles Stuart Parnell (1846–91) Kitty O'Shea

43, he died. A few months before it seemed that, if Ireland could be given some form of self-government, she had a united group of experienced parliamentarians and an acknowledged leader to help her over the first difficult stage. Now she had neither.

Although the Liberals narrowly won the election of 1892, it was on vague promises of social reform rather than on the platform of Home Rule; in fact they failed to get a majority of English seats, and owed their victory to the voters in Scotland and Wales. Nearly fifty Liberal Unionists now sat with the Conservatives, and Gladstone was entirely dependent on the support of Irish M.P.s. The Lords, now that most of the Whig aristocracy had changed sides, were almost solidly against Home Rule and certain to throw out any bill. Undaunted, **Second Home Rule Bill** Gladstone introduced his Second Home Rule Bill in February 1893. It proposed that, as well as having a Parliament in Dublin to deal with all Irish matters except defence, trade and foreign affairs, the Irish should also send eighty M.P.s to Westminster with the power to speak and vote only on issues affecting Ireland and the Empire. The bill passed the Commons by a majority of 34 in September, after a series of heated debates and an outburst of fisticuffs on the floor of the House. Predictably, the Lords rejected it by a massive 419 votes to 41.

Gladstone retired in 1894 for the last time. He still made long public speeches, kept up his writing on Church matters, and began a new project, the foundation, from his own books and money, of a library at St. Deiniol's, Hawarden, for public use. He died of cancer in May 1898 and was buried in Westminster Abbey; two future kings, the Prince of

Wales (Edward VII) and the Duke of York (George V) were among the pall bearers. For a man whose real interests were outside politics, Gladstone had had a remarkable influence on the life of his party and of his country. His obsession with Ireland eventually broke the Liberal party with the split over Home Rule. Yet, for Gladstone, Ireland posed the most important question of the time – how could its future relations with the rest of Britain be based on morality and justice? That question has still to be resolved; Ireland remains for Britain 'that Cloud in the West'. Gladstone made miscalculations in his Irish policy, as he did in his economic and foreign policies; he was not easy to work with; and though, as the 'People's William', he could sway the mass of the electorate with his sudden and passionate convictions, the results were not always what he intended. As a devout Christian he appealed to the better nature of his listeners, yet too often high hopes ended with disappointment; and this came to be the pattern of his efforts to solve the Irish Question.

After Gladstone's death, Rosebery, the new Liberal leader in opposition since 1895, announced that the Home Rule issue would not be revived until it had the majority of English voters behind it. The two factions of the Irish Nationalists reunited in 1900 under a new leader, John Redmond, but it was clear that it was useless to proceed with Home Rule plans so long as the House of Lords kept its power of absolute veto. In the meantime, the Conservatives made an all-out effort to solve the Irish land problem. Wyndham's Land Purchase Act (1903) made available a total of nearly £200 million to be paid out at £5 million a year to tenants wishing to buy their holdings. The repayments, at 3¼ per cent over 68 years, cost less than a normal rent. Within six years a further quarter of a million tenants were on the way towards owning their own land, while the rents of the remaining tenants were on average a fifth less than they had been before the 1881 Land Act. For a few years Ireland was relatively quiet. Some Conservative and Unionist leaders were optimistic enough to believe that Home Rule had indeed been 'killed by kindness'. They were sadly mistaken. It only needed the strong Liberal challenge to the House of Lords over Lloyd George's budget in 1909 to give a third Home Rule bill a real chance of success.

2 The Marquess of Salisbury and Joe Chamberlain

Irish Home Rule was the supreme issue of British politics in the 1880s, and the defeat of the First Home Rule Bill in 1886 was a major turning-point in the history of the United Kingdom. The great Liberal party which Gladstone had done so much to create and inspire was hopelessly split. A new political pattern appeared. The Liberal Unionists – those Liberals who believed that the Union with Ireland must be

Joseph Chamberlain (1836–1914)   Lord Salisbury (1830–1903)

maintained – broke with Gladstone. They came from both wings of the party; from the old Whigs of the Right, led by the Marquess of Hartington, and from the Radicals of the Left, led by Joseph Chamberlain. After 1886 these men moved gradually but inexorably into alliance with the Conservatives, and in 1895 together they formed a Unionist government under Salisbury.

On the Liberal side of the political stage Gladstone, the ageing crusader, was alone in his eminence. Two men dominated the new grouping on the other side. They could hardly have been more unlike one another. The first, Prime Minister in 1885 and 1886–92, was Robert Arthur Talbot Gascoyne Cecil, 3rd Marquess of Salisbury, descendant of Elizabeth I's minister William Cecil, lord of Hatfield House in Hertfordshire and its great estates. A big, bearded, stooping, short-sighted, untidy man, an aloof intellectual with probably the ablest mind among front-rank British politicians of the nineteenth century, he was a sharp and forceful speaker and writer who had never refrained from

Salisbury

criticism of his own party as well as of the Liberals. He had been the chief opponent of the Reform Act of 1867, for he had little belief in democracy and thought Disraeli a throughly unprincipled 'dodger'. Deeply religious and a devout Anglican, he nevertheless had a pessimistic and often cynical view of human nature. He had no enthusiasm for social reform (although indeed he was not hostile to change: as well as riding a tricycle to work in London, he was a pioneer of the domestic use of electricity, lighting his great mansion with it and using it to pump away the town sewage of Hatfield). He made his peace with Disraeli and as Foreign Secretary in the latter's second Cabinet had been the principal British negotiator at Berlin in 1878.

The second leading figure on the Unionist side in these years, Joseph Chamberlain, was a self-made and successful screw-manufacturer, a Unitarian in background, who had first made his name on the Liberal side in the local politics of Birmingham. A hard, masterful and ambitious man, possessing, in Beatrice Webb's words, 'energy and personal magnetism, in a word masculine force, to an almost superlative degree', he had also more than a touch of unscrupulousness. 'Joe' was single-minded in the pursuit of his political ends. The carefully-cultivated appearance, the monocle, the orchid in the button-hole; the flair for political organization, which gave him control of Birmingham as a base throughout his political career, whichever party he belonged to; the pugnacious style of his speeches, as in the famous onslaught on Salisbury in 1883 as 'the spokesman of a class .... who toil not neither do they spin' – all these things helped to win him national popularity and power in the years before 1886. He had been the founder of the National Education League of 1869, demanding a national system of free, compulsory, non-sectarian education, paid for out of local rates and government grants. As Mayor of Birmingham (1873–6) he had put through a model programme of social reform for a great industrial city. Under his leadership the corporation took over gas and water supplies, making the former efficient and profitable and the latter pure and plentiful; carried through a pioneering slum clearance scheme, driving a wide new 'Corporation Street' through the heart of the city; and developed such various new amenities as libraries, an art gallery, parks and swimming baths.

Such 'gas and water socialism' was an expression of Chamberlain's genuine radicalism, and in 1876 he was elected as a Liberal M.P. for Birmingham. He soon became prominent in the Commons; far more important, he organized in 1877 the National Liberal Federation, the first systematic party 'machine' in Britain. In 1880 Gladstone included him in his second ministry as President of the Board of Trade. There were already many who saw this vigorous politician of 44 as a future Prime Minister, leader of a radical and revitalised Liberal government after Gladstone, now in his 71st year, had left the stage. But the reality was to be very different, partly at least because the relations between the two men, both of them very self-willed, were never easy. Neither trusted the other. Gladstone seems to have thought 'Joe' no gentleman. Moreover he was not interested in the kind of social reforms Chamberlain wanted. The latter for his part was out of sympathy with the cautious Whigs who formed most of the Liberal cabinet. He was the prime mover in the Third Reform Act (1884) which increased the electorate from 3 millions to 5. For the election of 1885 he proclaimed to huge crowds in aggressive speeches his 'Unauthorised Programme', demanding such changes as free primary schools, local government for the counties, a graduated tax on property, rural smallholdings (with the celebrated slogan 'Three Acres and a Cow') manhood suffrage, the end of plural voting, payment of M.P.s, and repeal of the Game Laws. A century later these do not seem notably extreme; in 1885 they were very alarming, not only to Conservatives who called him 'Dick Turpin' or a 'Sicilian bandit', but also to many Liberals.

Yet it was not Chamberlain's radicalism that led to the final breach with Gladstone in 1886. It was his refusal to accept Irish Home Rule. Chamberlain, offended by Gladstone's failure to be frank with him about Irish policy, did not believe in Home Rule, which he thought dangerous to the security of the British Empire; perhaps more important, he thought (correctly) that a majority of voters in Britain did not favour it, and that it would be disastrous to the Liberal party whose leader he aspired to be. So in the critical debate of June 1886 on the First Home Rule Bill Chamberlain led 93 Liberals into the 'No' lobby, with Gladstone's followers crying 'Judas!' at him.

3 The years of Conservative supremacy

In 1886 Salisbury returned to office with a comfortable majority, and there began a spell of Conservative rule which lasted until 1905. It was interrupted only by a Liberal interlude from 1892 to 1895: Gladstone, Prime Minister for the fourth time at the age of 82, saw his Second Home Rule Bill rejected by the Lords and retired in 1893; his successor, Lord Rosebery, quarrelled almost at once with important groups in the party, and the government achieved little[1]. When he resigned in 1895 the Unionists won a handsome victory at the polls, and Salisbury remained Prime Minister until 1902.

For all his aloofness and seeming eccentricity, he was a skilful political operator. He was careful, for example, to ensure that nearly all the Liberals who had voted against Home Rule (the Liberal Unionists) had no Conservative candidates opposing them in 1886; he made very effective use of the Conservative Central Office as a means of controlling the work of local party associations; and within the parliamentary

[1]Although horses owned by the Prime Minister won the Derby in two successive years, an event unique in English history. It did him no good with the Nonconformists in the Liberal party.

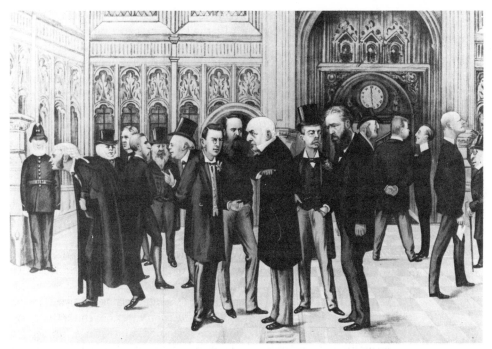

The lobby of the House of Commons, 1886. In the foreground, Chamberlain, Parnell, Gladstone, Randolph Churchill and Hartington

party he successfully outmanoeuvred an early challenge to his authority offered by Lord Randolph Churchill, the leader of that small 'Fourth Party' which had tormented Gladstone in the early 1880s, and got rid of him from his Cabinet with general approval. The Irish question kept the alliance between Conservatives and Liberal Unionists firm, and in 1895 some of the latter were given Cabinet posts – notably Hartington (now Duke of Devonshire) and Chamberlain, who became Colonial Secretary.

Salisbury's own main interest lay in foreign policy, where these years saw some highly important developments. In Ireland, as we have seen (p.180), Conservative policy was a blend of toughness and reform, with the firm line of 'Bloody Balfour' coupled with a scheme of Land Purchase. At home there were some important reforms, the most notable of which was the Local Government Act of 1888. This, pressed for by the Liberal Unionists, created County Councils elected on the same franchise as the Third Reform Act of four years earlier, and these took over most of the work hitherto carried out by local magistrates in Quarter Sessions. Sixty-one large boroughs with over 50,000 people each became County Boroughs with separate councils of their own. The new London County Council took over responsibility for an area which by 1901 contained some four and a half million people. The Act made possible great progress in problems such as health and housing, water,

Conservative reform

187

sewage and roads, where organization was urgently needed. Thus the demand for cleanliness which Edwin Chadwick had put forward half a century before could now be met; so too could the challenge of new types of transport, the tram, the bus and the motor-car. In the countryside the landowners and squires who had served on Quarter Sessions continued to dominate the County Councils; but in the County Boroughs many middle class radicals seized their chance of promoting reforms; while the London County Council was soon run by a vigorous Progressive Party which included people of all political opinions. Six years later Gladstone's fourth Liberal Ministry took reform further by putting through a second Local Government Act (that of 1894, sometimes named the Parish Councils Act) which created a pattern of lesser authorities called Urban and Rural District Councils, with responsibility for various matters of health, housing and highways, and also set up nearly 7,000 Parish Councils.

Other social reforms of these years included the virtual abolition of fees in elementary schools (1891) and the creation of the Board of Education (1899); the Workmen's Compensation Act (1897), by which the employer, for the first time, was compelled to compensate an employee injured at work, so long as the injury was not the latter's own fault; laws concerned with the land (e.g., on smallholdings, tithes, and the rating of farmland), appealing to the agricultural labourers lately (1884) given the vote and trying to tackle the problems caused by the depression in agriculture; and others on such varied matters as industrial arbitration and vaccination. In some, but by no means all, of these (notably workmen's compensation) the hand of Joseph Chamberlain may be seen; and he was also in the 1890s the first front-rank politician to put up proposals for Old Age Pensions. Any policy of social reform inevitably involved some interference by government, either national or local, with individual freedom, and often with private property. Both Salisbury and Chamberlain at this time saw limited action as a means of combatting the dangerous new doctrines of socialism which were beginning to win support in Britain in the final years of the nineteenth century.

4 Foreign affairs – Salisbury and 'splendid isolation', 1886–1900

Except in the Liberal administrations of Gladstone (1892–4) and Rosebery (1894–5) foreign affairs in the last fourteen years of the nineteenth century were in the experienced hands of Lord Salisbury, who combined the posts of Prime Minister and Foreign Secretary. He was well equipped for the task. Since the day when he had spoken against Palmerston in the 'Arrow' debate of 1856 he had had thirty years in public life. He had proved an able and industrious negotiator at the Congress of Berlin in 1878. Now his intelligence, his grasp of diplomacy and his calmness of temperament were invaluable at a time when international peace was threatened by national and imperial rivalries among the great powers. Salisbury once said that 'British foreign policy is to drift lazily downstream, occasionally putting out a boathook to avoid a collision'. Such a diplomatic statement concealed the considerable care and patience with which he laid his plans.

There was no doubt in Salisbury's mind that Britain's position in the world was deteriorating. Germany and the U.S.A. were overtaking her industrially and obtaining a greater share of world trade. The Concert of Europe, through which so many British Foreign Secretaries from Castlereagh on had tried to work, was now in shreds as Germany and France competed for allies. British naval supremacy was in danger now that technological progress made it possible for her rivals to build larger, faster and better armed ships. The continuing decline of Turkey increased the Russian threat in the Mediterranean. Africa was beginning to pose for Whitehall almost as many problems as Europe. International disputes had spread even to China. Salisbury was a realist who accepted these changes and tried to move with the times. He knew that British sea-power was still feared, and this encouraged him to follow, wherever possible, a policy of independence and neutrality. He was unwilling to commit Britain to formal alliances, preferring to keep her free to take sides as she thought fit on any issue as it arose. It was a policy which, down to about 1895, worked reasonably well.

Diplomatic problems

In 1886 Salisbury felt, as did most of his fellow countrymen, that the main threats to Britain came from Russia and France. A crisis with Russia had just arisen over Bulgaria. At the Congress of Berlin in 1878 Salisbury and Disraeli had prevented the creation of a 'Big' Bulgaria on the grounds that it might become a Russian satellite. Since then it had become clear to both Britain and Russia that the Bulgarians were fiercely independent. By supporting Turkey at the Congress, we had, as Salisbury himself said, 'backed the wrong horse', since a truly independent 'Big' Bulgaria now seemed a better bet than Turkey as a buffer against Russian expansion westwards. Accordingly, when the Bulgarians in Eastern Rumelia rebelled in 1885 and joined themselves to Bulgaria, Salisbury worked to gain the approval of the powers for the new state. Russia and Turkey both objected and, for a few months, there was a real risk of war; but the Russians were at that time rather more interested in Central Asia and the Far East than in the Balkans, so the crisis passed and Bulgaria was united. As a safeguard against interference by either Russia or France, Salisbury in 1887 made two Mediterranean Agreements, one with Italy and the other with Austria-Hungary, to defend, by force if necessary, the *status quo* in that area. Since these pacts were approved by Bismarck, Salisbury now had a good understanding with three Central European powers – Germany, Austria and Italy – who in 1882 had formed themselves into the Triple Alliance. This understanding smoothed the course of the colonial

Mediterranean Agreements

agreements of 1890 which made possible the peaceful partition of much of Africa (p.292), and also enabled Salisbury to persuade Germany to accept Heligoland in exchange for Zanzibar (1890). At the same time he twice rejected, in 1889 and 1891, offers of an alliance with Germany; his reason was that it was directed against France alone instead of against both France and Russia.

Meanwhile there had been trouble with France over Egypt. France resented the continued British occupation of Egypt, so, to improve relations, Salisbury suggested to the Sultan – who was still overlord of Egypt – that there should be a British withdrawal within three years. As he was far from certain that the Khedive could control his own country, Salisbury reserved the right to re-occupy if the Egyptian government broke down. France objected to this clause and, with Russia, forced the Sultan to refuse the British plan. So British troops stayed in Egypt; **Two power standard** France and Russia drew closer together, and in 1894 signed the Dual Alliance; and fear of combined Franco-Russian action led Parliament to pass the National Defence Act (1889) by which Britain adopted the Two-Power Standard, i.e. that her fleet should outnumber those of any other two powers combined.

When the Liberals were in office, between August 1892 and June 1895, Rosebery – who also combined the posts of Prime Minister and Foreign Secretary – abandoned Gladstone's brand of anti-Jingoism, and continued along Salisbury's lines. In particular, he was in sympathy **Imperialism** with a new wave of imperialism which was sweeping the country. Britain had long had an Empire and been proud of it. The Conservatives under Disraeli had fostered this pride, but now it grew into an obsession. The 'eighties had seen the start of a world-wide race for colonies, a race in which Britain's rivals further threatened her commercial supremacy. Colonies meant new sources of raw materials and new markets for manufactured goods, and Britain, though late in joining in the scramble, had no intention of being left behind. At the same time, the feeling grew that Empire-building was Britain's manifest destiny, that she should, in Kipling's words -

'Take up the White Man's burden –
Send forth the best ye breed –
Go bind your sons to exile
To serve your captives' need.'

The feeling of belonging to the greatest Empire the world had yet seen captured the imagination of millions; in a small way it helped to relieve some of the drabness of everyday life. As her rivals grew in strength it was a reassurance to many that Britain was not in decline. And although, as in all Empires, some made rich profits, this British Empire did seem to contemporaries, for all its military exploits, a humane institution. The Queen's Golden Jubilee of 1887, and even more her Diamond Jubilee of 1897, were spectacular proofs of the extent and variety of the Empire and of the affection for the old lady who was its head. *Rule Britannia* and *Land of Hope and Glory* were sung with the same fervour as the National Anthem.

'Wider still and wider may thy bounds be set.

God who made thee mighty make thee mightier yet,'
well expressed the mood of the country at the turn of the century, in spite of bad news from the South African front.

The politician most committed to this form of imperialism was Joseph Chamberlain. When the Conservatives came back to office in 1895 Salisbury gave him, at his own request, what was then the relatively minor post of Colonial Secretary. His aim was to build the Empire into a single economic unit capable of competing with Britain's strongest rivals. It was a policy which led both to beneficial reforms and to the Boer War of 1899–1902 (pp.227–33). Salisbury's own problems at the Foreign Office were world wide. In 1892 he had used arbitration as a method of peacefully settling arguments when he successfully submitted to a tribunal British claims, disputed by the U.S.A., to fishing rights in the Bering Sea. In 1895–6 the U.S.A. invoked the Monroe Doctrine (p.31) to protect Venezuela in a boundary dispute with British Guiana. External arbitration found in Britain's favour; but Salisbury was careful to mend any breach in Anglo-American relations by making public his support for the U.S.A. in the Spanish-American War of 1898.

During 1895–7 there was a further twist to the Eastern Question.

British troops entering Khartoum after the Battle of Omdurman, showing the effect of shelling upon the Mahdi's tomb

Salisbury had come round to the view that Egypt gave us an adequate base for defending the Eastern Mediterranean and our links with India. He had less and less faith in the Mediterranean Agreements, and any remaining ideas of bolstering up Turkey ended when Armenians were massacred by Turkish troops in 1896. From now on, in Conservative policy at least, it would be Egypt, not Constantinople and the Straits, that must be defended at all costs. The main threat to Egypt came not from Russia but from the south. After the death of Gordon in 1885 both Rosebery and Salisbury had postponed the reconquest of the Sudan, and had aimed, by diplomacy, to keep rivals out. In 1898 the French government, still smarting under the loss of Egypt, sent a Captain Marchand on an expedition to the White Nile which would have brought the French into the Sudan. Salisbury at once ordered an army under Lord Kitchener to reconquer the Sudan; the Dervishes, the followers of the Mahdi's son, were defeated at Omdurman and Khartoum was occupied. Kitchener learnt that Marchand, with half a dozen French officers and about a hundred Senegalese soldiers, had hoisted the French flag at Fashoda, 500 miles up the Nile. Kitchener pushed on to meet them and, after a polite but firm exchange, ensured that the French flag was replaced by the Egyptian. When the news of all this reached London it brought public enthusiasm for the new imperialism to its highest level. The popular press, led by the *Daily Mail*, made loud patriotic noises, and Salisbury was under pressure from Chamberlain and others in the cabinet to prepare for war. However, the French Foreign Minister Delcassé realized that, in this matter, France had no allies and that Salisbury held all the cards. Marchand was instructed to withdraw and the threat to Egypt was removed.

Yet, if France had no support over Fashoda, Britain herself seemed to be increasingly without friends. In 1895 the Kaiser Wilhelm II was quoted as saying, 'There is no question about it, the newspapers are right in saying – England is isolated. Now you have your hands full and everywhere you stand alone.' The Kaiser, grandson to Victoria, was young and ambitious; when Bismarck resigned as his chief minister in 1890 his actions became more reckless; and Anglo-German relations which had been friendly rapidly deteriorated. Immediately after the Jameson Raid (p.228) he sent a telegram to Kruger congratulating him on the failure of the Raid, an action which was extremely unpopular in Britain. In 1897 he appointed Admiral Tirpitz as German Minister of Marine, and it soon became clear that Tirpitz's aim was to build a navy capable of meeting the Royal Navy on equal terms. The German Naval Law (1898) approved the construction of twelve new battleships and ten large cruisers. The Kaiser also went on a tour of the Middle East, and Germany looked for backers, Britain included, to finance a railway from Berlin to Baghdad to increase her influence in that area. She was active in China, where Russia, Britain and Japan were also looking for bases; in 1898 she gained Kiao-Chow, with Russia gaining Port Arthur

Fashoda

Anglo-German rivalry

and Britain leasing Wei-hai-wei. When to all this was added Germany's rapid industrial growth and the political support she had from Austria and Italy in the Triple Alliance, then one of Britain's great fears was closer to being realized – the emergence of a single power strong enough to impose its will on the rest of Europe. Britain's other great fear had always been the loss of her command of the seas, and of the North Sea and the Channel in particular. The opening of the Kiel Canal in 1890 now gave the German Fleet easy access to these waters. To these threats Britain had to respond. To rub it in, she was the target for international hostility as a result of the Boer War, and she was isolated in a Europe dangerously divided into the two armed camps of the Triple Alliance and the Dual Alliance.

Triple Alliance

A later generation called this the period of 'splendid isolation.' The phrase, it is true, had first been used in 1896, picked up by Joseph Chamberlain from a speech made in the Canadian Parliament, and was revived by him in 1902. Everyone could see that Britain was isolated, but to call it 'splendid' gave the impression that this isolation was a deliberate choice made from strength. There was further confusion after the First World War when the phrase was used to describe Salisbury's foreign policy. Salisbury never thought of himself as carrying out a policy of isolation, splendid or otherwise. What he sought was not isolation but independence – freedom from committing Britain too deeply to either side. 'The British government', he said in 1902, 'cannot undertake to declare war unless it is for a purpose of which the electors of this country would approve'. In 1898 he had unsuccessfully tried to reach a general agreement with both France and Russia on all matters in dispute. Twice, in 1898 and 1899, Chamberlain approached Germany with offers of an alliance; the German answer was to introduce a Second Naval Law (1900) doubling the scale of her building programme. With Lansdowne as Foreign Secretary from 1900, due to Salisbury's failing health, Britain drew nearer to those countries who also felt menaced by Germany. The day of independent action was over.

12

Britain at the end of the nineteenth century

1 Queen Victoria and the Jubilees

Queen Victoria reigned until 1901. The Prince Consort's death from typhoid fever in 1861 had been a terrible blow: she had become 'the Widow of Windsor', living almost in seclusion, desperately cultivating his memory (the room where he died was kept entirely unchanged until her own death forty years afterwards). There was widespread criticism of her withdrawal, and some growth of republicanism. But in the 1870s, thanks to the devotion of her Scottish highlander servant John Brown and to the skilful management of Disraeli, she began to play a fuller part in public affairs. Her effective political influence was limited, for political parties were now far stronger than they had been in George IV's time. Yet her prejudices remained vigorous: thus she readily adopted Disraeli's jingoistic anti-Russian views at the time of the Treaty of Berlin, while in the 1880s she was firmly hostile to Irish Home Rule. Gladstone, indeed, she strongly disapproved of, as a dangerous radical who would lower British prestige abroad. After the Midlothian Campaign she thought him a 'half-mad firebrand who would soon ruin everything and be a Dictator'; and in 1885 she sent him an open telegram criticising his failure to send troops to Khartoum in time to save General Gordon.

In the later years of her reign Victoria, a formidable old lady in her widow's weeds, was deeply conscious of her role as a symbol of Britain's power in the world. She was no doubt encouraged in this by the fact that she was 'the grandmother of Europe', among whose descendants were princes and princesses galore throughout the continent (most notably the last Kaiser of Germany and the last Tsarina of Russia); and by the sheer extent of the British Empire at the end of her reign, when it included almost a quarter of the entire population of the globe. The theme of the British Empire in its glory was illustrated in her two Jubilees in 1887 and 1897, with their spectacular processions of foreign potentates, Indian princes, colonial chiefs and native soldiers, and their glittering reviews of army and navy. As the *Daily Mail* said of the Diamond Jubilee procession, 'Up they came, more and more, new types, new realms at every couple of yards, an anthropological museum, a living gazetteer of the British Empire. With them came their English officers, whom they obey and follow like children. And you begin to understand, as never before, what the Empire amounts to.'

Queen Victoria aged 78 (in 1897)

Certainly at the end of her 'sixty glorious years' Victoria was genuinely mourned by millions, for she had done much to make the British monarchy popular as well as respected. Certainly too her last Prime Minister indicated a main reason for this when he said that what the

The procession at the Diamond Jubilee

Queen thought on any topic was very likely to be what most of her subjects thought, 'particularly the middle classes of them'.

2 Economic affairs

The Diamond Jubilee of 1897 was a very different kind of celebration from the Great Exhibition of 1851 – and Britain's economic place in the world about 1897 was very different from that of 1851. The industrial and commercial supremacy which in the 1850s earned her the title of 'workshop of the world' remained until about 1870. At that date the total foreign trade of the United Kingdom and her colonies was greater than that of Germany, France, Italy and the U.S.A. put together. But thereafter the rate at which British trade was increasing slowed down quite sharply – while that of Germany (which became a united nation only in 1871) and of the United States (first linked by transcontinental railroad in 1869) went ahead fast. Such a development, given the greater resources both in population and in raw materials of these two countries, was no doubt inevitable at some time. The tables which follow show how the balance of economic power between the three countries changed from 1850 to 1914, in population and in the two vital industrial materials of the age, coal and steel.

Yet other circumstances too, all of them stressed by English critics at the time, contributed to the change. One lay in the different trading

Table 5: Population (millions)

United Kingdom	Great Britain		Germany[1]	USA
1851	27.4	20.8	1850	34.0	23.1
1861	28.9	23.1	1860	36.2	31.4
1871	31.5	26.1	1870	40.8	38.5
1881	34.9	29.7	1880	45.2	50.1
1891	37.8	33.1	1890	49.4	62.9
1901	41.5	37.0	1900	56.4	75.9
1911	45.2	40.8	1910	64.9	92.2

[1]1914 boundaries

Table 6: Coal Production (millions of tons)

	United Kingdom	Germany	USA
1850	57	6	–
1860	81	12	3.4
1870	112	34	10
1880	149	59	64.9
1890	184	89	143
1900	228	149	244
1910	268	222	356
1914	292	277	455

Table 7: Steel Production (millions of tons)

	United Kingdom	Germany	USA
1870	0.7	0.3	–
1880	1.3	0.7	1.3
1890	3.6	2.3	4.3
1900	5.0	6.7	10.0
1910	5.9	13.8	26.0
1914	6.5	14.0	32.0

policies adopted by the governments of the three countries. Britain since the budgets of Peel and Gladstone was committed to Free Trade, which meant that she lay wide open to the produce of every country. By contrast, Germany from 1879 and the U.S.A. from 1890 followed a policy of Protection, closing their doors by tariff barriers against imported goods. Secondly, many British manufacturers, just because they had been first in the field and prospered mightily, were now most reluctant to change their ideas and to install new machinery – whereas Germans and Americans alike were ready to pioneer new processes and techniques, as, for example, ring-spinning in cotton and various developments in chemicals and electricity. Thirdly, technical education was slow to develop in England, particularly by contrast with Germany.

It must be stressed that British decline was relative and not absolute: that is to say, British industry in general was not going backwards, merely going forwards more slowly than before and a good deal more slowly than that of its chief rivals. Nor of course did this change affect all industries equally. Some, like coal and steel, increased their output greatly; others, notably the great pioneering industry of eighteenth-century change, cotton textiles, grew, yet more slowly than before. Cotton goods had in the middle years of the nineteenth century been the biggest item in Britain's exports; and perhaps the most serious feature of these later years was the change in the kind of goods Britain was sending abroad. Earlier it had been ever-increasing quantities of manufactured articles – shirts, pots and pans, cutlery and other metal goods. By 1900 the proportion of such things in the export trade had fallen. Instead Britain was now sending abroad greater amounts of coal, machinery, and ships – which meant that her customers were becoming her competitors, aided by coal from British pits, engines from British foundries, and ships from British yards.

British achievements Such a development carried serious implications for the future. Nevertheless there was plenty of evidence of industrial and trading progress in late nineteenth century Britain. British technical advances of the time included, in steel making, the Gilchrist-Thomas Process (1878) which made it possible to use phosphoric iron ore; in marine engineering, the triple expansion engine (1881) and Sir Charles Parsons' invention of the steam turbine (1894); J. B. Dunlop's pneumatic tyre (1888); and Sebastian de Ferranti's development of electrical generating machinery (about 1890). Great enterprises were designed and completed, like the Severn Tunnel of 1886 and the Forth Bridge of 1890 on the railways, and the Manchester Ship Canal of 1894. Firms whose names became household words – Boots, Liptons, and Freeman, Hardy and Willis among them – started at this time, and this suggests how fast retail trade was expanding in the cities[1]. The railway network

[1]Among the goods advertised in the 1880s and 1890s were Hovis bread, Cadbury's and Rowntree's cocoa, Player's Navy Cut tobacco, Sunlight soap, Cherry Blossom boot polish, Bovril, Robertson's jams, Birds Custard, Beechams Pills, Scotts Emulsion, and Eno's Fruit Salts.

The Forth railway bridge (1890)

Transport in London, 1910

grew. The 7,500 miles of track in use in 1852 had become almost 22,000 by 1900; locomotives were heavier and faster, now running on steel rails and pulling corridor coaches, dining-cars and sleeping-cars. Underground railways were in use in London, the Metropolitan from 1863 and the first electric 'tube' from 1890. Electricity was also being used for lighting from the 1870s; to drive tramcars in the large cities from the 1880s; and to power engineering firms and shipyards (notably on Tyneside) and many small workshops by 1900. Finally, shipping and shipbuilding had undergone great changes, which had been stimulated by the completion (by a French company) of the Suez Canal in 1869. In 1870 there were less than 1,000,000 tons of British shipping under steam, compared with 4,500,000 under sail. Fifteen years later the figures were over 4,000,000 under steam and less than 3,500,000 under sail.

All this pointed to a prosperous commercial and manufacturing country – even allowing for the ups and downs of trade, the periodic spells when large numbers of workmen were unemployed, for example in the middle 1880s. Britain had lost her clear leadership in the world's economic affairs; yet her business was still expanding, even if not as fast as that of her greatest rivals, Germany and the United States. Indeed, as late as 1889 her foreign trade was as great as that of these two nations

Future risks combined. But, for the future, there were some disturbing elements in the situation. Britain's prosperity had become alarmingly dependent upon overseas trade. Her development during the nineteenth century had outgrown her own natural resources. By its end her people were importing considerably more goods than they exported – notably foodstuffs (by 1900 about half of all the food they ate came from abroad) and industrial raw materials other than coal. Two circumstances enabled them to pay their way in the world. One was that they provided services for other people: particularly in the form of shipping (British vessels formed about one-third of all the world's ocean-going tonnage) and banking and insurance (London remained the financial capital of the globe). The second, particularly during the second half of the nineteenth century, was the growth of huge overseas investment, interest upon which returned to the pockets of British people. These two items between them provided the great bulk of what have come to be called 'invisible exports' – items which filled the growing gap between the amount of goods Britain exported and the amount she imported – and thus gave her a 'favourable balance of trade'. Yet how long this situation could continue was uncertain. Above all, it would be at grave risk if a major war broke out.

Agricultural depression One section of British economic life was in serious trouble during the last quarter of the nineteenth century. This was agriculture, where the 'golden age' of the previous twenty-five years came to an end in the early 1870s. Three sets of figures indicate the situation. Wheat prices, 55 shillings a quarter in the early 1870s, were half that figure in 1900. Likewise the acreage of land under wheat fell from 3,600,000 in 1874 to just over half that total at the end of the century. The number of people employed in agriculture dropped from 1.6 million in 1871 to 1.3 million by 1901. Behind the bare figures lay a countryside of unpaid rents and emptying farms; of bankrupted farmers and of labourers compelled to seek jobs in the towns or to emigrate overseas; of fields abandoned to grass and weeds, hedges uncut, ditches uncleared. Agriculture, already by 1850 of declining importance in the national picture, seemed now to be failing fast. In the 1850s it had produced about 20 per cent of the total national income; by the end of the century its share was down to about 6 per cent.

The fundamental cause of this depression was the opening-up of the virgin soil of the world's greatest cornlands, the North American prairies. The construction of transcontinental railroads, the invention of new reaping and binding machines, and the building of ocean-going steamships – these developments, occurring simultaneously, made it possible to flood Britain with American wheat at prices well below those at which the home farmer could make a living. The flood began in the 1870s: within thirty years the amount of American wheat imported into Britain quadrupled. And there were now no tariff barriers at British ports to halt the flood. Since the Repeal of the Corn Laws (1846) Britain had been committed to Free Trade. Protection for farmers against foreign imports had gone, nor was it likely to come back. A nation of town-dwellers (by 1900 three-quarters of the population lived in towns) wanted cheap bread. Disraeli, who had given the vote to working-class householders in the towns in 1867 and who was now Prime Minister, said plainly that a return to Protection was out of the question (p.156).

Other circumstances made things even worse for the farmers. The weather itself was against them, bringing a succession of bad harvests in the later 1870s (1879 was the wettest year on record). Normally, bad harvests meant higher prices for corn, because it was scarce; now prices stayed low because of the American imports. Serious outbreaks of animal disease, foot and mouth in cattle and liver rot in sheep, also occurred at this time. In 1880 came a further threat, when *S.S. Strathleven* from Australia docked in London carrying the first success-ful refrigerated cargo, 40 tons of frozen meat. Before long there were regular shipments from Australia and Argentina as well.

The prospect looked bleak for farming, and it was certainly dark for most wheat farmers, especially in such areas as Essex and East Anglia. Moreover the value of land, the basic asset of farmers and of the landowning gentry and aristocracy to whom they paid their rents, declined. A further consequence of the depression was the collapse of the Agricultural Labourers' Union, launched in 1872 by Joseph Arch (see below p.203). Yet it is easy to paint too gloomy a picture of British agriculture as a whole at this time. The situation was far less bad in much of the midlands, in Cheshire and Lancashire and in the west of England, areas of mixed farming, than in the arable lands of the east.

The producers of beef and dairy produce positively benefited from low cereal prices, for it now cost them less to feed their livestock; and those near the growing cities did particularly well. Moreover in some areas, such as parts of Kent and Hertfordshire and the Vale of Evesham, market gardening and fruit growing developed fast in these years. The widening demands of the town-dwellers saved the day for many farmers. The rise of commercial jam making; a substantial increase in the consumption of beer; the expansion of the liquid milk trade – all these things benefited them, and must be set in the balance against the disappearance of the wheat farms.

3 Religion

For many English people organised religion was not as strong a motive force at the end of Victoria's reign as at its beginning. More people, indeed, were going to church or chapel in 1901 than in 1837; there were more churches and chapels, more clergymen and ministers and more people were taking communion. Yet the population of Britain in 1901 was over twice what it had been in 1837, and the number of people who did *not* attend church was now far larger. Particularly perhaps since the 1880s, many churches in the centres of large towns had empty pews on Sundays and in many villages churches too there was plenty of room. There were signs also that the political power of organised Christianity had grown less. Gladstone had disestablished the Church of Ireland in 1869, and by 1900 the Church of Wales was threatened with a similar fate. Jews had been allowed to sit alongside Christians in the Commons since 1858, and atheists also since the Speaker had in 1886 ruled that Bradlaugh could keep his seat. Religious tests for degrees at Oxford and Cambridge had been abolished by law in 1871.

Causes of change It is misleading to offer hard and fast reasons for such a change, for religion at bottom is a personal thing. Several different circumstances contributed. One certainly was the aftermath of the publication in 1859 of Charles Darwin's *Origin of Species*. The idea of evolution in this book clearly contradicted any literal belief in the account of creation contained in the opening chapters of the Bible and taught by the Christian churches. The controversy which followed, in which Darwin himself took no part, revealed widely-varied attitudes among the clergy. Its effect can be exaggerated. Most educated people probably accepted the idea of evolution within thirty years of Darwin's writing, and reconciled it with Christian beliefs. Yet the whole episode gravely shook the confidence of churchgoers, throwing doubt on the Bible and undermining the beliefs in which they had grown up. A second force turning back the tide of religion in these years was the growth of towns, and particularly of the large cities. By 1900 three-quarters of the people of Britain lived in towns. Even fifty years earlier the towns had scarcely been strongholds of religious faith, and now the situation was worse. Church-building and church organisation had failed, after the middle 1880s, to keep pace with the expansion of suburbs. Vast numbers of the very poor were scarcely touched by religion at all. There were London slum parishes where Anglo-Catholic clergy filled their churches by offering a mixture of ritualism and good works, and, sometimes, socialist opinions; areas (e.g., Liverpool) where Roman Catholic priests kept a watchful eye on their poor Irish flocks; northern towns where vigorous nonconformist preachers captured the millhands on Sundays. But these were exceptional. Working-class people on the whole were not so much hostile to religion as simply not interested in going to church – partly at least because church was a place where their well-dressed 'betters' went and where they did not feel at home.

In the villages of England the Anglican church which had so long been dominant was hit hard by the agricultural depression. This sharply reduced the tithes out of which much of the parson's income still came, and weakened the squire who usually backed the parson's work. Moreover radical ideas were spreading in the countryside, encouraged by the launching in 1872 of the Agricultural Workers' Union. Its founder was Joseph Arch, a labourer and Primitive Methodist preacher from Barford near Warwick, and by the end of 1873 it claimed 100,000 members. Arch was a deeply religious man, but he did not love the Church of England, and once told a crowd that 'the Church belongs to the rich men'. Many parsons and nearly all the bishops condemned the union, and the depression in farming almost destroyed it. Yet its ideas, and the bitterness towards the clergy, remained. Thousands of farm labourers were quitting the countryside anyway to seek work elsewhere, and many of those who stayed no longer went to church.

In various other ways the changing pattern of social life affected religion and churchgoing. Sunday excursions to the seaside towns like Brighton; the Sunday opening of museums and art galleries, the bands playing in the parks on Sunday afternoons; the vogue for cycling, spreading fast in the 1890s – these things all, directly or indirectly, affected the attitude to religion and the size of congregations. So too, at a different social level, did what has been called 'the invention of the week-end' by Edward, Prince of Wales, heir to the throne and leader of London 'society', whose attitude to Sunday observance was very different from that of his mother. Among the upper and middle classes, too, the custom of family prayers was during the 1890s beginning to lose its hold. The recruitment of clergy and ministers of suitable quality was becoming less easy. Other occupations – notably the growing home civil service, as well as the colonial service and missionary work in the overseas empire (below, p.266) were attracting many of those who might have become Anglican parsons in England. And some at least of those who might have become prominent nonconformist ministers

Rural changes

turned into working-class politicians instead: the chapels of South Wales and the north of England provided a useful training – in public speaking and in organising – for future Labour politicians.

Yet despite all these signs of change, the churches remained in 1900 an immensely powerful force in national life. Millions attended their services every Sunday, and a great many strove to put their teachings into practice during the week. Nearly all public men accepted their doctrines without serious doubt: Gladstone and Salisbury were both notably committed Anglicans. More children were being baptised than ever before. Sunday Schools were astonishingly full; in 1888, when they were at their height, it was reckoned that three children out of every four regularly attended one (quite a lot of those who did not belonged to the middle and upper classes, who tended to disapprove of them for their own young). The great majority of people in 1900 were still choosing to get married in church or chapel. It was still Christian belief that inspired most of the efforts of private individuals and groups to solve the social problems of the age. The homes for outcast and neglected children started by the London doctor Thomas John Barnardo (1845–1905); the housing projects in London of Octavia Hill (1838–1912); Bournville and the other philanthropic schemes of the Quaker George Cadbury (1839–1922) – these and countless less well-known projects rested upon a religious faith.

Salvation Army   One response to the social challenge of the time was so unconventional that it deserves special mention. This was the Salvation Army,

An assault on a Salvation Army procession in the 1880s

started in 1878 by William Booth, a former pawnbroker who had become an unorthodox Methodist preacher. It was a revivalist activity based upon preaching in the open air, where the poor felt at home; upon music from brass bands, originally used to drown the opposition (and, anyway, Booth said, 'why *should* the devil have all the best tunes?'); and upon military discipline, with Booth, a man of autocratic temperament, as 'General' and a newspaper called *The War Cry*. It survived hostility from Queen Victoria, publicans (all members had to be teetotallers), and a gang of thugs calling themselves 'The Skeleton Army', and within ten years it had over a thousand corps in Britain. Booth's initial aim was religious conversion, yet later in his career he turned also to social work among down-and-outs, prostitutes, discharged prisoners and the unemployed. By the time Booth died in 1912 'the Army' was a great world-wide organisation.

4 Education

Education and religion were inseparable in the minds of many Victorians, and this was reflected in the national system of elementary education which began with the Forster Act of 1870 (p.147). Alongside the existing Voluntary Schools run by the various religious bodies (most of which were Anglican) that Act established a second group of schools, the Board Schools run by locally-elected school boards. This Dual System certainly benefited the majority of children in England and Wales[1], especially after 1880, when Mundella's Act made education compulsory for all between the ages of 5 and 11, and 1891, when Salisbury's government virtually abolished the payment of school fees in elementary schools. It vastly increased the number of school places available, and so gave every child in the country the chance of an elementary education in the Three Rs. It led also to improved standards of teaching.

The Dual System

    Yet the thirty years after Forster's Act saw a prolonged conflict between the two kinds of school for the minds of English children. This conflict was at heart religious. The voluntary schools were predominantly Anglican (though there was a growing minority of Catholic schools in the big cities) mostly in rural England and in general backed by Conservatives, though the political divisions on education were by no means clear-cut. The board schools were required by the 1870 Act to offer only undenominational religious lessons, 'simple Bible teaching'; they were strong in towns and cities; and pretty warmly supported by the Liberals, many of whom were nonconformists. The conflict generated a great deal of heat, particularly in the elections to the school boards, which were often noisily and abusively fought by partisans of Church and chapel.

[1]It did not apply in Scotland, which had (and has) a totally separate system of education. An Act of 1872 reorganised the Scottish elementary schools.

W.E. Forster (1818–86)

Growth of Board Schools

One reason for the heat was the fact that the voluntary schools could not obtain money from local rates, whereas the board schools could; on the other hand, in many areas there was only one school, and that a C. of E. school, to which nonconformists had to send their children (although there was a 'conscience clause' which allowed them to be withdrawn from scripture lessons). The battle for numbers went in favour of the board schools. By 1902 over three times as many children were at elementary school as in the year of Forster's Act. Church schools still had most of them, but the board schools were overhauling them fast. They were town schools, and most children now lived in towns, and they had more money. Thanks to the rates, they had newer and better buildings – and they paid their teachers more, so they had better teachers (most of whom had in fact been trained in colleges maintained by the church). Inevitably pressure grew among churchmen, and among Conservatives, to 'put church schools on the rates'. Here lay the main cause of the next important act of Parliament about education, the Balfour Act of 1902 (below, p.236).

Eton College boys in the 1870s

Another cause was widespread dissatisfaction in the 1890s with the state of secondary education. The Public Schools, indeed, were flourishing, perhaps at the peak of their influence in these years. In the second half of the nineteenth century devout and strongminded headmasters, like Edward Thring (at Uppingham School, 1853–87) had developed the features that have remained characteristic ever since – the religious foundation, the emphasis on both discipline and independence, the 'House system', the organised games, the old boys'

Price £8 8s. Weight, 7 lbs. Size, 14 by 7 by 2½ in.
THE ONLY PORTABLE AND COMPLETE MACHINE EXTANT. UNIQUE IN ITS SIMPLICITY.

THE "HALL" TYPE WRITER

The "Times" referred to this Machine on March 11, 1884, as follows:—
" Messrs. Witherby may claim the credit of having introduced from America a New Type Writer, which is both cheap and portable. . . . . The principle of this beautiful little Machine. . . . It may be used in any position, on a desk, or in a railway carriage. A practised hand can achieve from thirty to forty words a minute, which is a good deal faster than most people can write. . . . . The plate is fitted with capitals and small letters, stops, numerals, &c."

An advertisement for an early typewriter, 1881

society. The curriculum had widened, to include modern studies and science. Their importance in British life was quite out of proportion to the number of boys in them. Most of the Anglican clergy; most M.P.s, civil servants, colonial administrators; most entrants to Oxford and Cambridge – these came from what was around 1900 a total of about 100 schools. In sharp contrast, other secondary schools, day schools in great cities and small country towns alike, were much criticised at this time, often on the ground that they were failing to train boys satisfactorily for work in commerce and industry. This criticism was strengthened by the relative decline of British industry in these years, particularly when compared with that of Germany. It led to official enquiries into the state of Britain's technical education, but to little else

Universities until 1902.

On the other hand the second half of the nineteenth century brought developments in university education. The reforms begun at Oxford and Cambridge before 1850 were taken further. Religious tests for admission to degrees were abolished (1871), and so were life fellowships attached to particular areas; fellows of colleges were allowed to marry; more professors were created, the system of studies was reorganised and its range widened and more serious research was undertaken. Outside the two older universities new ones arose, notably in great industrial cities, usually out of small local colleges and with the aid of a local benefactor. Birmingham University, for example, grew out of Mason College, opened on his eightieth birthday in 1875 by Josiah Mason, a pen manufacturer who also made a fortune out of electro-plate. It was later promoted by Joseph Chamberlain and financed by

George Cadbury the philanthropic cocoa manufacturer. Towards the end of the century there were notable additions to the University of London, including the foundation of the London School of Economics. By 1900 there were some 20,000 full-time students in British universities.

5 The coming of social change

In innumerable ways – in transport and housing, at work and at play – the pace of social change in England accelerated between 1850 and 1900. Old customs declined, new practices arose, swiftly changing the day-to-day lives of millions. Probably the principal reason for this lay in the remarkable growth of big cities. In the fifty years from the census of 1851 to that of 1901 the biggest of them grew as follows, with around each an ever-spreading ring of suburbs and satellites:

City	Population in 1851	Population in 1901	Percentage increase in 50 years
Birmingham	264,000	760,000	188
Liverpool	395,000	685,000	73
Manchester	338,000	645,000	90
Glasgow	363,000	904,000	149
Edinburgh	194,000	394,000	103
London	2,491,000	4,500,000	80

(Great Britain's population as a whole rose from 20,817,000 to 37,000,000 over the same fifty years, i.e. by 77 per cent.

The cities herded together great masses of people as never before, forcing upon them new ways of living and creating immense problems of health and police, of travel and leisure. Inevitably change came fast and plentiful. To chart it or measure its pace is impossible in short compass. The paragraphs which follow attempt to illustrate it by offering three different examples of what was happening.

Technological progress. A list of discoveries, inventions, or processes which first came into fairly widespread – though not necessarily general – use between 1851 and 1901, and which have been or are commonplace in twentieth-century Britain, must include the following:

anaesthetics	electric tramcars	refrigeration
antiseptics	gramophones	sewing machines
'safety' bicycles	combine harvesters	steam rollers
cameras	safety lifts (elevators)	telephones
contraceptives	linotype machines	torpedoes
dining cars on trains	machine guns	turbines
dynamite	margarine	typewriters
synthetic dyes	evaporated milk	pneumatic tyres
electric light bulbs	milk bottles	X-rays

Even brief reflection on so varied a collection will suggest some of the ways in which they altered the pattern of life for the later Victorians – in eating habits, clothes, use of leisure, business, health, agriculture, warfare, growth of empire, and many other matters.

Medicine and Public Health. As we have seen (above, p.93), the cholera epidemics of the 1830s and 1840s had sharply directed attention to the nation's health. They and other circumstances stimulated great

medical progress, on a very wide front, during the second half of the century – a progress only made possible for Britain by developments from other lands, for medicine was notably international. Anaesthetics, originating in the United States, ether and then chloroform, first tried in Edinburgh by the obstetrician James Simpson in 1847, came into use very rapidly. Antiseptics, made the more vital by the great increase in operations, followed with the experiments of Joseph Lister, in particular his carbolic spray of 1872. Lister's work, which steeply reduced the mortality rate in operations, was based on his belief in the 'germ theory' of the French scientist Louis Pasteur, first stated in 1864. Pasteur and the German, Robert Koch, who in 1882 isolated the germ responsible for tuberculosis, between them demonstrated how different bacteria cause different diseases. These various remarkable discoveries opened the way to rapid advances by surgeons and physicians in dealing with a wide range of diseases. At the end of the century their scope was widened yet further by the German Konrad Röntgen's discovery of X-rays, first used in England in 1896.

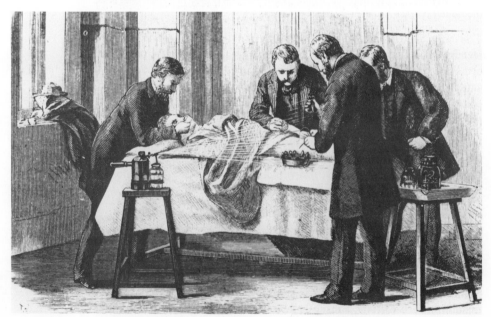

A surgical operation of the late 1870s (note the carbolic spray)

They were much aided by several other developments. One was the compulsory vaccination of children against smallpox, made law in 1853 but not effectively enforced until an epidemic of 1870, brought from France by refugees from the Franco-Prussian War, killed 40,000 people in this country. A second was the establishment of a genuine medical profession through the Medical Act of 1858, which created a General Medical Council whose first task it was to draw up a register of qualified practitioners. A third was the reform of hospital nursing, transforming an occupation hitherto looked upon as a low form of domestic service. This was the achievement from the 1860s onwards not only of Florence Nightingale, who opened a school of nursing at St Thomas' Hospital in London in 1860; but also of Sister Mary Jones, whose St John's House training school at King's College Hospital, started in 1857, quickly became internationally celebrated.

Hospital building expanded in these years, and included the con- **Public Health** struction of municipal infirmaries as a part of the provision for the poor. **reform** This was one element of a substantial movement towards public health reform, gradually carried through at both national and local levels. Parliamentary legislation like the Sanitary Act (1866) gave local author- ities greater powers to clean up towns; the Torrens Act (1868) was the first to enable them to compel landlords to keep property in order, and the Artisans' Dwellings Act (1875) the first to empower them to pull down slums and rebuild. The 'great' Public Health Act of 1875, as we have seen (p.154), gave local authorities the legal strength to attack a whole range of threats to health. These measures, by bringing pure water supplies and effective means of sewage disposal, were essential elements in getting rid of the terrible scourge of the water-borne epidemic diseases, especially cholera, typhoid and typhus. Such Acts were inspired and backed by a small group of civil servants, especially Sir John Simon, London's first medical officer of health and later the first medical officer of the Privy Council. To carry them out involved unseen feats of civil engineering, like that of Sir Joseph Bazalgette, whose sewerage schemes for London, constructed in 1859–66 (and still in use today) included 1300 miles of sewers and nearly a million cubic yards of concrete. The achievement of the reforming doctors and surgeons is most easily measured by one vital statistic. The death rate in England and Wales fell from 22.7 per 1000 in 1851–2 to 16.1 in 1901–5, a drop of almost 30 per cent.

Leisure and some of its uses. In 1871 Sir John Lubbock persuaded Parliament to pass a Bank Holiday Act which (together with another one in 1875) secured for the urban working class four days holiday each year. Originally designed for overworked bank clerks (hence its name), it was to prove of universal benefit to millions. Together with the custom of a Saturday half-day, which was fairly widely established twenty years earlier, and with the annual 'Wakes Weeks' and similar local customs, it marked some relaxation of the harsh pressure of nineteenth-century industry. Great numbers of industrial wage-earners and their families, living for the most part in smoky and grimy cities, came to have regular spells of leisure. Victorian working people used it in innumerable ways, from brass bands to drink, from reading novels to going to music halls, from singing Handel's *Messiah* to parading with the Volunteers. The four which follow may serve merely as varied examples.

Seaside resorts The rapid development of seaside resorts – some of which like Brighton and Scarborough had begun to grow earlier in the century – was a feature of the years 1850–1900. They were made possible by the extension of railways, which carried huge crowds on day trips on Bank Holidays and during Whit week from nearby industrial areas. So Skegness grew to cater for the east midlands and Rhyl for the Potteries and Manchester, New Brighton for Liverpool just across the Mersey and Blackpool, perhaps the most remarkable of them all, with its great Tower built in 1894 in imitation of the Eiffel Tower in Paris, for the entire Lancashire textile area. Piers, amusement parks and arcades, promenades, illuminations, theatres, donkeys on the beach, Punch and Judy shows – all these were well-established and widely-spread features of English life by 1900.

The beach at Margate in the 1890s

Sport Association football and cricket grew into organised and nation-wide sports in this period. The F.A. Cup was first competed for in 1871; the Football League began with twelve clubs in 1888. The County Cricket championship started in 1873; the first Test Match between England and Australia took place at Melbourne in 1877. They catered for the

The Australian touring cricketers, 1890

leisure needs of many thousands, the great majority of whom were
working men in the cities. This was an odd phenomenon, for both
games had earlier in the century been developed and given rules at the
Public Schools, spreading from them to church groups, works clubs
and the like before becoming professional and large-scale commercial
enterprises. The pedigree of famous football clubs illustrates the
change: Bolton Wanderers began as a group of young men at Christ
Church Sunday School, Stoke City with some old boys of Charterhouse
School who worked for the North Staffordshire Railway, Coventry City
with employees of Singers the cycle manufacturers. The change was
symbolised by the defeat of the Old Etonians in the Cup Final of 1882,
and the victories of Blackburn Rovers in those of 1884–6. Professional-
ism was legalised in 1885, and thereafter dominated the game. In
county cricket the blend at top level of amateurs and professionals,
'Gentlemen and Players', survived long after 1900. At that date both
games were attracting great crowds.

Technological progress in the 1880s – especially the inventions of **Cycling**
the Rover 'safety' bicycle in 1885 and of the pneumatic tyre by J. B.
Dunlop in 1888 – opened the way for cycling to become a widespread British enthusiasm. By 1895 there were perhaps 1½ million

213

An early chain bicycle, 1885

cyclists, enjoying the roads which the newly-established County Councils were improving. Most of them were probably upper and middle-class citizens, and a high proportion of them were women. Yet there were many workingmen's cycling clubs, including quite a few Clarion Clubs associated with the socialist newspaper of that name. Until the end of the century cyclists were little troubled by the motor-car, already being developed in France and Germany; for the ancient Red Flag law, which limited power-driven vehicles on the roads to four miles an hour, preceded by a man with a red flag, was not repealed until 1896. The motor-car remained a rich man's toy in England until after the First World War; it created a good deal of class hostility when it covered the poor man with dust, speeding by on roads not yet tarred.

Newspapers   The expansion of 'spectator sports' reflected on one side the growth of a big new 'mass market' of customers – and on the other a commercial enterprise ready to cater for them. This was also happening in a quite different way of using leisure, the reading of newspapers. 1896 saw the appearance of the *Daily Mail*, the first cheap national daily. The Victorians, especially the middle class and many artisans, were avid newspaper readers. As well as *The Times*, which was not cheap (copies were hired by groups of readers at a penny an hour) there were numerous solid and serious provincial papers, carrying, for example, full accounts of parliamentary debates. But technological change, particularly the invention of the linotype machine, which vastly increased the speed and output of the presses, opened up great new possibilities for newspapers; so too, in different fashion, did the rapid increase after 1870 of the number of children attending school. Alfred Harmsworth (later Lord Northcliffe), the young man of 34 who founded the *Daily Mail*, saw the chance of success for a different sort of paper – selling for a halfpenny, 'brighter', with arresting headlines and catchy personal stories, full of snippets of news and 'stunts', ready to seize on 'sensations' (and to invent them: the *Mail* printed in 1900 a totally fictitious account of a massacre by the Chinese during the Boxer Rising at Pekin). He himself intended his paper to appeal to '£1,000-a-year men', firmly middle class; Lord Salisbury once described it as 'written by office-boys for office-boys'. Certainly it was highly success-ful, with a daily sale of over 200,000 in its first year, rising – thanks in great part to the South African War, in which Harmsworth made the utmost of anti-Boer passions – to 750,000 in 1902. Its example, quickly followed, set a pattern for much of the national press, and helped to kill off many provincial papers.

13
New forces

1 Trade unions after 1851

Progress of
Trade Unions The second half of the nineteenth century was a period of progress for the British working class, and particularly for trade unions. They shared in the prosperity of the country as a whole, and they benefited from the general freedom and security of Victorian society. They developed in several ways. First, the group of relatively small unions of artisans, more skilled and better-off wage-earners, of which the Amalgamated Society of Engineers was the prime example, formed the Trades Union Congress, thus creating a kind of central organisation for the working class. The T.U.C. held its first meeting (at Manchester) in 1868. As well as dealing with employers, it served as a kind of pressure group, especially for lobbying Parliament to pass measures about conditions of work or about the rights of employees. So it contributed to a second way in which trade unions gained strength during this period, namely through the passage of important legislation concerning their own activities. They persuaded both Liberals and Conservatives to pass laws on their behalf. Gladstone's Trade Union Act (1871) gave legal security to their funds, while Disraeli's Conspiracy and Protection of Property Act (1875) protected them against charges of conspiracy and made peaceful picketing legal.

These laws heralded the 'arrival' of trade unions as one of the 'respectable' institutions of Victorian England. This is symbolised in contemporary photographs of their leaders, men like William Allan of the A.S.E. and Robert Applegarth of the Carpenters and Joiners, which show us grave-looking bearded gentlemen with gold watch-chains. A third way in which unions advanced between 1850 and 1900 was a great growth in membership. In 1874 the T.U.C. claimed to represent 1,100,000 members. By 1900 there were over 2,000,000 trade unionists. Many of these, in sharp contrast to the early days of the A.S.E., were unskilled workers, and with them came a new style of leadership. The leaders of this 'New Unionism' were more outspoken and more militant than those of the 'New Model Unionism' of a generation before; their funds were often solely for strike action; and they were closer to violence, for example in the bad times of the 1880s which brought an increase in unemployment, and in bitterness in relations between masters and men.

The great strike of dock labourers at the East End, 1889

The London Dock Strike of August 1889 was the central event in the spread of the New Unionism. It was preceded by two other surprisingly successful victories by workers in the London area. One was the outcome of a strike by a few dozen match-girls employed in dreadful conditions in the East End, who formed a union under the inspiration of Annie Besant, notorious in Victorian England both as a socialist and an advocate of birth-control; the other was won by 20,000 gas workers whose newly-formed union got its basic working day cut from twelve hours to eight. The London dockers, four-fifths of whom were Irish, wanted a rise of one penny to give them a wage of sixpence an hour, the 'dockers' tanner', and their strike effectively closed the Port of London for about a month. They were greatly aided by a long spell of fine warm weather and by the gift of £30,000 from sympathisers in Australia. Their campaign, with its daily speeches on Tower Hill by the three leaders (Tom Mann, John Burns and Ben Tillett, all of them rather flamboyant characters) and its orderly processions through the city carrying banners and such emblems of poverty as old fish heads and bits of stinking meat on poles to suggest what food dockers' families ate, made a great impression on middle-class Londoners. The employers, at first adamant against concession, eventually yielded the 'tanner', thanks in great part to the mediation of the Roman Catholic Cardinal Manning.

This remarkable event gave a great fillip to trade unionism, notably among unskilled workers. There were many strikes and lockouts during the 1890s, with engineers and miners prominent in them; the most notorious was the Miners' Lockout of 1893, during which two miners were shot dead at Featherstone by soldiers called in to keep order. At the same time socialist ideas began to spread fast among the more aggressive unionists, despite the opposition of the cautious leaders of the older unions on the T.U.C. It is scarcely surprising that in the 1890s opinion among trade unionists began to move towards the formation of a separate working-class political party.

2 The Labour Party to 1906

The years which saw the Liberals split over Home Rule also provided the background for the beginnings of a new political party, the Labour Party. Founded in 1900, it formed its first government in 1924, and in 1945 it took nearly 150 more seats in the Commons than all the other parties put together. But its origins were far from the House of Commons, nor had they anything to do with Ireland. They lay rather in widespread working-class dissastisfaction with the existing parties, particularly with the Liberals; in the activities of tiny groups of middle-class intellectuals; and, eventually, in the mass support of trade unions. The new party was from the start intended to be a distinct Labour group in Parliament; its purpose was to promote the particular interests of working-class people, just as the Irish Nationalist party existed solely to promote those of the Irish people. Many, by no means all, of those who launched it believed in socialism: that is, that the community should own for the benefit of all its members the main sources of national wealth, like the mines, the railways, and possibly the land itself.

The Reform Acts of 1867 and 1884, especially the latter, had given the vote to many thousands of working men. They also opened the way towards working men becoming M.P.s: two miners were elected for mining constituencies in 1874, and eleven working-class members sat in the Commons in 1885. Such men customarily voted with the Liberals (one of them, Henry Broadhurst, an Oxfordshire stonemason, was given a minor post by Gladstone in his third ministry). But in the last twenty years of the nineteenth century there were sound reasons why a separate working-class political party was likely to arise. Most working people were gaining in prosperity. 'Real' wages, it has been reckoned, increased by some 77 per cent between 1860 and 1900, for on the whole wages were rising and prices, particularly of imported foodstuffs, were falling. So they ate more meat, sugar, bread and butter. Ready-made clothing enabled them to be better dressed than their parents had been, workmen's fares gave them cheap travel on the railways, co-ops and the new big stores provided cheap groceries. They were better educated than the last generation: Forster's Act of 1870 and the coming of the Board Schools had maintained the advance of literacy which had been a feature of Victorian Britain. There was widespread political awareness among working men, on the evidence of the great meetings addressed by Gladstone and Chamberlain. Moreover, industry was growing in scale, with bigger factories and firms creating stronger class solidarity among employees. Such developments were sooner or later likely to make them dissatisfied with what Liberals and Conservatives were offering them, and lead them to create a party of their own.

There was, on the other hand, also plenty of terrible poverty and **Poverty** want in late Victorian England to provide material for social protest. The 1880s and 1890s brought the publication of considerable evidence, most of it from the great cities and much of it written by clergymen, about the atrocious conditions in which millions of British people lived. For example, in 1883 a Congregationalist minister, Andrew Mearns, wrote a startling pamphlet, *The Bitter Cry of Outcast London*, which led to widespread concern about slums. In 1889 the shipowner Charles Booth published the first section of his seventeen-volume enquiry into *The Life and Labour of the People of London*, in which he showed that as many as 30 per cent of them appeared to live below a tolerable subsistence level. The Dock Strike of that same year was itself in great part a revolt against appalling living conditions. The following year 'General' William Booth gave in *In Darkest England and the Way Out* a grim picture of the outcast poor whom his Salvation Army met in their daily work. Such evidence struck home to many middle-class consciences and led to an enormous range of local and national charitable activities, for waifs and strays, drunkards and prostitutes, for housing schemes and slum missions and countless other good causes. It also led a few to press for political action through the existing parties, Liberal and Conservative, to achieve such varied objectives as old age pensions and laws to promote temperance. And it led a very few to accept the ideas of socialism, particularly those propagated by Karl Marx (1818–83), the German Jew who had issued in 1848 the *Communist Manifesto* as a rallying-cry for revolution ('Workers of the world, unite! You have nothing to lose but your chains'). In 1867 he had begun the publication of his most celebrated book *Das Kapital*, in which he maintained that the coming of communism was inevitable, and that it should be hurried on by the revolt of the workers in industry against their masters.

Marx had many readers in Germany, where his ideas contributed much to the rise of a strong Social Democratic working-class party, but few in Britain. One of them was a London stockbroker named H. M. Hyndman, who in 1881 founded the Democratic Federation to spread socialist ideas, later (1884) renaming it the Social Democratic Federation. The S.D.F. was small, very middle-class, with **The S.D.F.** many cranks among its members; Hyndman was dictatorial and quarrelsome; and soon a group split away under the poet William Morris to form the Socialist League. In 1886–7, when unemployment was high, the S.D.F. caused consternation among the well-to-do of Victorian London, and got publicity for itself, by holding rowdy meetings in Trafalgar Square. After one of these a mob smashed windows in the Pall Mall clubs and looted shops in Mayfair (the Queen called it 'a *momentary* triumph of socialism and a disgrace to the capital'). But the S.D.F.'s lasting influence was slight – except that the Dock Strike leaders Ben Tillett and John Burns learned their socialism at its meetings. A more significant body with socialist leanings was the Fabian Society, also established in 1884. It took its name from the Roman general Quintus Fabius Maximus, who had worn down his enemies by his 'delaying tactics'. The Fabians intended to spread socialist ideas peacefully and gradually. They had both an academic and a drawing-room flavour about them. Their early members included the playwright George Bernard Shaw, the novelist H. G. Wells, the birth-control advocate Annie Besant and the social researchers Sidney and Beatrice Webb. They undertook careful enquiries into social problems and wrote tracts; they aimed to permeate both Liberal and Conservative parties with their ideas; and they were prominent in the early work of the London County Council (notably Sidney Webb). Fabian influence upon many members of twentieth century Labour governments was to be great; but for the moment the Fabians remained a small and somewhat 'superior' society remote from the working class.

The Fabians

    The most important working class contributor to the foundation of the Labour Party was a Scotsman who as a boy had worked as a trapper in a coalmine. James Keir Hardie (1856–1915), sacked for organising a trade union in his pit, began as a young man to see political, rather than industrial, action as the way to better conditions. He was led to socialism not by Marx but by the American Henry George who in 1879 had written *Progress and Poverty*, a book widely read in Britain, which maintained that a single tax on the 'unearned increment' of land would solve all economic difficulties. Hardie, independent and individualistic, was deeply sincere in seeing socialism not as a system of economics but, in the words of his programme as a Labour candidate at a by-election in 1888, as 'bread for the hungry, rest for the weary, and hope for the oppressed'. He wanted to get rid of the widely-accepted belief that working men could stand for Parliament only as Liberals. In 1888 he led the way in founding the Scottish Labour Party, and in 1892 he was elected Labour M.P. for West Ham, arriving in a cloth cap and homespun tweeds to take his seat among the top-hatted and frock-coated members of the Commons. In the House he saw himself as the champion of the common people, and was nicknamed 'the Member for the Unemployed'. He took the chair at the Bradford Conference of 1893, held by delegates from various socialist organisations, which established the Independent Labour Party. Its aim was to put forward

Keir Hardie

VOTE FOR

Home Rule.	Temperance Reform.
Democratic Government.	Healthy Homes.
Justice to Labour	Fair Rents.
No Monopoly.	Eight-Hour Day.
No Landlordism	Work for the Unemployed.

KEIR HARDIE.

Keir Hardie (1856–1915)

Labour candidates for Parliament who would be independent of all other parties; and its policy was avowedly socialist – 'the collective ownership [i.e. by the people] of the means of production, distribution, and exchange.'

This creation of a separate working-class party was a turning-point. Yet the I.L.P. was a small body, not very representative (most of the delegates at Bradford came from Scotland and the north of England), and it had few funds. During the 1890s Labour members won seats on local councils and on school boards; but these were quite offset by Hardie's defeat in the general election of 1895. To succeed the I.L.P. had to gain the support of the trade unions, by far the largest working-class bodies, with some 2 million members in 1900, and ample funds of nearly £4 million. Yet many trade unionists were hostile to socialism and to the I.L.P. – notably the two biggest groups, the cotton operatives, many of whom habitually voted Conservative, and the coalminers, who could elect their own men to Parliament anyway because they were so concentrated in the mining constituencies. But a change of front came about in the T.U.C. during the late 1890s. There was pressure from active socialists in the 'new unions', like the dockers, and from unions whose conditions of work were notoriously bad, like the railwaymen. There were growing fears about the effects of new machinery and foreign competition, especially in heavy industry; fears also that legal decisions, like those in Gladstone's day, might go against the unions and restrict their powers. Yet the main circumstances which brought trade union opinion round to favouring a separate Labour Party seems to have been a counter-offensive by the employers after 1895. This was shown in the formation of numerous employers' federations, especially in the huge and central engineering industry. Here in 1897 the employers won a notable victory after a six months' lock-out. So in 1899 the T.U.C. at last committed itself to support political action, and called in 1900 for a conference of Fabians, S.D.F., I.L.P., and trade unions. This conference set up the Labour Representation Committee, whose purpose, on a motion proposed by Keir Hardie, was 'to create a distinct Labour group in Parliament, who shall have their own Whips'. Almost at once the L.R.C. became known as the Labour Party. Its first secretary was James Ramsay MacDonald, later the first Labour Prime Minister.

Taff Vale   The new party, launched in February 1900, entered in the general election that May fifteen candidates (to whose expenses it devoted the total sum of £33), and won only two seats. At the next election, in 1906, it put up fifty-one, thirty of whom won seats; five times as many electors voted Labour as in 1900. This was a great advance, for which two events of the intervening years were mainly responsible. The first was the Taff Vale case. The law about trade unions, based upon the Acts of 1871 and 1875, was in a muddle. It was not clear whether they had full right to strike, or how far 'peaceful picketing' could go, or whether unions' funds were liable for actions committed by their members during a strike. Various judges had given contradictory decisions in various cases. This situation came to a head in 1901 when the Taff Vale Railway Company was awarded £23,000 damages against the Amalgamated Society of Railway Servants after a strike which that union had called. The implications of such a decision for trade unions were disastrous: it would soon lead them into financial ruin. So Taff Vale brought at once a demand that Parliament should change the law in their favour; and, more immediately important, a great increase in the number of trade unionists affiliated to the Labour Party. The figure rose from 187,000 in 1900 to nearly 550,000 in 1903, including the big and previously hostile cotton workers' association. Thus the Taff Vale affair not only gave the Labour Party a clear working-class issue to fight for, the right to strike; it also brought them a great deal more cash for their funds.

The second event which substantially helped them at this time was a political bargain. In 1903 Herbert Gladstone, son of the G.O.M. and chief whip of the Liberal party, and Ramsay MacDonald, secretary of the Labour Party, made a secret pact whereby in about thirty constituencies Labour candidates were to be given 'an open field against the common enemy', the Conservatives; no Liberal would be put up there at the next election. This agreement, deliberately kept secret by Gladstone and MacDonald, was highly advantageous to Labour. It was undoubtedly the key to victory in most of the thirty seats they won in 1906. On a longer view this agreement produced the cloud no bigger than a man's hand which was one day to blot out most of the Liberals' sky; twenty years on Labour would replace the Liberals as the main party opposing the Conservatives.

3 The emancipation of women

In the middle years of the nineteenth century women in Britain were second-class citizens – and this despite the presence on the throne of a fairly strong-minded woman (who, however, was in general unsympathetic to the cause of women's emancipation). They had no vote. Under English law a woman's property automatically became her husband's on marriage. It was virtually impossible for her to get a divorce. The education offered to middle and upper-class women was markedly inferior to that given to their menfolk. Men of every social class, and most women too, saw a woman's role as simply that of a wife and mother, obedient to the wishes of her husband and the needs of her children. The absence of effective contraceptives meant that families were very large, and the years of child-bearing long. Yet many working-class wives, from economic necessity, also had to go out to work. This was most obvious in the textile mills, yet it was also common in agriculture, shops and markets, and of course domestic service. There were a very few exceptional women whose work was of national significance. Queen Victoria was one; the novelists like Mrs Gaskell, the Brontë sisters and George Eliot (the male alias adopted by Mary Ann Evans) were others: so, in different senses, were Florence Nightingale, Frances Mary Buss and Mrs Beeton. But this scarcely touched the general plight of women.

In the second half of the century significant – though not revolutionary – changes came about, in several directions. In the long term probably the most important of these was in the secondary education of girls. Here the movement begun in 1850 by Miss Buss with the foundation of what later became North London Collegiate School (pp. 112–3) made substantial strides, much aided by a damaging report on girls' education by a royal commission in 1868. The Girls' Public Day School Trust formed in 1871 set up girls' grammar schools of high standard which served as examples to others throughout the country. Meanwhile women were slowly gaining entry to higher education. Bedford College for women was opened in London in 1848. After a long campaign run by Emily Davies (1830–1921), the demure and plump

Women's Education

223

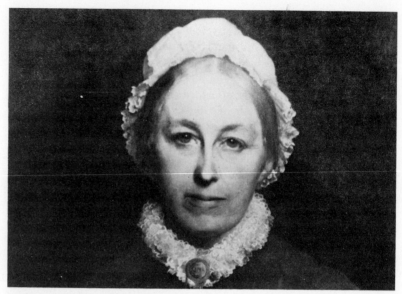

Emily Davies (1830–1921)

lady who was the leading woman emancipationist of the century, Girton
and then Newnham Colleges for women opened in Cambridge in the
1870s, followed shortly by Lady Margaret Hall and Somerville at
Oxford. The number of women students remained very small. At
Oxford and Cambridge they could go to lectures and sit for examinations, but not receive degrees until after the First World War. Medical

The Girton College Fire Brigade, 1887

education proved a tougher fortress to enter; many male students and doctors were violently hostile. The first woman to try to break in, Elizabeth Garrett Anderson, was eventually forced to obtain her medical degree in Paris, and not until the 1870s did the British medical profession begin to yield.

Changes in women's employment were a second force bringing emancipation. In 1851 30 per cent of all employed people were women. The proportion was little different in 1901; what had changed was the sort of work many of them were doing. On the one hand, factory and mines acts from the 1840s onwards had restricted some kinds of employment for them (though women factory inspectors were not appointed until the 1890s); on the other, a far greater range of jobs had come to be seen as 'respectable' for women. These included not only nursing and teaching, but also posts in the civil service, in the new department stores and as typists. It was now appreciably easier than fifty years before for a woman to be financially independent and socially respectable. Other circumstances outside work encouraged women to be, and to feel, independent. They took to the bicycle far more quickly,

A cyclist of the 1890s

and in far greater numbers, than men. Cycling, and also outdoor activities like lawn tennis (invented in the 1870s) did much to simplify women's dress, getting rid of the heavy petticoats worn by mid-Victorian ladies, and thereby contributing notably to a sense of emancipation.

Changes in the Law

The changes just mentioned mainly concerned single women – and the proportion of single women was growing quite fast in the later years of the nineteenth century. Yet most women were married, and they were affected by changes in the law at this time. A series of acts of Parliament, the earliest in 1857, was gradually to open the way for women to obtain separation or divorce on the same terms as men, but these were very far from complete by 1901, and anyway too costly for working women to use. For the middle-class wife, Married Women's Property Acts from 1870 to 1893 (notably that of 1882, which secured a wife's control of all she owned when she got married or acquired afterwards) were of substantial value; they undermined the activities of that familiar figure of Victorian melodrama, the scoundrel who married a wealthy heiress and, having acquired her money, promptly abandoned her. But for most wives and mothers changes outside the law were to be of greater importance. From about the 1870s the size of families in Britain began to decline; by 1900 it had fallen sharply, indeed almost halved. This quite radical change revealed the adoption of effective methods of birth control from about 1870, a practice given wide advertisement by the prosecution in 1877 of Charles Bradlaugh

Birth Control

and Annie Besant for publishing a pamphlet on the subject. It also suggested that middle-class parents – those whom these developments mainly affected before the twentieth century – were beginning deliberately to choose higher standards of living in preference to large families. Here was a social change of immense significance, clearly indicated by the fall in the birth-rate by about one-fifth from its peak in the 1870s.

'Votes for Women'

Yet for many late Victorian advocates of women's emancipation the central target was not social change but the parliamentary vote. They had little chance of success in this aim, for most Victorians, of both sexes, thought politics were not women's business. The Liberal philosopher John Stuart Mill during the debates on the Reform Act of 1867 introduced a motion for women's suffrage, but it was easily defeated. Forster's Education Act of 1870 allowed women ratepayers to vote for, and to be elected to, school boards; the County Councils Act of 1888 gave them the vote in local government elections. Various organisations agitating for the cause joined together in 1897 to form the National Union of Women's Suffrage Societies. Their members, called 'suffragists', were peaceful in their methods. They were also unsuccessful, and the new century was to see a more violent phase of the movement. Nevertheless the nineteenth-century developments, particularly those in employment and in education, had laid foundations which in the not very distant future would make 'votes for women' practical politics.

14
The Boer War and Conservative decline

1 The Boer War, 1899–1902

In 1899 Britain went to war with the two South African republics of the Transvaal and the Orange Free State. This Boer War turned out to be the biggest war fought by British forces between the Crimean War and the First World War of 1914–18. Its roots lay in the early nineteenth century – in the British acquisition of the Cape of Good Hope from Holland in 1814; in the Great Trek of the 1830s, the flight of thousands of Dutch white people from British rule; and in the rise of the two Boer republics beyond the Orange and Vaal rivers. In 1877 Disraeli's government had annexed the Transvaal; in 1881 Gladstone, beaten by an army of farmers[1] at Majuba Hill, had given independence back again in the Convention of Pretoria, subject to a vague British suzerainty. Majuba also gave the Boers under their leader Paul Kruger – who as a boy of ten had been in the Great Trek – a contempt for the British army. Here already was an unhappy legacy of bitterness between the two groups of white people in South Africa.

But the event which led to crisis came in 1886 – the discovery, on the Witwatersrand in the Transvaal, of the world's biggest goldfield. Within ten years the fifty miles of the Rand was producing more gold than the U.S.A., Australia and Russia put together. Into Johannesburg, transformed from a farming settlement into a great mining city, there poured many thousands of 'Uitlanders' (Afrikaans for 'foreigners'), the majority of them British. By 1899, although there may in the Transvaal have been more Boer men, women and children than Uitlanders, there were probably more Uitlander than Boer men. The Transvaal government, taxing heavily profits of the mines and essential supplies such as dynamite, became suddenly wealthy: its annual income rose twenty-fold in the ten years after the discovery of gold. The Uitlanders, who provided perhaps nine-tenths of the revenue, had no right to vote and no share in government. Inevitably feeling between Uitlanders and Boers ran high; inevitably too the former looked to Britain for help.

The man in Britain to whom they most readily turned was the Colonial Secretary, Joseph Chamberlain. He had surprised people by taking this office in 1895 rather than the Chancellorship of the

The Uitlanders

[1]The word 'boer' means 'farmer' in Afrikaans, and was originally used as a term of contempt.

Fig. 5 South Africa and the Boer War of 1899–1902

Exchequer, and he had done so because he believed passionately in the
British Empire and in its right to expand. Bold, impatient and
ambitious, frustrated by ten years out of office, now second only to
Salisbury in the Cabinet, he had a great popular following in England.
Such a man was scarcely likely to make relations with the Transvaal
smoother, and six months after he took office they became far worse
The Jameson   because of the Jameson Raid (1895). A group of Uitlanders planned an
Raid   armed rebellion against the Transvaal government. Cecil Rhodes

(p.295), head of a great gold-mining syndicate, chairman of the British South African Chartered Company and thus effective ruler of Rhodesia, and also Prime Minister of Cape Colony, was deeply involved in the plot. His lieutenant Dr Starr Jameson assembled an armed force of some 500 men, most of them officially policemen of the Chartered Company, at Pitsani on the Transvaal border to support the rising. The plot misfired lamentably. The Johannesburg rising never took place; but Jameson's force crossed the frontier and was easily rounded up by the Boers. President Kruger of the Transvaal correctly handed over the raiders to Britain for trial (Jameson got 15 months' imprisonment). Rhodes resigned the premiership of the Cape. A parliamentary committee of enquiry in Britain, containing leading Liberals as well as Conservatives, censured him, but no more. It exonerated Chamberlain, who denied his involvement in the plot. Contemporaries talked of the committee as 'the Lying-in-State at Westminster', and evidence which has been found since points clearly to Chamberlain's involvement.

The whole affair was disastrous in its impact on Anglo-Boer relations. In English eyes, not the least disturbing of its consequences was the provocative Kruger Telegram (1896) sent by Kaiser Wilhelm II of Germany to the Transvaal President five days after the Raid, congratulating him on having maintained the independence of his country 'without appealing to the help of friendly powers'. In the Transvaal itself the episode greatly revived the power of 'Oom Paul' Kruger, President since 1883, a shrewd old man bitterly hostile to the 'cursed English' whom he had seen gradually encircling his country during his lifetime (see Map on p.228). Moderate Boer leaders had realised the wisdom of compromise, and Kruger had only been narrowly re-elected in 1893; but in 1898 he had a great majority once more. The Raid gave him justification for military precautions, and during the years 1895–9 large quantities of arms, including Krupps guns from Germany, came in along the railway line, completed in 1895, which ran from the Rand through Portuguese East Africa to the sea at Lourenço Marques. The Raid also gave him, in the words of a contemporary Cape politician, every excuse to deny 'political rights and privileges to men who stand convicted of treacherously plotting to destroy the independence of the Transvaal'. It also shattered confidence in Britain among the Dutch people of the Orange Free State and of the Cape Colony.

Nevertheless British policy towards the Transvaal did not change. Powerful voices, especially in the London business world, were calling for the annexation of the backward and obstinate small state which included the gold mines of the Rand. There were those who, like Cecil Rhodes, wanted to see British territory extending the whole length of Africa from the Cape to Cairo. In 1897 Chamberlain had Sir Alfred Milner appointed as British High Commissioner in South Africa. Milner was a convinced imperialist and a stubborn man who seems to have come quickly to the conclusion that British military intervention would provide the only 'solution' of the 'problem' of the Transvaal. In 1898 he publicly denounced the 'unprogressive' policy of Kruger. The killing of an English mineworker by a policeman on the Rand led to a petition from 22,000 Uitlanders to the Queen asking for her protection. In May 1899 Milner and Kruger met at Bloemfontein to discuss the question of the franchise for the Uitlanders. Milner broke off the talks, despite advice even from Chamberlain not to do so. Both governments prepared for war, and it began that October, after the Orange Free State had thrown in its lot with the Transvaal. Milner later saw the war as a struggle not 'for the mines but for British supremacy in South Africa'. Chamberlain thought that what was at stake was 'the position of Great Britain in South Africa – and with it the estimate formed of our power and influence in our colonies throughout the world'. Many others, especially in Europe, saw only a ruthless attack by a great nation, greedy for gold, on a small independent people.

The Boer War   Nearly everyone in Britain expected that the war would be short and triumphant: it would be 'over by Christmas'. Great Britain contained about 36,500,000 people; the total white population of the Transvaal, the bigger of the two Boer Republics, was little more than that of Bradford, and many were Uitlanders. For all Kruger's rearmament, they had only about 70,000 potential flighting men. Britain had a skilled professional army, successful in a series of colonial wars, of which the most recent had been in the Sudan the previous year, where at Omdurman machine guns had slain 50,000 dervishes in five hours for the loss of a handful of British troops. With the Royal Navy in command of the seas, the Boers had no chance of outside help: European sympathy with them and hostility to Britain could get no further than words. The Boers fought alone, with a 'fifth column' of Uitlanders in their midst. Yet the military reality was very far from the expectation. In 1899 the British Army was by no means as strong as it seemed: Cardwell's reforms had not gone far enough. The reserves had been neglected and many units were below strength; the Boers at first even had superiority in numbers, putting 35,000 men in the field as against 27,000 British. There was no prepared plan of operations for a campaign in South Africa. Many of the officers lacked the flexibility and the imagination which was required in a struggle fought in novel conditions, so utterly different from battles against ill-armed natives. Although many thousands of recruits quickly offered themselves when war broke out, an appalling high proportion (e.g. 8,000 out of 10,000 in Manchester) turned out to be physically unfit. By contrast most Boers were expert horsemen and good marksmen. Fighting for their homes in terrain and conditions they knew well, and taking the initiative at the start, they were a formidable enemy.

The war fell into three distinct phases. In the first, from October 1899 to January 1900, the Boers won a succession of swift victories, notably along the line of the Tugela River in Natal. They encircled

British forces in Kimberley, Ladysmith, and Mafeking. In one 'Black Week' in December they defeated three British armies. Had their forces at this stage driven south into Cape Colony, where perhaps half the white inhabitants were of Dutch stock, they might have pushed the British into the sea. Instead they turned east into Natal, with its largely British population, and wasted men and time on the three besieged towns, so losing the momentum that might have given them victory.

A second phase of the war began in January 1900 with the replacement of the Commander-in-Chief, Sir Redvers Buller, whose nerve had gone, by Lord Roberts. The victor of Omdurman, Lord Kitchener, was chief of staff. Roberts launched a counter-offensive in February. A Boer field army was defeated at Paardeburg and Ladysmith was relieved. Bloemfontein, capital of the Orange Free State, fell in March. The Transvaal was invaded in the summer, and both Pretoria and Johannesburg were captured. President Kruger fled to Europe, in an unavailing attempt to get help from Germany and other continental powers. In October his country was formally annexed to the British Crown. Roberts went home, leaving Kitchener in command. The war seemed over, apart from the mopping-up. Nothing of the sort was true: the third and, from the British point of view most tedious and humiliating, phase was about to begin.

In October 1900, with British victory seemingly complete, Salisbury held what came to be known as the 'khaki election'. The Unionists repeated their success of 1895 – with a slightly smaller (18 seats fewer) majority. The war had been very popular to begin with, particularly perhaps among the lower middle class. A lot of people were noisily warlike, encouraged by the *Daily Mail*. Some later episodes aroused hysterical enthusiasm, notably the relief of Mafeking in May 1900 after a siege lasting 217 days[1]. The early defeats did something to sober opinion down, as well as evoking Queen Victoria's comment, 'Please understand that there is no one depressed in *this* house; we are not interested in the possibilities of defeat; they do not exist'. There was scattered opposition to the war throughout, from various sources ranging from Quakers and other pacifists to those of anti-Semitic opinions who believed the war was being fought mainly to benefit Jewish financiers with investments in the Rand mines. The Liberal Opposition in Parliament was much divided. A few were among the 'pro-Boers', like the young Welshman, David Lloyd George, who once had to escape from an anti-war meeting in Birmingham Town Hall disguised as a policeman; rather more were 'Liberal Imperialists', firm supporters of the war like Lord Rosebery the former Premier and H. H. Asquith a future one; in between was a group headed by the official leader of the party, Sir Henry Campbell-Bannerman, who

British attitudes

[1]The occasion, celebrated especially in London by wild crowds, added a new word to the language – to 'maffick', meaning to 'exult riotously'. The commander at Mafeking was Colonel Robert (later Lord) Baden-Powell, founder (in 1907) of the Boy Scouts, a movement the idea for which sprang from his South African experiences.

believed that the war was the outcome of disgraceful policy, particularly by Chamberlain (it was frequently called 'Chamberlain's War'), even though it must now be fought through to victory. Labour and trade union opinion was similarly divided: Keir Hardie opposed the war as a pacifist, John Burns because he was against the Jews, other working-class leaders supported it. There was little evidence of widespread jingoism amongst industrial workers. These varying attitudes were no doubt reflected in the fact that the government's majority declined even in a wartime election.

In the final phase of the war, which lasted twenty months, the Boer commandos turned to guerrilla warfare, making full use of the great spaces of the veldt, of their skills with rifle and horse, and of their ability to melt into the civilian population. They found ingenious and daring generals in such men as De Wet, Botha and Smuts. Eventually Kitchener turned to drastic measures. He stretched great belts of barbed wire, with blockhouses at intervals, across the countryside, and swept the areas between the wire clear of all inhabitants, killing the animals and burning the farms (Boer generals did the same, to frighten farmers out of surrendering). Concentration camps were set up into which women and children were herded. Conditions in these were so bad that one-sixth of their inmates died before reforms (after ceaseless agitation from Emily Hobhouse – 'that bloody woman' as Kitchener called her) were undertaken. Campbell-Bannerman in the Commons denounced these policies as 'methods of barbarism'. But eventually the 'elusive bands of bearded farmers' were worn down by sheer weight of numbers; the British government employed altogether 450,000 troops in this war. A peace treaty was signed at Vereeniging in May 1902. Thanks in great part to the soldier Kitchener, it was not ungenerous; the civilian Milner would have had it otherwise. The Orange Free State and the Transvaal were both annexed to the British Crown. Their white peoples were to be given self-government as soon as practicable; the question of the franchise for non-whites was postponed until after self-government. Although English was to be the official language, Afrikaans was to be allowed in schools and law courts. The British government gave £3,000,000 towards the rebuilding and re-stocking of farms.

Results So ended a war between the two white peoples of South Africa which had cost Britain some 22,000 lives and £222 million. About 4,000 Boers died. In several different ways the Boer War was an event of high and varied importance in British history, a turning point indeed. It had been a traumatic experience; despite the ultimate victory, British people would never again regard a policy of imperialism with great confidence – certainly not one of imperial conquest. In South Africa itself, despite the terms of the treaty and the creation of the Union of South Africa as a self-governing dominion in 1910, the gulf between Briton and Boer was never really bridged. Although some of the Boer generals of 1899–1902, notably Jan Christian Smuts, were to become leading imperial statesmen, others among them established the tradition which led to the creation in 1961 of the Afrikaaner-dominated Republic of South Africa. In the wider world, the Boer War exposed with alarming clarity the truth that Britain had few friends in Europe, and thereby encouraged the coming of the ententes from 1904 onwards. At home the military mismanagement of the campaigns led straight to Haldane's Army Reforms. In the party struggle the war also led, not quite so directly, to a sharp decline in the fortunes of the Conservative party.

2 Foreign affairs – the search for allies, 1900–5

The first country with whom Lansdowne, the new Foreign Secretary, negotiated an alliance was Japan. The initiative came from the Japanese. Russia had first forced them to give back Port Arthur which they had taken from the Chinese, and had then seized it for herself: and this was followed by a Russian invasion of Manchuria in 1900. Japan was prepared to take on Russia but needed an ally with a fleet capable of keeping other powers out of the China Sea while the war was on. Britain had that fleet, and, since Britain herself wished to see Russian power in the Far East curtailed, the Anglo-Japanese Alliance was signed in 1902. Britain promised military help to Japan if Japan were attacked by more than one power. In the Russo-Japanese War of 1904–5 Russia was unexpectedly defeated, its fleet so battered that, ironically for Britain, the Germans replaced the Russians as the third great naval power after Britain and France. A new alliance, to last ten years, was signed between Britain and Japan in 1905, and this time it was Britain who took the initiative.

Anglo-Japanese Alliance

Though Britain now had an ally in the Far East, it was in Europe that her isolation was most dangerous. Under Balfour, who became Conservative Prime Minister in 1902, a Committee of Imperial Defence had been set up to advise the cabinet, and pressure from this body and from the Admiralty produced two important decisions. The first was to seek an alliance with France. Anglo-French relations were still cool, though the French Foreign Minister Delcassé had long had hopes of a France-Russia-Britain axis to save Europe from German domination. A three-day visit to Paris by the new king Edward VII helped to change the atmosphere, and talks began between Delcassé and Lansdowne. In April 1904 the Anglo-French Agreement was signed. It settled all the minor disputes outstanding between the two countries from Newfoundland to Siam and Madagascar, and, more importantly, the related problems of Egypt and Morocco. France agreed to recognize British control of Egypt in return for French claims to treat Morocco as a sphere of French influence. The Entente, as it was called, was not a

Anglo-French Entente

The Entente Cordiale, 1904

military alliance, nor was it meant necessarily to commit Britain to supporting France in any future war. Germany took it very calmly. The German Ambassador in London reported – 'The British Government has the satisfying feeling of having one opponent fewer. But reconciliation with one opponent does not necessarily mean emnity with a third. On the contrary, I know it does not wish to destroy but to maintain the line to Berlin'.

It was a different matter with the second decision taken by Balfour's cabinet. This was to reform and expand the British Navy, a policy put into effect by Sir John Fisher, First Sea Lord from 1904 to 1910. Obsolete ships were to be scrapped and the Fleet, instead of being dispersed over the high seas, was now concentrated in three commands – Mediterranean, based on Malta; Atlantic, based on Gibraltar; and the Channel, based on home ports. It was a move clearly meant to strengthen the defence of Britain against either France or Germany. And since we had just come to an understanding with France, it could only be against Germany that the move was intended. Even more pointed was the decision to build a new type of battleship and cruiser, each faster and more heavily gunned than any other ship afloat. This programme of naval expansion was begun by Balfour's government and continued after 1905 by the Liberals (see Chapter 15).

3 Tariff reform and Conservative defeat

Salisbury, old and ailing, retired from the premiership six weeks after the end of the Boer War. His successor was his nephew, Arthur Balfour

Arthur Balfour (1848–1930) outside No. 10 Downing Street. Balfour was an early motoring enthusiast

– acceptable as leader, whereas Chamberlain was not, to the Conservative majority in the Unionist coalition. Balfour, an adroit debater who was tougher than his lath-like appearance and weary manner suggested, was already engaged in steering through Parliament what was probably the most far-reaching domestic reform carried by the Unionists during their long spell of power, the Education Act of 1902. This had two main elements. First, it 'put church schools on the rates': that is, it enabled schools run by the various religious denominations to receive assistance from local rates, hitherto given only to board schools (p.147). Thus it remedied a grievance strongly felt by many Anglicans and Roman Catholics, and enabled their schools to survive, alongside those provided by the community. Secondly, the Act abolished the elected school boards created by Forster's Act of 1870. Henceforward the undenominational board schools were to be run by education committees of county and county borough councils, the Local Education Authorities (LEAs). Further, whereas the school boards could provide only elementary education, the LEAs were given authority to organise secondary and higher education for older pupils and students. (A number of smaller boroughs and councils received the power to run elementary schools but not secondary). The debates on the Act were prolonged, with bitter words from nonconformists among the Liberal Opposition, in which the pro-Boer David Lloyd George, M.P. for Caernarvon Boroughs, was prominent. The framework of local authority management of education thus created by the Act has, broadly, lasted ever since. Yet its most significant result was the effective and rapid establishment of a national system of secondary schooling. By 1906 the number of secondary schools receiving government grant was twice what it had been in 1902, and the number of pupils had quadrupled. Here was the start of a social revolution which transformed the quality of English secondary education as well as its quantity.

Although the 'land war' in Ireland was ended by Wyndham's Act of 1903 (p.183) the remainder of Balfour's term of office was disastrous. The Education Act had a stormy passage. But far worse trouble lay ahead for Balfour – worse because it came within his own party and from the most formidable politician in the land. Since taking over the Colonial Office Joseph Chamberlain had tried, for example at the Colonial Conferences of 1897 and 1902, to strengthen the unity of the British Empire, notably in matters of defence and trade. Ministers from Canada and Australia had been cautious in their response, but Chamberlain continued to press his ideas. In particular he was moving towards a trade policy of protection, coupled with preferential treatment for colonial produce in this country. From time to time during the previous twenty years, especially when trade was depressed, men had talked about the weakness of Free Trade – particularly when they saw how the industries of Germany and the United States seemed to prosper behind tariff walls; and trade was depressed in 1902–3. Chamberlain was anxious to link his policy of 'Tariff Reform' with belief in the Empire. Moreover, he did not like the Education Act, which he knew would offend his nonconformist followers in Birmingham; and he believed that the Unionists needed a new programme to appeal to the public. Tariff Reform would provide this. In May 1903, on his return from a tour of South Africa where he had preached his gospel of imperial unity, he proclaimed his new policy in a great speech in Birmingham. The result was chaos in the Cabinet and in the Conservative party, and widespread opposition in the country. For Tariff Reform would mean the reversal of the established policy of Free Trade, by now the traditional belief of millions of the British people; and dearer food, for the principal exports of the colonies were foodstuffs (like Canadian wheat), so tariffs would have to go on similar foodstuffs from foreign countries if the Empire were to benefit.

Political reaction was swift. In the Commons Chamberlain was attacked alike by Liberals and by Free Trade Conservatives. His most prominent enemies included two rising parliamentary stars: Lloyd George among the Liberals and Winston Churchill (who was soon to change parties on this issue) among the Conservatives. Free Traders resigned from Balfour's Cabinet, and so before long did Chamberlain himself. Balfour tried to steer a middle course to hold his party together, on occasion even leading his followers out of the Commons in order to avoid voting on the issue. For their part the Liberals, so divided over the Boer War, now had in Free Trade an excellent policy on which to close ranks, and in 'No Food Taxes' and 'Your Food Will Cost You More' splendid slogans on which to appeal to the public. Chamberlain meanwhile formed a Tariff Reform League and threw himself into a great nationwide speaking campaign; his cry was 'Tariff Reform means Work for All'. Unluckily for him, business improved during 1904, and undermined the case for a change from Free Trade to Protection. It was ominous that the Conservatives, hopelessly divided on this issue despite Balfour's desperate negotiations to unite them, did badly in all the by-elections that year. Chamberlain and Tariff Reform

Eventually in 1905 Balfour resigned as Prime Minister. His successor, the Liberal leader Sir Henry Campbell-Bannerman, called a general election early in 1906. The result was a foregone conclusion. The Unionists went into the ring split into three rival groups – Tariff Reformers, 'Free Fooders', and a handful of 'Balfourians'. The Liberals, reunited and confident in the prospect of triumph, had little need to put a positive policy before the voters. They had plenty to denounce. There was the Education Act; a Licensing Act of 1904 which seemed to be unduly generous to the brewers; 'Chinese Slavery', a scheme by which Milner had permitted the importation to the Rand of 50,000 Chinese coolies to work in the mines; Balfour's apparent lack of resolution throughout his government; and above all Chamberlain's Tariff Reform, with the only too easy contrast between the 'Big Loaf' The election of 1906 of Free Trade and the 'Little Loaf' of Protection. So the Liberals won a resounding victory, one of the biggest in British parliamentary history, taking 377 seats. Conservatives and Liberal Unionists together got 157, 109 of whom were Tariff Reformers. The Irish Nationalists won 83, and there were now 53 Labour members, 29 of whom formed a separate party under the Labour Representation Committee. Balfour himself was beaten in Manchester, and several other ministers also lost their seats. Chamberlain, by contrast, retained his hold on Birmingham, where seven other Tariff Reformers were elected as well, some with increased majorities. He had not triumphed in the nation – yet he seemed to have captured the Conservative party. But his career was almost over. Within six months of the election he was laid low by a stroke, and he took no further part in politics, dying in 1914.

15
The Liberals in power 1905-14

1 Campbell-Bannerman's ministry 1905–8

Sir Henry Campbell-Bannerman, Prime Minister from 1905 to 1908 and leader of the victorious Liberals in the election of 1906, was a genial Scottish millionaire who had become the party leader when abler politicians were too quarrelsome or too idle. 'CB' was a poor speaker, and offered no new political ideas. But he was personally popular, a kindly, trustworthy man with plenty of humour and common sense; his Boer War phrase 'methods of barbarism' had won him wide public approval; and he was radical enough to satisfy a Liberal party which had not forgotten Gladstone's reforms. His ministry contained three future Prime Ministers, all of them brilliant men. H. H. Asquith, heir apparent to CB (who nicknamed him 'The Hammer'), a superb debater and imperturbable chairman, in the words of a colleague 'like a great counsel in whom solicitors and clients have faith', became Chancellor of the Exchequer; and David Lloyd George, the vigorous Welsh radical and pro-Boer, was made President of the Board of Trade. The third was Winston Churchill, son of Lord Randolph and a renegade from the Conservatives over Free Trade, who held minor office until 1908. Other Cabinet members included John Burns, the former dockers' leader; Sir Edward Grey at the Foreign Office; and R. B. Haldane at the War Office. The government contained far fewer landowners and more professional men, especially lawyers, than had been customary during the nineteenth century.

By common consent among historians the Liberal Cabinets from 1905 to 1914 were among the most able of all British governments. The Liberals in 1906 won a great majority, capturing 84 more seats than all the other parties combined (220 of the Liberal M.P.s had never sat in Parliament before). Yet they also faced great problems. There were growing demands for a great range of social reforms, to cope with poverty and unemployment, with the needs of the very young and the very old. There was much discontent among industrial workers, since for most of the period after 1900 wages were not rising as fast as prices. The old problem of Home Rule had been reawakened by the victory of the British allies of the Irish Party; a new one had arisen, with the 'suffragettes' using 'nuisance tactics' to gain political equality. Across the Channel the advance of German power presented a new threat to British security. In politics at home, two matters were of particular

H.H. Asquith (1852–1928)

concern to the Liberal leaders. One was plain enough: the Conservatives, heavily outnumbered in the Commons, had a gigantic majority in the Lords (they had thrown out the Second Home Rule Bill in 1893 by 419 votes to 41), and little hesitation in using it. The second, less immediate yet deeply disturbing, was the arrival of the Labour Party. Its single-minded demand for reform to benefit the working class was, like Irish Home Rule, a challenge from a section of the community. Behind it lay the threat of socialism, very frightening to the well-to-do middle-class men who filled the Liberal benches at Westminster. It was no wonder that Lloyd George, not the least radical of the Liberals, was emphatic in his speeches about the need to satisfy such demands of labour as the reform of trade union law, in order to undermine the challenge from the left.

In just over two years in office CB's government put through some **Reforms** useful and important reforms. A Workmen's Compensation Act (1906) simplified the law and added six million people to those able to claim compensation for injury at work. Lloyd George was responsible for a Merchant Shipping Act (1906) which limited pilots' certificates on British ships to British subjects, and required better conditions for their crews, and for a Patents Act (1907) which compelled all new holders of British patents to use them within three years or forfeit their rights. He also devised a scheme, carried out in 1908, to create a single Port of London Authority to replace the existing jungle of private dock and wharf companies. The Qualification of Women Act (1907) allowed women to become county and county borough councillors. In 1906 local authorities were given power to pay for free school meals out of the rates, and an Act of 1907 set up a medical department in the Board of Education and provided for the compulsory medical inspection of schoolchildren, a great stride in preventive medicine. These two measures for education have been described as 'the first elements of the welfare state'. Finally, perhaps the most noteworthy of these first Liberal reforms at the time was the Trade Disputes Act of 1906, which reversed the Taff Vale decision, and laid it down that trade unions could not be sued for damages arising from their members' actions during a strike. This indicated that the Conservative leadership in the Lords could be selective about the Liberal bills it declined to pass; it also gave the trade unions a privileged legal position from which they have continued to benefit ever since.

Yet by contrast these same years also saw a series of Liberal bills **Lords'** either rejected by the Lords or so mutilated that the Commons **opposition** abandoned them. The catalogue of casualties included important Education and Licensing Bills intended to reverse those passed by Balfour's government; a Plural Voting Bill whose purpose was to end the situation whereby electors who owned property in several constituencies could vote in each one; and a small crop of bills about land. Men talked of the Lords 'filling up the cup' and of the government 'ploughing the sands'. Campbell-Bannerman responded by carrying through the Commons in 1907 with a majority of nearly 300 a resolution that 'the power of the other House to alter or reject bills passed by this House must be so restricted by law as to secure that within the limits of a single Parliament the final decision of the Commons should prevail'. The Lords ignored what seemed an empty gesture, while the voters appeared to blame the government for what was happening. The Liberals lost a series of by-elections, including two humiliating defeats by Labour. And those who had no vote added insult to injury, if that is an accurate description of the tactics adopted by the suffragettes in those years. Striking particularly at the Liberals, the party which alone had the power to give them the vote, shrieking women persistently interrupted Liberal meetings, or chained themselves to ministers' railings and threw bricks through their windows (p.255). When CB resigned through serious illness and Asquith took over in the spring of 1908 the Liberal cause seemed at a low ebb.

2 The expansion of social reform from 1908

Yet a new approach was at hand. Already in 1906 Asquith as Chancellor of the Exchequer had promised to introduce Old Age Pensions, the first of the great social reforms for which his Liberal government is above all celebrated. These reforms ranged widely and benefited groups as various as old people, schoolchildren, coal miners, overworked dress-makers, shop assistants and workers in heavy industry. They reached something of a climax in the National Insurance Act of 1911. Their development coincided with a bitter constitutional conflict between the Liberal majority in the Commons and the Conservative majority in the Lords, whose outcome was the Parliament Act of 1911 reducing the powers of the Lords. Indeed the problem of financing the social reforms was a central element in Lloyd George's Budget of 1909 which set off that conflict (pp.250–3).

State aid to poor and aged

The Liberals in these reforms were using the power of the state to help members of certain groups in the community who were not strong enough to help themselves. This was not in itself novel: children in factories and mines, for instance, had been helped from over sixty years before. The novelty lay partly in the great range of the reforms, mainly in the kind of responsibility which the government was undertaking. Old Age Pensions, planned by Asquith and carried through by Lloyd George in 1908, offer a good example of the new approach. Many thousands of old people were unable to save enough from their wages to avoid entering the dreaded workhouse, or being a great burden upon their children. Joseph Chamberlain had advocated Old Age Pensions in 1892 (p.188), and they would probably have been introduced earlier but for the Boer War. Opposition to them had come from the Friendly

The first old age pensioners

Societies, suspicious of any scheme which seemed to compete with their own savings activities. Only gradually did they accept Asquith's plan, even though it was non-contributory, with pensions paid out of general taxation. Under it old people over 70 were to receive 5/- per week if their income was less than £26 a year (this original sum was in fact altered to a sliding scale between £21 and £31). There was an unexpectedly large demand; the cost was underestimated by £2 million on the first year's working alone; and in 1914 there were 970,000 pensioners. The scheme pointed to a changed attitude in the community – to a positive recognition that the nation as a whole had a responsibility to prevent the old from spending their last years in poverty, either inside or outside the workhouse. Pensions, provided out of national funds, could be claimed as a right[1]. The belief behind them began also to be applied during these years to the needs of the poor and the hungry, of the very young, the unemployed and the 'sweated labourer'.

Many circumstances contributed to this change of attitude. In the later years of the nineteenth century central government had increasingly taken action in social matters vital to general well-being, like health and housing, and people were getting used to its intervention. The Boer War had jolted British self-esteem, leading many to talk about 'national efficiency', and to wonder in particular about the physical well-being of a nation 40 per cent of whose volunteers were rejected as unfit. Middle-class opinion had grown more hostile to the 'official' remedy for poverty, the poor law workhouse. There was far less readiness than a generation earlier to link poverty with sin, to say that it was a man's own fault if he was poor; it was far more widely recognized how much people were at the mercy of the environment in which they lived and worked, how easily they could be hit by unemployment, sickness or poverty. Stern Victorian assumptions about self-help were being undermined. Moreover at the same period other countries were offering examples of a new approach. Germany in the 1880s had launched a system of national sickness and accident insurance; and in 1898 New Zealand had started Old Age Pensions.

Yet the immediate forces behind the Liberal reforms may be put under three headings. First, around 1900 a notable series of social enquiries, by private citizens and official committees, demonstrated beyond doubt that millions of British people lived in dire poverty, permanently on the margin of destitution. The most massive of these was by the shipowner Charles Booth, who carried out between 1886 and 1903 an immense investigation, published in seventeen volumes, of *The Life and Labour of the People of London*. This showed about one-third of the population of the Empire's greatest city living below 'the poverty line', and in conditions of overcrowding and squalor, with an average of two or three to a room. Old people especially were in this plight, and Booth was an early champion of old age pensions. All the good works of such private bodies as the Charity Organisation Society did practically nothing to improve the situation. Likewise in 1901 Seebohm Rowntree, of the Quaker chocolate firm, published *Poverty: A Study of Town Life*, which revealed that about 28 per cent of the population of York lived at a standard below that necessary for the mere maintenance of physical health.

[1]They were relieved of anxiety ... At first when they went to the Post office to draw it ... they would say as they picked up their money 'God bless that Lord George ... and God bless you, miss!', and there were flowers from their gardens and apples from their trees for the girl who merely handed them the money.' (Flora Thompson, *Lark Rise to Candleford*, 1939).

Booth and Rowntree offered abundant evidence, but few remedies. The most notable of the official enquiries tried to do so. From 1905 to 1909 a royal commission investigated the working of the Poor Law, and in 1909 it produced two reports. Both condemned the existing system. The Majority Report recommended putting all social services under a remodelled poor law; the phrase 'poor law', with its unpopular 'guardians', was to be replaced by 'public assistance'. But it was the Minority Report, the work largely of the Fabian Beatrice Webb, which secured more readers. Its aim was to use the resources of the nation to prevent people from becoming destitute. The Poor Law was to vanish; in its place were to come special services for particular needs like health and pensions, run by local councils. Unemployment, which under modern industrial conditions was the chief cause of poverty, was to be tackled by an office of the central government, a Ministry of Labour, which would provide Labour Exchanges; insurance against it would be voluntary, and operated through the trade unions. The details of the Minority Report had little immediate influence; it was clearly in tune both with the aims of the Liberals and with later developments of the Welfare State.

Secondly, in the first decade of the twentieth century there was political pressure from several quarters demanding reforms. Organised labour, in the shape of the tiny parliamentary party and of the TUC, was calling for old age pensions, for education, and for action against unemployment – though many ordinary working people were deeply suspicious of government action, which they identified with the Poor Law and the police. For their part, Liberals, with an eye after 1906 on the Labour threat to their left, had in Lloyd George's words 'to cope seriously with the social condition of the people, to remove the national degradation of slums and widespread poverty in a land glittering with wealth'. Unless they did so they might be overtaken by the new party. Moreover Liberals and many Conservatives regarded social reform as an antidote to socialism, a means of saving Britain from the doctrines of state control preached by many continental Marxists. There were immediate political pressures, too. 1908 was a good year in which to introduce pensions, as a counterblast to the failures and the by-election losses of the last two years.

Thirdly, policies and their timing reflect the personalities of those who launch them and carry them through. The growth of social reform in Britain would surely have taken a different course if Asquith had not had David Lloyd George and Winston Churchill as his chief lieutenants. Both were relatively young in politics: in 1908 Lloyd George was appointed Chancellor of the Exchequer at 44 and Churchill President of the Board of Trade at 33. Each was a remarkable blend of idealism and realism; each was ambitious, full of energy, and a superb orator. Both at this stage of their careers were committed deeply to social reform. Lloyd George was an 'outsider' in the Edwardian parliament, a poor

David Lloyd George (1863–1945)

boy brought up by his shoemaker uncle in Llanystumdwy, profoundly moved by the contrasts he saw between immense wealth and extreme poverty in Edwardian society; Churchill the grandson of a duke, born in Blenheim Palace, yet seeing Liberalism as 'the cause of the left-out millions'. Together they did more than any others to promote the cause of social reform and to win it widespread public support. They were fortunate in the backing of a group of outstanding civil servants, of whom Robert Morant and William Beveridge are merely the best-known.

Children's Charter

The year 1908 brought three other important reforms besides Old Age Pensions. The Children Act (or 'Children's Charter') ranged widely in its attempts to safeguard children. It strengthened the laws for protecting them from cruelty and for maintaining illegitimate children; forbade the sale of alcohol and tobacco to children; created special juvenile courts, stopped the imprisonment of offenders under sixteen and set up remand homes for those awaiting trial; and established at the Home Office a Children's Branch dealing with those rescued from neglectful parents as well as with delinquents. The Miners' Eight-Hour Day Act achieved a reform for which coal-miners had been campaigning for nearly half a century. Its passage reflected the presence in the Commons of sixteen M.P.s sitting for mining constituencies, most of them 'Lib-Labs', backing the Liberal rather than the Labour Party. Thirdly, an act to establish Labour Exchanges, already working in Germany, was passed in 1908, largely as the result of pressure by the young economist William Beveridge whom Churchill had appointed to his staff. Nationally-financed, voluntary rather than compulsory, they provided places where employers could report vacant jobs and where employees could find out about them. The first 83 were opened early in 1910. From the start Churchill and Beveridge intended that they should form the first section of a wider scheme to tackle the vast problem of unemployment. The second was to come in the National Insurance Act of 1911.

During 1909–10 politics were dominated by the great issue of Lloyd George's Budget and the Lords (p.251), and the single notable other reform of that time was Churchill's Trade Boards Act (1909), an attempt to help workers in the 'sweated trades', who laboured very long hours in bad conditions for low wages. It set up in four such trades (tailoring, making of paper boxes, lace-making and chain-making; four more were added in 1913) boards with power to fix minimum rates of wages, and was a useful beginning.

The National Insurance Act of 1911 was probably the most significant achievement of Asquith's ministry and of what has been called 'the New Liberalism'. Part I of this act, which dealt with the problem of sickness and ill-health, was the responsibility of Lloyd George; Part II, concerned with unemployment, that of Winston Churchill. Both parts rested upon insurance, inspired by the German example, which had greatly impressed Lloyd George on a visit in 1908, in contrast to Old Age Pensions, which were non-contributory (until 1925). Contributions, in the form of stamps stuck on cards – as in Germany – built up a fund upon which the contributor had the right to draw when he was in need of help. Both Lloyd George and Churchill – like Bismarck in Germany – saw social insurance of this kind as a means of heading off the challenge of socialism.

National Insurance for sick and unemployed

Part I was entitled 'Insurance against Loss of Health and for the Prevention and Care of Sickness.' It was compulsory for all wage-earners. They had to pay 4d a week and employers 3d, to which the state added 2d: hence Lloyd George's slogan 'ninepence for fourpence'. In return they received 10s. a week in sickness benefit, together with free medical attention from a doctor on an official list called a 'panel'. A

Part I of the National Insurance Act

30s. maternity benefit was also payable. The scheme was supervised by the state, though the sickness benefits were paid through 'approved societies', that is Friendly Societies, trade unions and the commercial insurance companies like the Prudential. Other details of National Health Insurance included the provision of £1,500,000 for setting up sanatoria for the cure of tuberculosis (which at this time killed 75,000 people a year), and of one penny per insured person towards research, which made possible the creation of the Medical Research Council.

This was in its author's words 'a great social experiment', embodying a new pattern of social responsibility. Yet it fell well short of what Lloyd George had originally envisaged, and he himself called it 'driving an ambulance wagon to the relief of the distressed'. It was far from universal; it gave no treatment to the wives and children of workers; it made no provision for hospital treatment or for the use of consultants; it said nothing of widows' and orphans' benefits. Lloyd George abandoned the last of these items – what he called 'the most urgent and pitiable case of all' – in face of the organised pressure not only from Friendly Societies but also from the commercial insurance groups, whose business might well have been ruined and whose 80,000 door-to-door collectors could exert enormous political influence. There was other opposition. Some Labour leaders, Keir Hardie among them, condemned the contributory principle as 'unjust and wasteful'. Trade unions were against any payment of contributions. Fashionable ladies complained about licking stamps. Far more seriously, the doctors, whose fees would depend on the number of patients on their panels, feared that they might lose both income and professional independence.[1] Eventually they accepted and indeed many of them did well out of the new scheme. Nevertheless, incomplete as it was and with its further expansion soon blocked by war, the scheme became a permanent and vital feature of British life, of real and daily benefit during the thirty-five years which passed before it was replaced by a National Health Service incorporating many of Lloyd George's original proposals.

Part II of the National Insurance Act Part II of the Act, about unemployment, was far less complicated and controversial. It upset fewer vested interests than Part I, and concerned, at first, far fewer people. Large-scale unemployment, the outcome of industrial expansion dependent upon world-wide trade, was at last being recognized as a problem which only governments could begin to cope with. Churchill had said in a famous speech at Dundee in 1908 that its causes were as 'independent of our control as the phases of the moon', and that it was the responsibility of the central government to help its victims. In 1909 Beveridge wrote *Unemployment: A Problem of Industry*, maintaining that only by some system of insurance could workers be protected against the periodic spells of unemployment

---

[1]After one meeting with the British Medical Association Lloyd George said 'I do not think there has been anything like it since the day when Daniel went into the lions' den.'

which occurred in times of trade depression, and that this could only be organised by the state through some system of Labour Exchanges. By regular small payments, with governmental help, a fund could be created by which all contributors could be protected against this risk.

Unemployment insurance was, in Churchill's words, 'the untrodden field'; the Germans had not entered it. So Churchill and Beveridge drafted the scheme of unemployment insurance which in 1911 (by which date Churchill had moved to the Home Office) was passed as Part II of the National Insurance Act. It was compulsory, but at first it applied only to some 2¼ million workers in a group of industries (including shipbuilding, ironfounding, mechanical engineering and building) where wages were low and fluctuations in trade serious. Employer and employee each paid 2½d a week to the fund, and the state added one-third of that total. In return the workman got 7s. a week while he was unemployed, for a maximum of fifteen weeks in any one year. The unemployed man had to sign on and receive his benefit at the Labour Exchange. Clearly the amount of relief this scheme provided was limited, as were the jobs it covered (munition workers were added during the war of 1914–18, and all manual workers except farm labourers and domestic servants in 1920), and it was to run into grave trouble with the depression of the 1930s. Yet, as a benefit clearly in return for money paid in, it was utterly different from the hard charity of the Poor Law, and acceptable to the pride of the worker. It was also respectable in the eyes of those who had opposed non-contributory old age pensions. Taken as a whole, the Act of 1911 marked the beginning of insurance as the central element of British social security.

It also marked the peak of the Liberals' social reforms. There were other lesser measures during these last pre-war years, like the Shop Hours Act (1911) which secured a weekly half-holiday for shop assistants, or the Coal Mine Minimum Wages Act (1912). But Asquith's government was at this time heavily preoccupied with urgent immediate problems, and it put through no more constructive reforms. Its achievement was substantial. It is commonly claimed that the Liberals between 1908 and 1914 laid the foundations of the later British Welfare State – the state in which, certainly since 1945, it is generally assumed to be the duty of the central government to ensure that all citizens have the opportunity to live a full life in decent conditions – conditions which involve health and education, housing and employment. There is truth in this claim: later governments, working deliberately towards that goal, have built on what the Liberals did, especially in the years 1908–11. The Liberals of that time, however, saw things differently. They had a more limited aim, namely to provide minimum standards of life for the poor and other weaker groups of people – what some historians have called a 'social service state'. In doing this much they were also opening the way to wider future development. Certainly Lloyd George and others had in mind far more radical and comprehensive policies than the Liberals actually achieved.

3 The People's Budget and the Lords

When Lloyd George introduced his budget in 1909 he was demanding more money than any previous Chancellor of the Exchequer. He proposed taxes amounting to £15 million – £3 million more than the budget of 1900 in the middle of the Boer War. The main reasons for this high taxation were two, of quite different kinds, one involving the armed forces, the other social reform.

Army and Navy reforms

The Liberals between 1905 and 1914 carried out major reforms in both army and navy. Those in the army were largely the work of R. B. Haldane, the Scottish lawyer who was Secretary for War from 1905 to 1912. The Boer War had shown that thoroughgoing changes in the organization of the army were required. Even more important, Haldane had no doubt, after the Anglo-French Entente of 1904 (p.233), that Britain now needed an army ready to fight on the European mainland. So in 1906 he created a General Staff, on the German model, and in 1907 he formed an expeditionary force of seven divisions, equipped to cross the Channel at short notice. For home defence he established a Territorial Army of part-time trained volunteers. Finally in 1908 he started an Officers' Training Corps (the ancestor of the present Combined Cadet Force) in the public schools and universities. These measures, opposed by pacifists on the left and by advocates of conscription on the right, were to prove of vital importance in 1914.

Haldane's reforms were surprisingly cheap: the army estimates were lower when he left office in 1912 than when he entered it in 1905. By contrast the naval developments of these years were extremely costly, for they involved great technological change – in particular the construction of new battleships of the *Dreadnought* class. The first *Dreadnought*, built in secret and with great rapidity in 1906–7, was the first 'all-big-gun' ship and the first turbine-engined battleship. Her fire-power and speed made every other naval vessel in the world second-class, and gave Britain several years' strategic lead over her nearest naval rival, Germany. The man behind her construction, Admiral 'Jackie' Fisher, First Sea Lord 1904–10, helped to whip up a newspaper 'scare' campaign in 1908 for a large-scale programme for the building of dreadnoughts. Asquith yielded to the music-hall cry 'We want eight and we won't wait.' The eight dreadnoughts contributed to Britain's supremacy in capital ships in 1914. Meanwhile they had to be paid for, and they formed the largest single item in Lloyd George's budget of 1909.

The 'People's Budget'

The second reason why that budget was so big was the Old Age Pension, costing far more than expected and about four times as much

H.M.S. Dreadnought

as in 1908. But there was much more in this particular budget than the mere paying of bills. For Lloyd George deliberately used what he chose to call 'the People's Budget' as a weapon of social policy. Describing it as a 'war budget ... for raising money to wage implacable war against poverty and squalidness', he imposed upon the rich what by the standards of the time were heavy taxes in order to provide for the needs of the poor. As a party politician, he saw the budget as a golden opportunity for the Liberals to press home their initiative in social reform. His proposed taxes would appeal to the working class, for they would hit landlords and other rich men; to the middle class, because they would pay for social reform without introducing socialism; and to free traders, because they were a means of providing both battleships and pensions without placing tariffs on imports.

The Chancellor spread the net of taxation wide. Income tax was to go up from 1s. to 1s. 2d; a new 'super tax' was placed on incomes above £3000 a year; death duties (first imposed only fifteen years before) were increased on all estates between £5000 and £1 million. Extra duties were placed on tobacco, spirits, and liquor licences. A special Road Fund – to finance improvements made necessary by the rising tide of motor-cars[1] was created by taxes on petrol and on motor licences. Finally, all land was to be valued, and there was to be a new series of taxes on land, the most noteworthy of which was one of 20 per cent on the 'unearned increment' of land whenever it changed hands: that is, on any gain it had made in price without effort on the owner's part, e.g. if it was sold for housing on the outskirts of a city.

Lords vs. Commons
The sheer scale of the budget as a whole, and the land tax proposals in particular, aroused a storm of hostility among Conservatives. They had during the nineteenth century used their great strength in the House of Lords to reject many bills passed by a Liberal majority in the Commons; and they had resumed this process against Liberal bills since 1905. Now it was suggested that the Lords should reject the entire budget, the central financial measure of the year, upon which the operations of government depended. Such a step would be unprecedented; it would also be a complete denial of the supremacy of the Commons as representatives of the people. No elected government could tolerate it. Wiser heads among the Conservatives advised against such a move. Moreover, it gave Lloyd George an opportunity, which he seized with relish, to denounce the peers. In a series of hard-hitting speeches he displayed them as selfish defenders of class privilege and luxury. At Limehouse he proclaimed 'A fully-equipped duke costs as much to keep as two dreadnoughts, and dukes are just as great a terror, and they last longer'; at Newcastle-upon-Tyne he asked 'Should five hundred men, chosen accidentally from among the unemployed [i.e., the House of Lords] override the judgement of millions of people who are engaged in the industry which makes the wealth of the country?' Balfour had called the House of Lords 'the watchdog of the Constitution'; Lloyd George scorned it, as 'Mr Balfour's poodle'.

The Parliament Act. 1911
Nevertheless the Lords in October 1909 threw out the budget by 350 votes to 75. Asquith declared their action 'a breach of the Constitution and a usurpation of the rights of the Commons', and appealed to the people in a general election held in January 1910. The campaign was lively, with Liberal posters depicting decayed-looking peers grasping bags full of unearned gold, and the proportion of the electorate that voted (over 86 per cent) was the highest in British history. The results were not easy to interpret. The Conservatives got more of the votes (46.9 per cent) than the Liberals (43.2 per cent), but slightly fewer seats (273 against 275). Labour (40 seats) supported the Liberals both over the budget and over the need to limit the powers of the Lords. The Irish Nationalists (82 seats) were against the budget, which increased the tax on whisky – but they above all wanted to curb the Lords, the

---

[1]The 18,000 cars registered in 1903 when licences were first required rose to 389,000 by 1914.

great barrier against Home Rule. Asquith, thus dependent upon the Irish and anxious to convince them that he meant business about the Lords, introduced three resolutions in the Commons saying that (a) the Lords could not touch a bill which the Speaker of the Commons ruled was a money bill (b) any bill passed by the same House of Commons three times in successive sessions would become law whether the Lords agreed or not (c) the life of a Parliament would be shortened from seven years to five.

The Commons quickly passed the budget, and the Lords accepted it. But the great issue now was the reform of the Lords themselves. Would they pass the Parliament Bill containing the three resolutions?

In May 1910 the sudden death of Edward VII interrupted the crisis. His successor George V encouraged the party leaders to meet in secret conference to see whether they could reach any compromise on the question of the Lords. Despite almost five months effort, they failed to do so – mainly because of the problem of Irish Home Rule, which any effective reform of the Lords would make inevitable; and a proposal canvassed by Lloyd George at this time for forming a coalition government also came to nothing. Asquith thereupon obtained from the King a promise, kept secret, that he would, if it were necessary, create enough peers to overcome opposition to the Parliament Bill in the Lords; and another general election was held (December 1910), this time with reform of the Lords as the main issue. Although a good many seats changed hands, the party totals (Liberals 272, Conservative 272, Labour 42, Irish Nationalists 84) differed little from those of January, and Asquith's government was still at the mercy of the Irish. Would the peers yield now? The Conservatives divided into 'hedgers', prepared to give way; and 'ditchers', ready to die in the last ditch, even after Asquith made public the King's pledge to create new peers[1]. Eventually after a long and tense debate in the exceptionally hot August of 1911 (the temperature at Greenwich reached 100°F., the highest ever recorded in Britain), the Parliament Act with its three clauses went through the Lords by 131 to 114. The votes of 37 Conservatives and 11 bishops in its favour were needed to defeat the diehards. It was a victory for the House of Commons and for the representatives of the people over the hereditary peerage; for the Liberals over the Conservatives; and for the skilful management of Asquith. In the long run it meant a steep decline in the significance of the House of Lords in the British system of government. In the short run it led in 1911 to the fall of Balfour from the Conservative leadership and to his replacement by an altogether harder and more limited personality, Bonar Law. Most important of all, the passage of the Parliament Act at once reopened the Irish Question, with alarming consequences. Home Rule, effectively in cold storage since the fall of Parnell and the defeat of Gladstone's bill in 1893, came back to the centre of British politics.

[1]Lists of about 250 worthies upon whom peerages might be conferred were actually drawn up, though not published until some twenty years later.

4 The Liberals' time of troubles, 1911–14

The Parliament Act was passed in August 1911. That same month dockers, coal miners and railwaymen were out in the biggest strike movement so far seen in Britain. A relentless campaign, involving arson and violence, by the Women's Social and Political Union demanding the vote was in full swing. Across the Irish Sea the prospect of Home Rule for Ireland was rousing the Protestants of Ulster to prepare armed resistance to what they saw as 'Rome rule'. The constitutional problem of the House of Lords had been solved. But these three other developments – the activities of the organised working class, of the 'suffragettes', and of the Ulstermen – dominated the three years that passed between the Parliament Act and the outbreak of war with the German Empire in August 1914. All three had, in varying measure, a flavour of illegality and violence. So the orderly development of a series of social reforms tended to fade from view. Some continental observers, indeed, were inclined to believe that government in the United Kingdom was breaking down, and that anarchy was taking the place of the traditional British moderation and compromise.

Labour unrest   The five years 1910–14 were a period of widespread labour unrest. About ten million working days were lost in strikes or lockouts in every year except 1912, when over forty million were lost. Many trades and industries were involved, above all the three big groups of coal miners, dockers and railwaymen. The national miners' strike of 1912 brought out nearly a million men. With these strikes came riots and violence, not entirely discouraged by the readiness of the government to send troops into the industrial areas (two men were shot in disturbances at Liverpool and two at Llanelli in 1911). The reasons for this outburst were various. Prices were rising, and wages were not keeping pace. Employment was plentiful, so 'blacklegs' were not easy to find and trade unions were in a stronger position to bring their members out on strike. The Labour Party in Parliament did not appear at this time to be achieving much; the elections of 1910 had done little to increase its representation. So workers were ready to turn to industrial action instead. This was encouraged by some spread of 'Syndicalist' ideas, especially from France, which argued for the formation of a single union for each industry and for workers' control of industry. Tom Mann, the dockers' leader of 1889, was their chief advocate. Yet their influence seems to have been quite limited.

Trade Unions prospered in these years, if numbers of members are the yardstick: they went up from 2,500,000 in 1910 to over 4,000,000 in 1914. Moreover, they won a second legal triumph comparable with that arising from the Taff Vale Case (p.241). In 1908 W. V. Osborne, Secretary of the Walthamstow Branch of the Amalgamated Society of Railway Servants and a member of the Liberal Party, brought an action against his union to stop it from contributing to the funds of the Labour

Party. He won his case, and thereby dealt what might well have been a knock-out blow to the party, many of whose M.P.s depended on payments from the unions for their keep. The TUC protested strongly, and the Liberals were not unsympathetic. In 1911 Lloyd George introduced the payment of a salary (£400 per annum) to M.P.s, and in 1913 Parliament passed the Trade Union Act, which permitted unions to establish, after a ballot of their members, a separate fund out of which they could support M.P.s. Members not willing to pay this 'political levy' had the right to 'contract out' of it. Finally, the following year saw the formation of the so-called 'Triple Alliance' of three great unions (coal miners, railwaymen, and transport workers) with the aim of co-ordinating their strike pressure. This was a portent for the future, suggesting the possibility of something like a 'general strike'. At the time, however, it could scarcely be seen as a step towards revolution. The purposes of members were firmly limited to the improvement of wages and working conditions.

The second, and certainly the most infuriating, of the Liberals' troubles during these years was the militant behaviour of the suffragettes, the Women's Social and Political Union. Votes for women was a teasing problem for the politicians. Each of the three parties was divided about it. Mainly for this reason, yet partly also because they had higher priorities (social reforms, the Lords, the Irish) the Liberal government did not put it at the head of their agenda. This aroused the furious antagonism of the WSPU, a body dominated by the extremist and highly autocratic mother and daughter Emmeline and Christabel Pankhurst. Their campaign, opening in 1905 with interruptions at Liberal meetings, grew more violent. They chained themselves to railings, smashed windows, and attacked ministers: in 1909 Churchill was assaulted with a dog-whip at Bristol railway station, and Asquith jumped on while playing golf. From 1909 many of them went on hunger-strike in prison and were forcibly fed. In 1912 they started to set fire to pillar-boxes, and in 1913 went in for widespread arson, burning railway stations, pavilions, private houses and churches. That same year one threw herself in front of the horses running in the Derby at Epsom and died of her injuries. The so-called 'Cat and Mouse Act' of 1913, enabling the authorities to release prisoners whose health was suffering and then rearrest them virtually at will, had only limited success. But on balance the evidence strongly suggests that the campaign did far more harm than good to the cause of women's suffrage. The Pankhursts' methods undermined the work of the more moderate body, the National Union of Women's Suffrage Societies, who up to 1905 had been gaining support; turned mild sympathisers among politicians into opponents; and antagonized much public opinion, to judge from the attitude of crowds in the later stages of the campaign, particularly among the working class and among women themselves.

The Suffragettes

A suffragettes' demonstration

Ulster

The suffragettes, for all the high importance of their cause and the bravery of many of its supporters, were primarily an irritant to the Liberals. The third of their problems, that of Ireland, was a major political issue which came within sight of causing a civil war. There was nothing new about 'the Irish Question', clearly; and two of its nineteenth century ingredients, religion and Home Rule, were at the heart of the crisis which followed inevitably upon the passage of the Parliament Act in 1911. For that Act had been made possible only by the votes of the Irish Nationalist party in the Commons; and the Irishmen now demanded their price – Home Rule. The barrier of the Lords was down, or would be within two years for, thanks to the Parliament Act, the peers could delay Home Rule no longer than that. But many of the people of one part of Ireland, the mainly Protestant region of Ulster, were of Anglo-Scottish stock and were determined to resist it. When Gladstone had introduced his first Home Rule bill in 1886 Lord Randolph Churchill had said 'Ulster will fight and Ulster will be right'. The crisis had been postponed for twenty-five years; but now the prospect of Home Rule was real. There were many Catholics in Ulster – in parts of the countryside in the south of the province, and above all in Belfast (and to a smaller extent Londonderry) where they had come in their thousands with the growth of shipbuilding and other industries in the late nineteenth century, and where they lived in virtually separate areas from the Protestants. Yet their presence merely

Edward Carson (1854–1935) and Bonar Law (1858–1923)

made the Protestant majority, led by such associations as the Orange Order (commemorating William of Orange who had delivered them from the Catholics at the Battle of the Boyne in 1690), the more determined to oppose Home Rule. For in doing so they saw themselves as defending both their Protestant faith and their link with Britain. In their minds religion and loyalty to the Crown united in the cause of Ulster. Nor would opposition be limited to words, for there was a tradition of violence in Ireland in which Ulstermen fully shared. In the Irishman Bernard Shaw's words, when the Ulsterman 'sings O God our help in ages past, he means business'.

So in 1911 when Asquith's government prepared to frame its Home Rule bill, Ulstermen set about creating a provisional government to take over the province 'the moment Home Rule passes.' Its two chief leaders were James Craig, an Ulster M.P., and Sir Edward Carson, a Unionist from Dublin, one of the most brilliant barristers of the day, grim in appearance and formidable in speech. They roused loyalist opinion throughout the province, getting almost half-a-million signatures in 1912 to a solemn Covenant to 'defeat the present conspiracy to set up a Home Rule Parliament in Ireland . . . and to refuse to recognize its authority'. They formed in January 1913 an Ulster Volunteer force, drilled and trained ready to fight Home Rule, and they collected arms

Ulster's Solemn League and Covenant.

Being convinced in our consciences that Home Rule would be disastrous to the material well-being of Ulster as well as of the whole of Ireland, subversive of our civil and religious freedom, destructive of our citizenship and perilous to the unity of the Empire, we, whose names are underwritten, men of Ulster, loyal subjects of His Gracious Majesty King George V., humbly relying on the God whom our fathers in days of stress and trial confidently trusted, do hereby pledge ourselves in solemn Covenant throughout this our time of threatened calamity to stand by one another in defending for ourselves and our children our cherished position of equal citizenship in the United Kingdom and in using all means which may be found necessary to defeat the present conspiracy to set up a Home Rule Parliament in Ireland. ¶ And in the event of such a Parliament being forced upon us we further solemnly and mutually pledge ourselves to refuse to recognise its authority. ¶ In sure confidence that God will defend the right we hereto subscribe our names. ¶ And further, we individually declare that we have not already signed this Covenant.

The above was signed by me at_____
"Ulster Day," Saturday, 28th September, 1912.

God Save the King.

Ulster's Solemn League and Covenant: Carson was the first to sign

for it wherever they could – most notably through a celebrated gun-running at Larne in 1914, when they put ashore 30,000 rifles. Such developments led inevitably to similar activities in the remainder of Ireland. In 1913 a rival National Volunteer Army was formed with headquarters in Dublin, and it too set about running guns into Ireland, in support of Home Rule.

The Curragh Mutiny

These events in Ireland – as the bill made its three slow journeys through Commons and Lords during 1912–14 – were alarming enough. British opinion was even more disturbed by two other developments. In 1912 Bonar Law, the Conservative leader in Parliament, himself the son of an Ulster Presbyterian minister, said in a speech at Blenheim Palace

'I can imagine no length of resistance to which Ulster can go in which I should not be prepared to support them, and in which, in my belief, they would not be supported by the overwhelming majority of the British people'. Conservative leaders took the salute at a review of the Ulster Volunteers. This conduct by the Opposition sounded like incitement to rebellion, and the undermining of parliamentary democracy. Secondly, in 1914 there occurred the so-called 'Curragh Mutiny'. Many officers in the army sympathised with Ulster[1]. At the military camp at the Curragh in Ireland fifty-eight of them, under the leadership of General Sir Hubert Gough, offered their resignations rather than face the prospect of having to take part in forcing Ulster to accept Home Rule. The affair was sorted out and the War Minister resigned; but the episode suggested strongly that the Army could not be relied on in this crisis. By now Asquith was making desperate efforts to find some compromise acceptable both to Ulstermen and to southern Irishmen. But John Redmond, the moderate who led the Nationalist M.P.s at Westminster, declined to accept what seemed to most Englishmen the obvious solution, the exclusion of Ulster from Home Rule. For to him and his followers Ireland was one and indivisible; and many of them believed that all the activities of the Ulstermen were just bluff anyway. More important still, Redmond was only too well aware of the rise in Ireland of the movement called Sinn Fein ('Ourselves'), which intended to go beyond Home Rule to the creation of an independent republic. Home Rule would have given Ireland a separate Parliament, controlling most of its own internal affairs – but not finance, defence, or foreign policy, and still subject to the British Crown. To accept the exclusion of Ulster would play into the hands of Sinn Fein. Nor was it easy to define 'Ulster', and to decide exactly where a boundary between the province and the rest of Ireland could run. In July 1914 Asquith yielded to George V's pressure and called a conference of party leaders (Liberals and Conservatives, Ulster Unionists and Irish Nationalists) at Buckingham Palace to try to find an eleventh-hour compromise. It failed. Two days later the Irish National Volunteers carried out a successful gun-running at Howth in Dublin Bay. Civil war in Ireland seemed to be growing daily nearer.

But the day before the Buckingham Palace meeting broke down the Austrians sent to Serbia the ultimatum which led to the outbreak of the First World War in August 1914 (p.264). The war brought an abrupt end to the Liberals' domestic troubles. Trade unionists and suffragettes joined in the war effort. Ulstermen flocked to the colours. In Parliament Redmond pledged the support of Ireland in the conflict with Germany (a promise that was later to be his political ruin in Ireland). The Home Rule Bill, officially becoming law in September 1914, was not to come into operation until the war was over and until Parliament had been able to make special provision for Ulster.

[1] Sir Henry Wilson, an Anglo-Irishman who was then Director of Military Operations at the War Office, happily gave advice to the Ulster Volunteers. In 1922 he was murdered by the IRA on his own doorstep.

16
Foreign affairs 1905-14
the road to war

When the Liberals returned to office in 1905 the new Foreign Secretary was Sir Edward Grey, later Viscount Grey of Falloden. A 'frank and straightforward man', as the German Ambassador called him, he was related to the Earl Grey of the 1832 Reform Act. He was the first Foreign Secretary to publish a full account of his work in office; and he had a deep and lifelong love of the countryside – his spare time was devoted to weekend walks in Hampshire, or holidays in his native Northumbria and, until his sight failed, to bird-watching. His record of eleven years continuous service at the Foreign Office saw a much closer relationship develop between Minister and officials. Since most of the cabinet were heavily involved in domestic reforms, he and his colleagues were able to go very much their own way, and during his time senior civil servants – the 'mandarins' of Whitehall – considerably

Sir Edward Grey with Winston Churchill and Lord Crewe in 1910

increased their influence on the conduct of foreign affairs. In politics Grey was, like Asquith and Haldane, a 'Liberal Imperialist' – their critics called them 'Limps' – much more in the tradition of Rosebery than of Gladstone. There was little difference between Grey's policy after 1905 and the previous Conservative policy of Lansdowne. The main opposition to Grey came from within his own party, from the Prime Minister Campbell-Bannerman and from the Radical Lloyd George, both anti-Imperialist.

The hardest problems facing Grey, however, were European, not imperial. Europe was each year more clearly dividing into the two hostile power groups of the Triple Alliance and the Dual Alliance. The Anglo-French Entente, which Grey had inherited from the Conservatives, and the recent Anglo-German naval rivalry had virtually ended any hopes of Britain remaining strictly neutral. Grey still held to two main aims which he hoped were not incompatible – to keep the peace and to stand by France. He knew that support for France would have to fall short of a binding military alliance since public opinion in Britain would not back such a move; but he hoped that the Entente might act as a deterrent to German aggression. He therefore tried to remain on good terms with all the powers and, at the same time, to make sure that, if the British government was forced into war, it would have a united country behind it. It was a policy of which, not unnaturally, the Germans were suspicious, and this mood showed itself in two crises involving Morocco.

Germany provoked the first Moroccan crisis (1905–6) without being sure of where it would lead her, though it was a clear attempt to test the strength of the recently signed Entente. The Kaiser landed at Tangier in 1905 and declared that, so far from France having special influence in Morocco, Germany herself had 'great and growing interests' there, and that he proposed to deal direct with the Sultan over them. It was a gesture meant to show that Germany should not be ignored in international matters, and to prove to France perhaps that, under pressure, Britain would desert her. Grey's reaction was to tell the German Ambassador that the Entente was popular in England and that, if there was war between Germany and France over Morocco, 'any British government, Conservative or Liberal, would be forced to help France'. Yet, at the same time, when the French Ambassador Paul Cambon asked Grey if he could guarantee armed support for France if she were attacked, Grey would give no firm promise. A confrontation between Germany and France was avoided when the American President Theodore Roosevelt suggested an international conference to discuss the future of Morocco. This met at Algeciras in January 1906 and decided to give France control over the Moroccan Bank and part control over the police. The decision was a rebuff for Germany who saw that, in a crisis, she could not count on the support of the powers, and it strengthened the Entente. It also impressed Russia, now recovering from her defeat by the Japanese.

Crises in Morocco

Grey had always hoped that one of Salisbury's later aims, an agreement with Russia, might be possible. 'I am impatient to see Russia re-established as a factor in European politics' he wrote at the time. In August 1907 the Anglo-Russian Agreement was signed. It marked a revolution in British foreign policy, far more so than the Anglo-French Entente. It upset the Radicals who did not wish to see Britain in league with a repressive régime, though it was really a commitment to France rather than to Russia. It was, again, an entente rather than an alliance, an attempt to settle outstanding disputes over Persia, Tibet and Afghanistan. Persia was divided into three zones; one in the north under Russian influence, one neutral, and one in the south under British influence – an arrangement which by no means ended friction. Tibet was recognized as an independent buffer state under Chinese suzerainty, Afghanistan as being under British influence. The Anglo-Russian Entente was bound to increase German suspicions of Britain since what had been a Dual Alliance was now a Triple Entente. Britain was not yet Germany's enemy but at least she had friends in the enemy camp.

Behind the scenes, Grey had early in 1906 taken the step of making official the informal talks, begun by Lansdowne, between French and British army and navy staffs. He told Campbell-Bannerman and Haldane but not the rest of the cabinet because, he said, there was a general election at the time. Few people knew, therefore, that actual plans were being laid. By 1912, for example, the French Fleet had first-line responsibility in the Mediterranean, the British in the Atlantic and the Channel; and a British Expeditionary Force was established which could be used, if required, to protect France's northern front. Such plans, in Grey's view, did not bring Britain closer to war because, up to 1914, whatever the tension between France and Germany, there was no compelling reason for Britain to be drawn in. When such a reason did appear, with the invasion of Belgium in 1914, then the Anglo-French plans were seen as wise precautions.

The second Morocco crisis blew up in 1911 when the Sultan asked for French help in putting down a rebellion, and French troops were sent from Algeria to occupy Fez, the capital. The German government demanded their early withdrawal, and two months later, with the French still in Fez, a German gunboat, the *Panther*, was sent to Agadir, a port on the Atlantic coast of Morocco. The reasons given were 'to protect German interests' and 'to rescue endangered Germans'. As soon as one could be found, many miles away in Mogador, he was duly rescued! Public opinion in Britain hardened against Germany, and even Lloyd George, known to be both pro-German and in favour of strict neutrality, felt it necessary to give Germany a public warning. At his own suggestion, he included in his speech at the annual bankers' dinner at the Mansion House these words – 'If a situation were to be forced upon us in which peace could only be preserved by the surrender of the

THE ELASTIC ESTIMATES,

OR, BEATEN IN THE STRETCH.

Anglo-German naval rivalry, 1912. In the caption 'Fritz' is saying 'Himmel! De more I squeeze to stretch mein own boat, de bigger it makes de odder one!'

great and beneficent position Britain has won by centuries of heroism and achievement ... then I say emphatically that peace at that price would be a humiliation intolerable for a great country like ours to endure.' They were strong words for a man with his views, but they helped to decide the Germans to withdraw the *Panther* and begin negotiations; as a result, Germany recognized Morocco as a French Protectorate in exchange for part of the French Congo. She also accelerated her naval building programme so that, as the Kaiser said, 'we can be sure that no one will dispute our rightful place in the sun.'

It was in Eastern Europe, however, that the delicate balance between the Triple Alliance and the Triple Entente was finally destroyed. In 1908 Austria annexed the two provinces of Bosnia and Herzegovina, breaking the terms of the Congress of Berlin (1878) and infuriating the neighbouring Slav state of Serbia (the greater part of modern Yugoslavia). In 1912 four Balkan states, Greece, Serbia, Montenegro and the newly independent Bulgaria (p.189), joined together in a league against Turkey, and the First Balkan War (1912) saw the Turks virtually driven out of Europe. Thanks largely to Grey's diplomacy, a peace treaty was signed in London, only for Bulgaria to fall out with her

Crises in the Balkans

partners in the Second Balkan War (1913). Serbia grew stronger and bolder as a result of the two wars, and clamoured for a new Greater Serbia which should include Slavs not only from the fast disintegrating Turkish Empire but also from the Austrian Empire. As in 1876 Slav patriots called on Russia to help them. It was the turn of Austria, and indirectly her ally Germany, to feel threatened. Austria therefore looked for an excuse to get in the first blow against Serbia, and she had not long to wait. On 28 June 1914 the Archduke Francis Ferdinand, heir to the Habsburg Empire, was murdered by a Serbian student, Gabriel Princip, in a street in Sarajevo, capital of Bosnia.

For a month little happened. Then, on the very day, 23 July, that Lloyd George told the House of Commons that Britain's relations with Germany were 'better than they had been for years', Austria sent an ultimatum to Serbia to be answered within forty-eight hours. The Serbs were required to allow Austrian officials to enter Serbia to bring to justice those reponsible for the murder; and to this provocative demand the Serbs mildly agreed within the time limit. Austria, however, had already been given *carte blanche* by Germany to take whatever action she thought fit, and the action Austria intended was war. Over the last ten years Europe had lived in fear of a major clash between the two armed camps, and now one power after another was pulled into the conflict. Austria declared war on Serbia; Russia mobilized; Germany declared war on Russia and then on France when France refused to remain neutral. All this took place between 28 July and 3 August. Grey worked vainly to get a conference under way. He warned Germany not to count on Britain's neutrality, and France and Russia not to rely on her support. For safety's sake, the major Fleet squadrons of the Royal Navy had, thanks to Churchill, been at their battle stations since 31 July.

The invasion of Belgium

In London Grey was under intense but conflicting pressures – to fight or not to fight. Two cabinet ministers, Morley and Burns, resigned rather than be associated with a possible declaration of war. What ended the dilemma for Grey, and for most of his countrymen, was the German decision to push ahead with their Schlieffen Plan, involving the invasion of Belgium. On 3 August the Belgians received an ultimatum demanding free passage for German troops; the Belgian King Albert appealed to George V; and Grey and Asquith, the Prime Minister, finally persuaded Lloyd George and the strong anti-war group of Liberal and Labour M.P.s to accept the Belgian issue as a reason for going to war. By the Treaty of London of 1839 (see above p.60), Britain and the other powers had guaranteed Belgian neutrality, and, for Grey, this was the means of uniting the Commons and the country behind him. The German Chancellor Bethmann Hollweg complained that 'just for a scrap of paper Britain was going to make war on a kindred nation who desired nothing more than to be friends with her.' A more unfriendly act than the occupation of Belgium by Germany could hardly be imagined by the British public. On 4 August an ultimatum was sent to Germany to respect Belgian neutrality; at midnight, Britain was at war.

No one dreamed in 1914 that Britain's entry into the war would result in conscription and the loss of nearly a million soldiers from Britain and the Empire. What was expected was a naval war in which it was hoped Britain would hold some advantage. As the war lengthened, criticism of Grey's policy grew. Some felt that if he had committed Britain to military alliances rather than to ententes, Germany might have been deterred from escalating the Balkan problems into a world war. Others felt that even an entente with France meant that we had no choice but to help her when attacked. Grey's answer to the first argument was that he did not have sufficient support within his own party or in the country to form a military alliance with either France or Russia. His answer to the second lay in the invasion of Belgium. In Grey's words, the possibility of 'the whole of Western Europe opposite to us ... falling under the domination of a single power' was brought suddenly nearer. It was Belgium, not the Anglo-French Entente, which decided the Commons vote on 3 August 1914. It was a Bank Holiday Monday and, at its close, Grey observed 'the lamps are going out all over Europe; we shall not see them lit again in our lifetime'.

17
The British overseas
Canada and Australasia

1 The Second British Empire

The period 1815 to 1914 very nearly covers the duration of the Second British Empire, the most extensive and populous the world had yet seen. The Thirteen American Colonies had broken away in 1776, but a substantial part of the first colonial Empire remained in 1815 – notably in the West Indies, in Canada, and in the East India Company's possessions in India. Few in Britain in 1815 positively wanted to see this Empire extended, except perhaps in India. The belief that all colonies would eventually hive off as the Americans had done was widespread. The cost of colonial defence was constantly criticized; it was argued that the Empire was an encumbrance; and in 1815 it was not easy to see how the expansion of overseas possessions could help Britain's prosperity. Such views persisted well into the 1860s.

Reasons for growth

Nevertheless the Empire grew during the nineteenth century, mainly by circumstances, a little by design. Much of the growth was due to remarkable men, like Edward Gibbon Wakefield, Lord Durham, Sir Stamford Raffles (founder of Singapore), military governors in India, explorers in 'Darkest Africa'. Missionaries seeking to convert 'the heathen' in India and in Africa, convicts 'sent to Botany Bay' because Britain could not cope with them – each helped to extend the Empire. So, for example in Southern Africa, did British Governors and local officers, far beyond the leash of Whitehall, who went in for a 'forward policy' against 'the natives', and put thousands of square miles under the Union Jack regardless of the views of the government at home. Yet the government itself from time to time took a hand in expansion for strategic reasons – as, in 1815, acquiring the Cape of Good Hope and Mauritius to protect the old route to India, and in the 1880s occupying Egypt to safeguard the new route through the Suez Canal. All these activities extended British imperial responsibilities and the amount of red on the maps.

But in general the most continuous and important reason for the spread of the British Empire in the nineteenth century was trade. As Britain's industrial output expanded she needed ever greater supplies of raw materials, and ever wider markets to absorb her production. Business men began to see colonies in a new light. At government level Huskisson in the 1820s encouraged the idea that colonies and 'mother country' had identical interests, and, with Canning, adapted the tariff system to include colonial preference (see above p.26). So trade with the Empire grew. In steadily increasing amounts wool came from Australian sheep to Yorkshire mills, and cotton garments from Lancashire went to clothe Indian peasants. By 1850 30 per cent of British exports went to the Empire and 23 per cent of her imports came from it. And trade brought imperial expansion in some odd ways – not least through those many merchants whose enterprise (including the sale of guns and liquor) led in one way or another to 'trouble' with the natives, and so to the arrival of British ships or soldiers to 'protect' them – and sometimes, as in parts of West Africa, to lasting occupation.

The Dominions

British colonies, or some of them, attracted settlers from Britain as its population grew during the nineteenth century. They were not numerous until the 1870s, yet they were important, for they laid the foundations of British customs, speech, and ways of government in the later 'White Dominions'. Emigration was not cheap, and often those who would most benefit from emigrating were those who could least afford to do so. Before 1850 there were already private and some government schemes to help particular groups. Edward Gibbon Wakefield and the 'Radical Imperialists' launched a system of the controlled emigration of small but complete communities to fertile land bought from the government. Money from the sale was then used to give assisted passages to new settlers. The new settlers became suppliers of raw materials and customers for manufactured goods, and

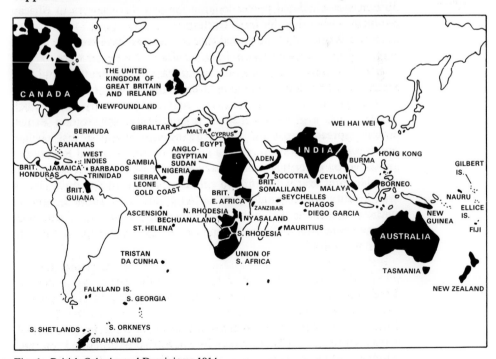

Fig. 6 British Colonies and Dominions, 1914

in time they attracted British money for investment. Wakefield's plans, put into practice in South Australia and New Zealand, were limited in achievement; and they were only part of a great migration which took, in the years 1815 to 1854, some four million people from Britain, of whom more than half went to the United States.

If this Second Empire was not to go the way of the first then Britain had to make political as well as economic concessions. The man who made clear that the colonists must be trusted to manage their own affairs was Lord Durham. The advice given in his Report of 1839 (p.270) led to a new relationship between Britain and the colonies of white settlement which held the new Empire together. In India, the most jealously guarded of all the British possessions, the stated aim of giving the Indians some share in their own government remained an ideal. In the West Indies, economically ruined by the great social reform of the abolition of slavery (p.46), Britain's once prized possessions became, as Lloyd George later described them, the 'slums of Empire', their native inhabitants not to be trusted with real political power. The other imperial possessions, fortresses and islands like Gibraltar, Malta, Hong Kong and Singapore, were vital for trade and defence and had to remain dependent. Thus they remained Crown Colonies while India became an empire and the white colonies of settlement were given Dominion status. South Africa required its own solution because of the presence of the Boers. By the time the 'Scramble for Africa' came Britain was a satiated power looking for peaceful answers to African problems rather than for fresh territory.

Towards the end of the period there was, as we have seen, an intense interest and pride in Britain in imperial affairs. No longer were colonies 'millstones round our necks', or 'fruits that cling to the tree until they ripen'. Without undue government interference, with fewer wars than most imperial powers in the past had found necessary, with much idealism and a growing sense of responsibility, the Second British Empire spread across the globe. In essence it was a vast civilian enterprise in business overseas, a product of the Industrial Revolution protected by government diplomacy and the armed forces. In 1914 its population of nearly 400 million still accepted a common unity, but it was a unity which would not last long into the twentieth century without further changes in the relationship of its members. When those changes came after 1918 the Second British Empire became the British Commonwealth.

2 Canada

Pitt's Canada Act (1791) had divided the area into two provinces – Upper Canada, or Ontario, mainly English speaking and Protestant with its capital at Toronto, and Lower Canada, or Quebec, mainly

French and Catholic with its two cities of Montreal and Quebec. Each province was given an elected assembly but this had no control over a legislative Council nominated by the Lieutenant-Governor, himself appointed by the Crown. It was a constitution ill-suited to that country at that time. Most English-speaking Canadians were what George III described as 'United Empire Loyalists', about 80,000 of whom had moved north from the Thirteen Colonies during the War of American Independence. They were not anti-British, but they had been used to some measure of self-government. They complained that the new Council was dominated by an old-established clique called the Family Compact. They objected to large areas of land being kept idle as 'clergy reserves' for the upkeep of a Church which had few active clergy; and they felt that Ontario was given too small a share of the customs revenue. French-speaking Canadians had a major grievance in that they were excluded altogether from the Council; they were mainly farmers and trappers who felt they were being exploited by British merchants. In neither province did the settlers feel that they themselves had enough say in government. Pitt's Act had given representation without responsibility. It provided 'a fire without a chimney'. And although the French remained loyal during the Anglo-American War of 1812–14, there was constant friction, both between province and province and between assembly and Governor.

In 1837 there was a rebellion in Ontario led by W. L. MacKenzie and another in Quebec led by Louis Papineau. Though timed as a joint enterprise they were easily suppressed. Nevertheless, they alarmed the Prime Minister Melbourne sufficiently for him to tell Lord Durham in 1838 to 'go out and put it right'. Durham had recently been Ambassador at St Petersburg. He was at once an aristocrat and a radical, capable of saying seriously that 'a man could jog along on £40,000 a year' and of helping to draft the 1832 Reform Bill. In 1838 he was pushing for a post in the government. Melbourne, who privately thought him second-rate, wanted him out of the way. It turned out to be the right choice for the wrong reason. Durham's brief was to find the causes of discontent and to suggest remedies and, to assist him, he took a Radical lawyer Charles Buller, and Edward Gibbon Wakefield, not long out of prison for abducting his second young heiress. Durham started off on the wrong foot. He took so much personal luggage that it took two days to unload and, once in office, he promptly broke the law. He deported some of the French-Canadian ringleaders to Bermuda for trial since he was sure no Canadian jury would convict them of treason. Melbourne disowned him and within a year he was back in England; and it was then that his contribution to Canada and to the British Empire really began.

For all his faults, Durham had vision. Unlike Melbourne and most contemporary statesmen, Durham sensed, even from his brief visit, the potential of Canada's vast natural resources 'to supply the wants of our surplus population, to raise up fresh consumers of our manufactures,

The Durham Report

and producers of a supply for our wants'. He was also sure that the Canadians should be given greater liberty if they were not to go the way of the Americans. On his return, therefore, he inspired the Durham Report (1839), written by Buller and Wakefield, and proposing two remedies. The first was that Ontario and Quebec should be reunited under one government to safeguard British interests. This was effected by the Reunion Act (1840) which set up a single Parliament for a united colony of Canada. In the Lower House, Ontario and Quebec each had 42 members, but the Upper House was still nominated by the Governor. The second remedy, more liberal and far-seeing, was that the Canadians should be given a degree of responsible self-government, not including control over foreign policy, defence and external trade. At home, the Tories attacked this as 'Chartism for the colonies', but officials on the spot saw it differently, particularly when Durham's son-in-law, Lord Elgin, became Governor-General. In March 1848 when the government was defeated on a vote in the lower house, Elgin invited the opposition to form a ministry. He felt it quite impossible to withhold self-government from 'such a pushing and enterprising people, unencumbered by an aristocracy and dwelling in the immediate vicinity of the United States'. By this vital step he made ministers responsible to the electorate and produced a new model of colonial government. Durham's second remedy had been applied.

At the time of its writing the Durham Report had been an attempt to keep Canada British. To this end Durham and his successors were prepared to give the smoking fire a chimney in the shape of what Durham called 'municipal self-government,' i.e. over internal affairs. But, as Canadian interests increasingly diverged from British interests, the Canadians pressed for greater independence. For example, by the Repeal of the Corn Laws, Canadian wheat had lost the advantage of low duties compared with other foreign corn. By 1859 the Canadian assembly had gained the right to opt out of imperial Free Trade and to put tariffs on British imports. Both Canada and Britain were nervous of expansion by the U.S.A. Boundary disputes had been settled peacefully in 1818, 1842 and 1846 (p.8 and p.69) but in 1854 the U.S.A. had ended a commercial treaty vital to Canadian trade. Fears of an American invasion grew, especially after the victory of the North in the Civil War. Now the Canadian need was for unity – 'a vigorous government of British Americans under the British sovereign' was one phrase used.

British North America Act The result was the British North America Act (1867), passed during the Derby-Disraeli ministry. It created a federal 'Dominion of Canada' – rather than 'Kingdom' which might have offended the U.S.A. – to include Ontario, Quebec, New Brunswick and Nova Scotia. Manitoba was added in 1870, British Columbia in 1872 on the understanding that a rail link would be built, and Prince Edward Island in 1873. Only Newfoundland, Britain's oldest colony, stayed out. Ottawa eventually became the new capital. Canada was now virtually self-governing. Even more important, a precedent had been set for the other colonies of settlement – Australia, New Zealand and South Africa. It was not quite what Durham had foreseen, but it was Durham's report which had made it all possible.

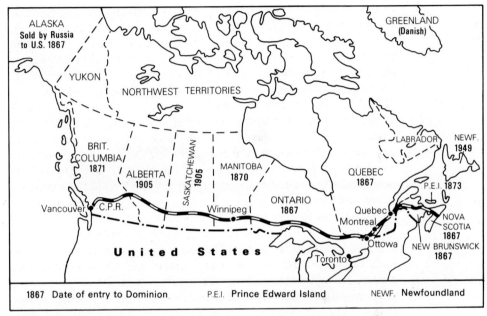

Fig. 7   Canada

By 1870 Canada had about 3¼ million inhabitants of whom all but about ¾ million lived round the Great Lakes or along the St Lawrence. The Maritime Provinces of the eastern seaboard tended to go their own way, but the Federal government pushed ahead vigorously in its efforts to open up the west. In 1869 it proposed to buy out the rich and powerful Hudson's Bay Company for £300,000, a plan which alarmed the half-breed fur trappers and led them, under Louis Riel, to try and set up a revolutionary republic. Colonel Garnet Wolseley, later to become British Army Commander in Chief, put down this rebellion with a force transported to Fort Garry, later Winnipeg, by canoe. An official of the Hudson's Bay Company, Donald A. Smith, who subsequently became Lord Strathcona, played a vital part in this stage of Canadian development. By shrewd business deals he became Chief Commissioner of the Company and from fur trading moved to railways. With his cousin George Stephen he bought up the bankrupt St Paul and Pacific Railroad, put it into operation to connect Minneapolis to

Economic Expansion

Winnipeg in 1872

Winnipeg as it is today

Manitoba and, in 1880, founded the Canadian Pacific Railway Company. Within five years, at a spot west of Kicking Horse Pass, Smith himself drove in the last spike of this ambitious project.

Smith was helped financially by the Conservative government in Ottawa of John MacDonald: railways were seen as the quickest way to bring law to the prairies. Riel had started a second rebellion in Saskatchewan and the authorities feared the spread of unrest among French-Canadians and Amerindians. Other rail networks appeared but, by 1914, the C.P.R. had only one effective rival in the Canadian National Railway. MacDonald's government also introduced tariffs and encouraged new industries to promote economic growth. Firms like Massey-Harris produced goods of such efficiency that their agricultural machinery found a ready market in Europe. Perhaps the biggest factor in Canada's rapid expansion came from great waves of immigrants from the U.S.A., Scandinavia, Central Europe and, to a lesser extent, from Britain. Expansion reached a peak under the Liberal government of Sir Wilfred Laurier (1896–1911). In 1896 gold was found at Bonanza Creek in the Yukon, and between then and 1914 three million immigrants poured into the far west and to the wheat farms and cattle ranches of the prairies. Newly-formed provinces of Saskatchewan and Alberta joined the Federation in 1905, though the bulk of the country's population was still in the east. Relations with the U.S.A. had greatly improved and while most Canadians were happy to keep close ties with Britain, Canada was now strong enough to go her own way – as she did at the Colonial Conference in 1902, when she stood out against a joint imperial system of defence. When war came in 1914 600,000 Canadians were to fight alongside the British – a far cry from the days of Papineau and MacKenzie.

First train into Calgary, 1883

3 Australia

In January 1788 the first white settlers in Australia sailed into Botany Bay, site of Captain Cook's landing eighteen years earlier. They came less to found a colony than to establish an open-air prison. Some 750 were convicts who 'had left their country for the country's good', with another 200 officials and marines to supervise them; their first headquarters was at Port Jackson, now Sydney, in what Cook had named New South Wales. The first shipload of free settlers arrived in 1793 but for nearly forty years convicts outnumbered the rest. The 'canaries', as they were called from their yellow uniform, were set to work either in chain gangs or 'assigned' to free settlers for ten hours a day. Conditions were primitive with rum the common currency. Only slowly did settlements spread along the coastal strip from Perth in the west to Brisbane in the east.

Early settlement and exploration

Two Scotsmen helped to put white Australia on the road to prosperity. The first was John Macarthur who, in 1797, began the successful breeding both of Spanish merino sheep – which had been imported from the Cape – and of his own crossbred Bengal ram and Irish ewes strain. Compared with most British sheep their wool was long and fine, and the British government gave Macarthur 5,000 acres of grazing land in New South Wales to help meet the ever growing demands of the British textile industry. Macarthur's sheep farm at

The Burke and Wills expedition

Parramatta – where he also planted the first Australian vines – was the model for hundreds of other colonists; and once across the Blue Mountains (1813) they found on the Bathurst Plains the finest grazing grounds in the world. In three years land prices rose eightfold, and many settlers, unable to buy land, became squatters. The other Scot was Lachlan MacQuarie, Governor of New South Wales from 1809 to 1821. He developed Sydney as a capital and did the same for Hobart in Tasmania. He freed many convicts whom he thought would make honest settlers. Most important, he encouraged the exploration of both coast and interior.

Those who ventured into the Australian interior faced vast distances, almost continuous drought, and little help from the native aborigines; the bodies of some have never been found. The first voyages round the entire continent were made between 1817 and 1822 by Phillip King, born in Norfolk Island and the first Australian to reach the rank of admiral in the Royal Navy. Charles Sturt explored the Murrumbidgee-Murray-Darling river system in 1828–30, thus opening up the coastal region which later became South Australia. The daunting South to North crossing of the continent was made in 1860–1 by Robert Burke and William Wills; they missed their relief party by a few hours and died of starvation. In 1882 John Stuart reached the geographical centre of Australia, and it was his route from Adelaide to Darwin which was followed when the Overland Telegraph system was opened ten years later. John Forrest, later Prime Minister of Western Australia, charted an overland route from Perth to South Australia in 1870. Distances, terrain and lack of equipment made the spread of a transport system painfully slow. The bush coach, introduced by American settlers, was one answer to the poor, convict-built roads; at their peak, the leading firm of Cobb and Company was harnessing 6,000 horses a day. When the railways came in the 1870s, financed largely by British investors, industry and farming benefited enormously. But it was the explorers who had made it all possible.

If wool began Australian prosperity gold kept it moving. First found at Bathurst, N.S.W. in 1851, then in larger deposits, at Bendigo and Ballarat in Victoria, gold attracted thousands of prospectors over the next ten years before big companies took control. In their way the 'Diggers' were more unruly than the convicts. Their defiance of authority was notorious; a group of 150 fought a famous battle with Victoria state troops at the Eureka Stockade in 1853. The Diggers resented the cost of licences to prospect, the introduction of 20,000 Chinese by the companies to develop the goldfields, the influence of the big agricultural interests; even in 1880 fewer than a hundred sheepmasters controlled more than eight million acres of land. In the ten years after 1851 the population of Victoria rose from 77,000 to 540,000. Many of the new settlers had left Britain as Chartist sympathizers; in Australia they demanded a more democratic government.

Economic growth

The ending of transportation in 1849, further reducing the proportion of convicts to free settlers, smoothed the way to self-rule. In 1850 Parliament permitted the Australian colonies to grant themselves constitutions. By 1859 five of the six states had their own responsible government on the Canadian model – N.S.W., Tasmania, South Australia, Victoria and Queensland: the exception was Western Australia where, until 1868, the convict system was used to meet labour shortages. By the end of the 1860s Australia was progressing enough to attract foreign investment. It supported through its own agriculture a population of one and a half million. In the 1870s and 1880s new mineral resources were developed – another gold strike in Queensland, zinc at Broken Hill, coal in N.S.W. Sugar and cotton became profit-making crops. The invention of refrigerator ships revolutionized the meat trade. Victoria, N.S.W. and, to a lesser extent, Queensland became predominantly industrial with urban populations. The other states remained largely agricultural. South Australia, for example, many of whose early settlers had been attracted there by Edward Gibbon Wakefield's schemes, was now the main wheat growing area.

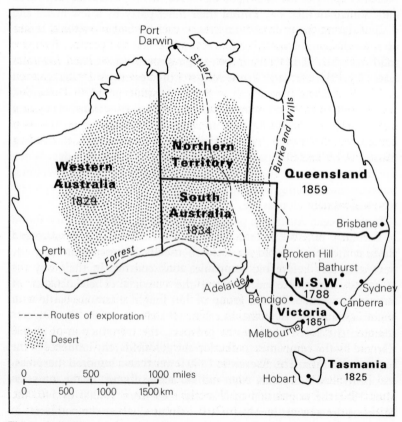

Fig. 8 Australia

276

Federation came slowly, forced on the jealously independent states by a common fear of Japanese and German infiltration into the Pacific and, in particular, of the growing Japanese naval power. After almost a century of cheap, effective protection by the British Navy, the Australians realized that their country, whose states could not agree even on a common railway gauge, needed union quickly. The Commonwealth of Australia came into being on 1 January 1901 as a Dominion of six federated states. Each state had its own Parliament, but the Federal Parliament, sited after 1927 at Canberra, controlled major issues such as foreign affairs. A 'White Australia' policy, first inspired by the introduction of the Chinese in 1857, was strengthened in 1905 by a compulsory language test for all would-be immigrants – a device to exclude non-Europeans. As in Britain, a Liberal government under Labour pressure began schemes of social welfare. Trade Union power was strong in the industrial areas, well organized and democratically run. The Australian cult of outdoor sport grew rapidly; cricket has been a strong link with the mother country ever since, in 1878, an all-white Australian XI had trounced the M.C.C. in England. When war came in 1914 the country would fight, as one politician put it, 'to the last man and the last shilling'.

Considering the enormous deserts of the Australian outback, it had been a century of impressive political and economic growth. Even by 1850 over half of Britain's imports of raw wool came from Australia alone; by 1913 over half the world's wool supply came from Australia and New Zealand. Instead of a small aborigine population and one convict settlement there were over four million white Australians in a free society democratically governed yet still retaining its ties with Britain. Small wonder that its inhabitants claimed that they lived in 'Australia Unlimited'.

4 New Zealand

In the early nineteenth century white visitors to New Zealand were either missionaries, hoping to convert the native Maoris to Christianity, or dubious traders dealing in muskets, gunpowder and rum. There was no serious attempt at settlement until Edward Gibbon Wakefield, with the aid of Francis Baring, founded the New Zealand Association to begin 'systematic colonization'. The British government was not anxious to involve itself in the defence of yet another colony, and referred the scheme to a parliamentary committee. Wakefield went ahead on his own. The Association's first emigrant ship landed in 1839, and Wakefield's brother, who was in charge, bought land from the Maori chiefs. But fear of French designs on the islands convinced the British government to send Capt. Hobson, the senior officer in Australian waters, to bring New Zealand under the authority of the

Governor of New South Wales. An agreement was made with the chiefs in 1840 called the Treaty of Waitangi. The Maoris accepted British rule in return for a guarantee of possession of their land; the British were to have first refusal of any land coming up for sale, though negotiations had to go through the Government. The new colony was given its own Governor and nominated assembly.

The Association settlers had little respect for the treaty or for the rights of the Maoris, and were soon involved in disputes. Serious trouble was avoided by the appointment of Captain, later Sir George Grey as Governor in 1845. He had already served as Governor of South Australia and enjoyed a good relationship with the Maoris, a brave and intelligent race. He did not want them to become 'lawless borderers' and he applied the terms of the Waitangi Treaty firmly and fairly, stopping the illegal acquisition of land by the Association. A more settled atmosphere encouraged emigrants from Britain, especially when South Island was bought from the Maoris. The Free Church of Scotland helped to establish one group at Otago, the Church of England another at Christchurch. In 1850 the Association was bought out and its charter ended.

As in Australia, the increase in white settlers – there were 60,000 by 1856 – led to stronger demands for responsible government. On Grey's advice, the existing six provinces were each given an elected Council to deal with local affairs, while an elected Assembly, to include four Maoris chosen by their own people, dealt with national issues. In 1856 ministers were made responsible to the Assembly rather than to the Governor; self-government had been won in less than twenty years. By

The Treaty of Waitangi, 1840

1876 the provincial Councils had disappeared and the country was governed from the capital, Wellington.

Grey had moved to South Africa in 1854 and at once tension had **Maori War** increased. The Maori chiefs in North Island resented their loss of power and the threat to tribal institutions; the white man's civilization had brought disease; under a new leader, self-styled Potato I, they began in 1860 to fight the British. It was not a large-scale war – though the Maoris could ill afford their 2,000 dead – and the main resistance was over by 1864. Guerrilla fighting by a fanatical group, who thought they were invincible if they chanted *Hau Hau*, prolonged the war until 1872. Many British troops sympathized with the Maoris against the land-hungry settlers, but were wary of opponents whose recent forebears had in 1843 killed and eaten one of Gibbon Wakefield's sons and the settlers at Wairau. Once the war was over, the Maoris lost half their territory in North Island but white attitudes to them became more liberal. Relations improved and the Maoris were given opportunities for education and direct representation in the Assembly.

Not until the 1890s did New Zealand's economy begin to prosper. Profits from pastoral farming soared with the coming of refrigeration ships. Canterbury lamb and New Zealand butter became increasingly familiar to the British housewife. In 1914 foreign trade totalled £45 million, 60% of it with the United Kingdom. In politics, power passed from the old colonial gentry to the leaders of a strong socialist movement. Under Richard Seddon, Prime Minister from 1893 and a Radical Imperialist, New Zealand pioneered the welfare state. Votes for women, non-contributory old age pensions, the start of a health service, labour exchanges, compensation for industrial injury, and compulsory arbitration in industrial disputes were some of the important reforms smoothly achieved. In 1907 New Zealand was recognized as a Domin- **Dominion Status** ion. Small in population, vulnerable in its dependence on overseas markets, it had the advantage of a progressive, self-reliant society in which the Maoris had managed to keep their identity. It had been Wakefield's favourite colony. Though he died there in obscurity its progress was all that he could have wished.

18

The British overseas India

1 Crown and Company 1815–56

India occupied the constant attention of British politicians throughout the nineteenth century. The reasons for this were largely commercial, and grew stronger after Parliament in 1833 finally ended the East India Company's trading activities in India. Within twenty years India's exports had nearly trebled in value and her imports, with Lancashire cotton goods to the fore, had more than trebled. The Company itself remained the agent through which British India was governed. It appointed the Governor-General who with his Council was in charge of Indian affairs, subject to a Board of Control in London whose President was a member of the Cabinet. In foreign policy, there was a conviction that Russia (two thousand miles from British India, beyond Persia, Afghanistan, and the independent Sikh state of the Punjab) was determined to annex India, and that there was an overriding need to protect her frontiers and trade routes – hence the acquistion in 1815 of the Cape of Good Hope and Mauritius.

Annexations   Within India the British were unquestionably the 'paramount power'. The main threat to them came no longer from European rivals but from native rulers. The annexation of one territory often led to trouble with another new neighbour. So successive Governors-General fought wars to secure or 'round off' the frontiers. The Marquess of Hastings (1813–23) was involved in two ferocious campaigns. One, to protect Bengal from the north, was with Nepal (1814–16), the western part of which was annexed by Britain; its Gurkha soldiers were later to fight for Britain with exceptional courage and loyalty not only in the Mutiny but also through two World Wars. A second war, against the
Hastings   Pindaris and the Marathas, led to annexations in central India. By 1823 virtually the whole continent, except Sind and the Punjab, was directly or indirectly under British control. Lord Amherst (1823–8) secured the eastern frontier of Bengal by invading Burma and taking Assam and Arakan.

Auckland   For a while there was a lull in military expeditions until the arrival of the aggressive Lord Auckland (1835–42). He was a nominee of Palmerston and, like him, feared that 'if we do not stop Russia on the Danube, we shall have to stop her on the Indus'. It now became British policy to ensure that at least the Punjab and Afghanistan had pro-British rulers. So when Ranjit Singh, the Sikh ruler of the Punjab, asked for help against Dost Mohammed, the Amir of Afghanistan,

Palmerston and Auckland decided to strengthen British influence by deposing the latter in favour of Shah Shuja, an unpopular Afghan prince deservedly exiled if only for his habit of blinding political opponents. The First Afghan War (1839–42) was a disaster. British troops and sepoys – native troops in British service – deposed Dost Mohammed and installed Shah Shuja as Amir with an army of occupation. But in 1841 the Afghans revolted; Shah Shuja and the British Resident were murdered; and the army of occupation, promised a safe conduct to India, was destroyed in the mountain passes. From an army of 15,000 men one survivor reached India. A new force, sent to avenge the massacre, sacked Kabul and then withdrew. Before long Dost Mohammed was back as Amir. British influence in Afghanistan had declined, at a cost of an entire army and £15 million.

During the years 1843–56 British power in India increased considerably, thanks to some remarkable generals and administrators – larger than life characters like Napier and the Lawrences. Sir Charles Napier, a descendant of Charles II, had served under Wellington. At the age of 68 he could write in his diary – 'Got up at four o'clock but rode my elephant till daylight; galloped my Arab horse for ten miles, had breakfast at seven, wrote until five, then reviewed two regiments.' With an army of only 2,000 men and 12 field guns he annexed Sind in 1843, and set about reorganizing its government, attacking abuses like slavery, and making Karachi a great port. Another entry in his diary read – 'We have no right to seize Sind, but we shall do so, and a very advantageous, useful, humane piece of rascality it will be'. It might have served as an epitaph on the whole of British India.

Napier

The remainder of the vast Indus valley – the Punjab – fell into British hands as a result of the First (1845–6) and Second (1848–9) Sikh Wars. The Koh-i-noor Diamond was sent to the Queen as a symbol of conquest. Sir John Lawrence and his brother Henry were as dynamic in the Punjab as Napier in Sind. They simplified the laws, built roads and irrigation schemes, and ended feudal dues and the payment of taxes in kind; so strong was their influence that, when the Mutiny came, North-East India remained loyal to the British. The Marquess of Dalhousie (1846–56) was perhaps the most positive of the Governors-General. 'At school' he said, 'I did little but smoke, drink and dawdle', yet his death at the early age of forty-nine was due mainly to over-work in India. He carried through the Sikh Wars and, in the Second Burma War (1852), annexed Rangoon and Lower Burma. In 1856 he deposed the ruler of the Ganges valley state of Oudh for misrule, and took over the whole country with its capital Lucknow. Finally, he made use of the so-called 'doctrine of lapse' by which, whenever an Indian ruler died without natural heirs, his state conveniently lapsed to the overlord – now the British; the Hindu practice of adopting heirs was no longer accepted without approval of the Governor-General. Among the states annexed by this means were Nagpur and Jansi.

The Lawrence brothers

Dalhousie

If the forty years before the Mutiny were years of conquest they were also years of reform. The Evangelical and Benthamite ideas which produced the changes in the 1830s and 1840s in Britain were carried to India by missionaries and administrators. Lord William Bentinck **Westernization** (1828–35) was in office when the Company's renewed charter declared that employment should be denied to no one on the grounds of race, creed or colour. He felt strongly that the only justification for the rule of the British was that they could contribute something to India's benefit **Bentinck** which the Indians themselves could not achieve. He hoped, as did the historian Lord Macaulay, who joined his Council in 1834, that in time there would emerge an Indian élite, educated in western ideas and capable of sharing in the running of a modernized India. He attacked those Hindu practices most outrageous to Christians, such as female infanticide; 'suttee', where widows were burned alive on their husband's funeral pyre; 'thuggee', in which travellers were strangled by dedicated fanatics in honour of the goddess Kali; and the 'meriahs', kidnapped victims buried to ensure good crops. Such customs were gradually put down. Education was used as a weapon against superstition. Largely on Macaulay's advice, English became the official language of instruction; while this proved of immense benefit to the economic development of India, the fact that the more intelligent Indians were now brought up on western ideas encouraged many to demand political liberty and national independence.

Under Dalhousie the Indians felt the full force of 'westernization'. Four thousand miles of roads were built, chiefly for military purposes, like the Grand Trunk road from Calcutta to Peshawar. A telegraph system and a cheap postal service were introduced. Schemes to improve irrigation, forestry, mining, port facilities and the training of engineers were carried through with typical Victorian energy and initiative. The first lines of an Indian railway network were laid. The Indians already had an alien government. Now an alien culture was imposed on them whose material benefits did not compensate for the loss of their religious customs and taboos. In Ireland the British were blamed for giving too little too late; in India it seemed too much too soon. The brisk changes made by well-intentioned reformers threatened the accepted way of life of millions; in particular, they cut across the caste system which controlled Hindu society. They created an atmosphere of resentment, not strong enough to unite all Hindus, much less Hindu and Moslem, yet sufficient to encourage part of the sepoy army to mutiny.

2 The Mutiny, 1857–8

Causes   The Mutiny was spearheaded by the relatively well paid, high caste Brahmin troops from Bengal. Bengali sepoys had mutinied in 1823 by refusing to serve in Burma since their religion forbade them to cross the sea or to mix with lower castes in crowded troopships; almost a regiment of mutineers was shot. Now Hindu fears were increased by proposals to form new units of mixed Hindu and Moslem troops. Soldiers from the former Oudh army were bitter at being redrafted as sepoys. Vague rumours increased tension – that Christianity was to be forced on all Indians and that British power would end a hundred years after the battle of Plassey (1757). It was known that British troops had not been invincible in the Crimea, while among those left in India discipline was growing lax. There was a dangerous shortage of British troops – at most 45,000 to almost 250,000 Indian. Into this magazine of explosive materials the British in 1856 dropped two lighted matches. The first was a regulation demanding an oath from all recruits that they should agree to serve overseas. The second was a War Office decision to issue to the Indian Army cockades of leather and cartridges greased with fat, the ends of which had to be bitten off before they could be used in the new Lee-Enfield rifles. Hindus revered the cow as sacred and refused to use either cockades or cartridges which they were sure were covered in cow-fat. Moslems were equally sure that the grease was pig-fat, unclean in their religion. The cartridges were quickly withdrawn but the excuse for mutiny had been provided. When 85 sepoys at Meerut refused the suspected cartridges and were sentenced in May 1857 to ten years in prison, three regiments mutinied, murdered their officers and marched on Delhi.

The Mutiny quickly spread but only to a limited area, to the upper and middle Ganges valley (roughly between Patna and Delhi). It was confined to the Bengal army; the other two provincial armies of Madras and Bombay were scarcely affected. Less than 100,000 soldiers rebelled, compared with a civilian population of some 200 million. But for six months British power in India was under serious threat. Only the mistakes of the mutineers and some remarkable British exploits saved the day. The Meerut mutineers captured Delhi, murdered all the Europeans they could find, and proclaimed the aged Mogul as Emperor. The British Commander-in-Chief was in Simla but the sepoys delayed for three weeks, omitted to cut the telegraph link, and so gave their enemy the chance to organize. Meanwhile there were risings at Cawnpore and Lucknow in Oudh and in Jansi; but outbreaks further afield, as in the Punjab, petered out with sepoys in some places being disarmed by civilians. The British moved into the Ganges valley both from Calcutta and from the Punjab where Sir John Lawrence found no difficulty in enlisting Sikh and Hindu regiments. From June to December Delhi was besieged, finally to be taken by an army under Sir John Nicholson. This time it was the British troops who massacred the defenders.

At Cawnpore one of the few rulers to take advantage of the Mutiny, Nana Sahib, led the mutineers. The defending garrison held out for

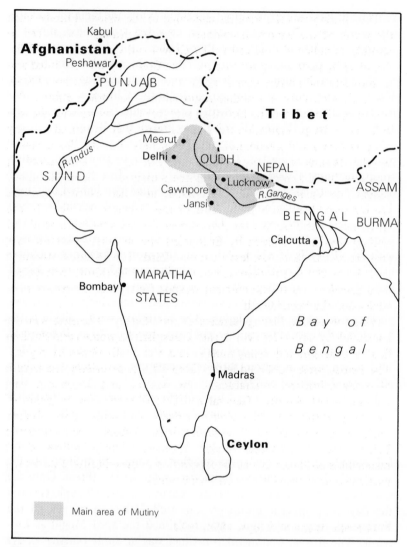

Fig. 9   India at the time of the Mutiny

three weeks, surrendered on being promised safe conduct, and was
promptly wiped out. Palace servants then murdered the women and
children with knives and threw over two hundred bodies down a well.
In nearby Lucknow a small garrison was besieged by 60,000 Indians. In
Jansi the Ranee, a girl of 20, led a civilian rising. After two tremendous
marches by forces under Havelock and Outram, first Cawnpore and
then Lucknow were relieved, and the impetus of the Mutiny was over.
The Bengali sepoys fought back and, for a while, regained lost ground,
but the combination of British, Punjabi Sikhs, and Gurkhas under an
able Commander-in-Chief in Sir Colin Campbell was too strong. By
July 1858 the Mutiny was officially over.

The Mutiny was the greatest challenge to the British Empire since the revolt of the American colonies. The government was forced to rethink its policy of dual control by Crown and Company. The India Act of 1858 made sweeping changes. The Company was abolished and its property and powers transferred to the Crown. A Secretary of State for India took over in London responsibility for Indian affairs. The Governor-General became the direct servant of the crown with the title of Viceroy. By proclamation the Indians were again promised equality of opportunity and freedom of religious beliefs. But the shock caused by the Mutiny made equality of opportunity a hollow promise; educated Indians in government service remained as 'babus' in minor posts. The Viceroy, on the other hand, now had executive powers greater even than those of the Tsar or the Emperor of China. In the Army too it was clear that the British meant to keep the whip hand. All artillery was now manned by Europeans and in other branches their proportion was to be not less than one third. The Indian Army, now paid for by the Indian taxpayer and reinforced by troops from home, soon became a cheap and efficient weapon for fighting British wars in Africa and the Persian Gulf.

There were two lasting legacies of the Mutiny. The first was the hatred felt by both sides over the atrocities; British women and children had been slaughtered, sepoy mutineers ceremonially blown from guns. The British press published letters from officers describing the torture of sepoy prisoners, congratulated the writers, and denounced Earl Canning – last Governor-General and first Viceroy – for his policy of clemency. Bitter memories sowed suspicion and soured Anglo-Indian relations for generations. The second legacy became apparent as the British, fearful of another rising, continued to keep Indians out of responsible positions. It was the frustration of the educated élite denied participation in the rule of their own country.

3 The rule of the Viceroys, 1858–1914

After the Mutiny India settled down to a period of consolidation under the 'raj' or government of the Viceroys. With powers like the Roman pro-consuls of old, with a salary of £16,000 a year and an expense account of £73,000, they controlled seven provincial governors each with an area larger than Britain. The administration of the provinces, now about three-quarters of the continent, was in the hands of some 1300 district commissioners. They acted as magistrates, chiefs of police and tax assessors, and coped as best they could with the frequent natural disasters of floods, famines and epidemics over areas as big as English counties. Many Indians still spent their lives without ever seeing a European, yet India was peaceful and reasonably well governed by a handful of men whose public school background moulded them for the task. Behind them, of course, was an Indian Army now 250,000 strong, and the ever growing vested interests of British business.

The need to protect Anglo-Indian trade was now even more at the heart of British foreign policy than in Palmerston's time. Disraeli sought to protect trade routes by the purchase of the Suez Canal shares and to strengthen Indian loyalty to the Crown by making the Queen Empress of India. He revived the 'forward' policy of Lord Auckland by trying to control Afghanistan to counter the Russian threat. The Viceroy, Lord Lytton (1876–80), was instructed to ensure that the Amir Sher Ali should reject Russian 'advisers' in favour of British. Lytton, by nature neither patient nor diplomatic, sent a military mission to Kabul. When it was turned back, an army under General Roberts invaded Afghanistan and replaced Sher Ali by his son. In May 1879 the new Amir gave Britain control of the passes and of Afghan foreign policy, and accepted a British Resident. In September, the Resident and his staff were burnt alive by mutinous Afghan soldiers. It was 1841 all over again. Roberts returned with another army, recaptured Kabul and hanged those responsible. There was a British defeat at Maiwand, but in July 1880 Roberts led an epic march of 313 gruelling miles in 23 days to rescue the garrison at Kandahar. By 1881 a new and anti-Russian Amir was in power and Gladstone had reversed the 'forward' policy. But in 1885, with Britain preoccupied with the news from Khartoum (p.174) the Russians crossed the River Oxus and defeated an Afghan force at Penjdeh. Gladstone denounced the attack, Parliament voted £11 million military credit, and the cabinet drafted a declaration of war; the Russians withdrew and resumed boundary negotiations. Afghanistan, with its mainly Pathan Moslem tribesmen, maintained its precarious independence.

India's North-West frontier was now secure and the rest of Burma was annexed in 1885. Much of the pre-Mutiny brand of 'westernization' had disappeared after 1858 but India continued to be ruled mainly in the interests of Britain. British investment in India almost doubled in thirty years – from £160 million in 1870 to £305 million in 1900 – although it was still less than half our investment in the United States. Jute and cotton mills, built with British money, provided employment for the fast growing population, though the scale of Indian production was never allowed to threaten the Lancashire industry. Between the two, however, the Indian village spinners and weavers lost their livelihood. India's balance of trade showed a serious deficit while Britain's huge surplus from her Indian trade financed some 40 per cent of her total deficits. At the same time, British rule brought immense material benefits. The new roads, railways and canals were the best in Asia. A single irrigation scheme, the Sukkur barrage on the River Indus, was by 1909 watering an area half the size of Great Britain. Under the forceful Lord Curzon (1899–1905) as Viceroy, the 'raj' was in its heyday. He created the North West Frontier Province, ensured

Second Afghan War

Curzon

The visit of an Indian nobleman to the Viceroy of India (the Earl of Mayo, 1889)

British control of the Persian Gulf, encouraged Indian education from village school to university, set up an efficient police force, and suggested co-operatives to give credit to farmers. He also found time to restore ancient monuments and to attempt – without much success – to increase Western contacts with the Dalai Lama of Tibet and the 'forbidden city' of Lhasa.

Peace and a benevolent despotism, however, could never satisfy the growing number of Indian nationalists. In the 1830s Macaulay had looked forward to a governing Indian class 'Indian in blood and colour, English in taste, opinions and morals'. The Mutiny had ended all thoughts of power sharing, but western education had continued. Fifty years after Macaulay a radical politician commented 'Under our present system of excluding natives from the Indian Civil Service, the more boys we educate the more vicious and discontented men we have beneath our rule.' Gladstone felt that we should have been able 'to give to India the benefits and blessings of free institutions'. The Indian National Congress Party was formed in 1885. Inspired by sympathetic members of the I.C.S., its members wanted for India the same sort of responsible government as that found in Canada or Australia. Little progress was made until 1909 when Morley, the Secretary of State, and Minto, the Viceroy, brought in some limited concessions. The Vice-regal Council and the Provincial Councils of Bengal, Madras and Bombay already included some co-opted Indian members. This representation was now to be widened to give a majority of Indians on all Provincial Councils. They were to be elected, though the franchise was

Morley-Minto reforms

to be restricted to men who could read. Moslem interests were to be safeguarded. It was representation without responsibility and not intended to lead to self-government or Dominion status. In the same year as the Morley-Minto proposals the first terrorist bomb appeared, thrown at the Viceroy by a Hindu extremist. Nearly a million Indian Army troops fought for Britain in the 1914–18 War. Yet when it was over, the India so painstakingly united by Company and Crown moved behind Gandhi towards the goal of independence.

19
The British overseas Africa

1 The Partition of Africa

Few Englishmen in 1815 knew much about Africa. British possessions there, a handful of tiny spots on a great map, included former slaving stations on the Gambia and the Gold Coast; Sierra Leone, recently founded as a refuge for freed slaves; and the Cape of Good Hope, just taken as a naval station from the Dutch. A hundred years later Britain claimed and incorporated in her Empire vast tracts of territory in the south, east and west of the continent – altogether over 2,000,000 square miles, some twenty times the size of the United Kingdom. Thus she became the ruling power responsible for millions of native Africans, hitherto organized in numerous tribal kingdoms.

Nearly all this expansion took place between 1860 and 1900. The Britons most prominent in its beginning were explorers, missionaries and traders, and of the explorers the most celebrated was David Livingstone (1813–73), the mill-boy from Lanarkshire who became a medical missionary. His journeys of 1852–6 (across the continent from Angola and down the great Zambesi to Mozambique, the first crossing of Africa by a European) and 1858–64 (when he discovered Lake Nyasa) awakened the interest of Victorian Englishmen in 'the Dark Continent'. He also aroused their consciences by revealing the continuing horror of the slave trade in the heart of Africa. There were numerous others, some German but most of them British (such as John Speke, Samuel Baker and the Welshman H. M. Stanley), as intrepid as Livingstone, yet not commanding such attention from the Victorian public. Their initial aims were scientific, in particular to trace the sources of the Nile and the other great rivers of Africa, and humanitarian.

The explorers

They were quickly convinced – and convinced others – of the need to take the blessings of European Christianity and commerce to the peoples of Africa. So missionaries, for example the Universities Mission to Central Africa (which arrived in 1861), and traders, like those who bought palm-oil in the Niger Delta with guns and liquor, followed hard on the heels of the explorers. British governments in the 1860s and 1870s showed no desire whatever to occupy land in Africa for its own sake. But the activities of Britons on the spot often led to government intervention, to support their missions or to protect their trading interests and their persons. So, in West Africa, Lagos at the mouth of

Causes of British intervention

the Niger was occupied in 1861 as part of the policy of killing the slave trade, while in 1873–4 a military expedition led by Sir Garnet Wolseley defeated the proud and ferocious Ashantis of the Gold Coast under King Kofi. Yet the great extension of the British Empire in Africa came during the 1880s and 1890s, and for wider and different reasons. One was an economic challenge from other European powers, beginning to see colonies as a source of minerals and other raw materials (and also perhaps of fighting men), and as potential markets for their manufactured goods. A second was strategic – the threat to areas which seemed vital to Britain, most notably Egypt after the opening of the Suez Canal in 1867, Disraeli's purchase of its shares in 1874, and Gladstone's occupation of 1882. There was much British anxiety in the late nineteenth century lest the French or the Germans get hold of the head-waters of the Nile, and so control the water supplies and the entire economy of Egypt.

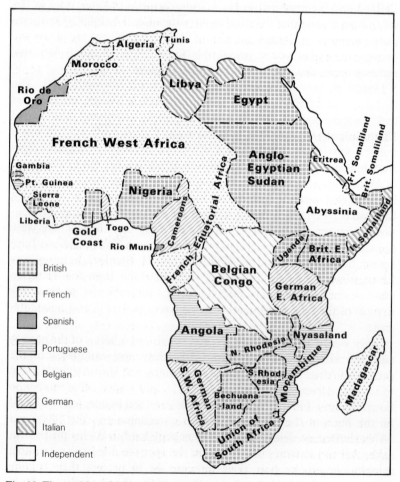

Fig. 10 The partition of Africa before 1914

Here was the background for the European 'Scramble for Africa' of the late nineteenth century. In 1870 only one-tenth of Africa was under European control; by 1900 scarcely one-tenth remained independent. France gained more land than any other power – vast areas in West Africa (including the Sahara, in Salisbury's words 'much of it very light soil') and on the Equator; in the north Tunis and Morocco added to the old colony of Algeria; Djibouti at the gateway to the Red Sea; and the great island of Madagascar in the Indian Ocean. Germany took Tanganyika in the east, a great area around Angra Pequena in the south-west, Togo and part of the Cameroons in the west. The Portuguese extended their sixteenth-century coastal settlements inland into Angola and Mozambique; the Italians secured Eritrea and part of Somaliland in the east – and were deeply humiliated by failing to secure Abyssinia in 1896. King Leopold II of Belgium created a private empire in the Congo Basin which he was forced to hand over to the Belgian Parliament after revelations of appalling treatment of native Africans on his rubber plantations. This astonishingly rapid partition of an entire continent was at least carried out without any wars between the European conquerors – although there was not infrequent warfare with Africans defending their tribal lands, and much exploitation of black labour.

2 Britain's share in West and East Africa

Britain's part in these proceedings was sorted out in a group of treaties which Salisbury made with France, Germany and Portugal in 1890; these settled disputed European claims and determined the fate of millions of black people who had no share in the diplomacy. Broadly, in West Africa the frontiers of the older British colonies (the Gambia, the Gold Coast and Sierra Leone) were pushed far inland. Nigeria was created by a huge northward extension from Lagos, conducted by the Royal Niger Company under Sir George Goldie, chartered in 1886. This device of the 'chartered company' meant in practice that the British taxpayer did not have to meet the costs of government; the company footed the bill, in return for a virtual monopoly of trade in the area. In the later 1890s Anglo-French rivalry grew heated in the Niger region, and Joseph Chamberlain (Colonial Secretary from 1895) pursued a vigorous 'forward' policy, organising a West African Frontier Force to compel the French to yield. But war was avoided by the Niger Convention of 1898, and the big Nigeria of the present day became a British Protectorate in 1900. Likewise a much-enlarged Gold Coast (modern Ghana) came decisively under British rule with the final defeat of the Ashanti in 1901. In East Africa, where great territories were also at stake, it was the Germans who were the rivals, under their most famous explorer Carl Peters. An Anglo-German bargain of 1886,

West Africa

East Africa

however, put Kenya under British rule and Tanganyika under German, and in 1888 another Chartered Company – the Imperial British East Africa Company – was created to look after British claims in the area. In 1890 Salisbury's treaty with Germany gave her the tiny yet strategically important North Sea island of Heligoland, and recognised the German claim to a strip of land stretching from South West Africa to the Zambesi (the 'Caprivi Strip'); in return the Germans recognized British control of Uganda and of the island of Zanzibar. A third treaty of that same year, with Portugal, led to that country's acknowledgment of British control of Rhodesia and Nyasaland – but this is more properly part of the story of southern Africa.

3 South Africa and Rhodesia

Cape Colony

Cape Colony, the southern tip of Africa, was occupied by British forces in 1806 during the world-wide campaigns against Napoleonic France, and became part of the British Empire in 1814. The Netherlands received £6 million in compensation. Its area was substantial, yet small set against the immense continent to the north; its population tiny (perhaps 25,000 whites, most of them Dutch; 20,000 native Hottentots; and 30,000 slaves). Its sole value to Britain lay in the naval base at Simonstown, standing sentry over the route to India. British settlers began to arrive after 1815, some 4,000 of them in 1820. The Dutch farmers, the Boers, did not welcome either them or their new British masters in Cape Town. The Boers were Calvinists in religion, with an outlook reminiscent of the Old Testament, particularly on matters of race. They regarded native Africans as inferior beings, and the ownership of slaves was a normal feature of their way of life. But British opinion at this time was moving fast against slavery, and the London Missionary Society, deeply critical of the Boer treatment of non-Europeans, had great influence at the Colonial Office in London. Nor did the Boers like the introduction of English criminal law (which allowed slaves to give evidence against their masters) and the adoption of English as the official language. It is scarcely surprising that the Emancipation Act of 1833, abolishing slavery in the British Empire, aroused intense hostility in Cape Colony.

The Great Trek

The Boers were worried also about other matters. They complained bitterly of their losses – of livestock, of burned and plundered homesteads, and of lives – from large-scale raids by African tribes across the frontiers and in the Kaffir War of 1834. They felt short of land within the limits of the colony. As owners of great herds of cattle in a dry land, Boer farmers expected estates of some 6,000 acres apiece on which to settle each of their sons. Beyond the frontiers was ample land which the British would not let them occupy. Such grievances were at least as real as the effects of Emancipation. Yet it may be that, as a Boer

The Great Trek

writer put it, the deepest hostility of all arose from 'their [i.e. the coloured peoples] being placed on an equal footing with Christians, contrary to the laws of God and the natural distinction of race and religion.' These varied motives led in 1835–36 to the start of the Great Trek, the planned movement of many hundreds of farmers and their families, native servants and belongings, out of the Cape to find a promised land in the great spaces to the north of the Orange River. The 'Voortrekkers' in their ox-wagons went through high and wild country, endured great hardships, and inevitably came into conflict with the native peoples, including the Matabele, the Basutos and the formidable Zulus. In 1837 the Zulu chieftain Dingaan lured Piet Retief, the principal leader of the Voortrekkers, and many of his followers unarmed into his kraal, and killed them all. A year later 'Dingaan's Day' was avenged at the Blood River, where Boer rifles destroyed 3,000 Zulu spearmen at the cost of three Boers slightly wounded.

The Great Trek, the exodus of the Afrikaner people, quickly became a legend, and the future inspiration of their nationalism. Meanwhile it set a problem for the British who, unable to stop the emigration, had to find a policy to deal with its results – with the native wars the Voortrekkers provoked, and with the small states they set up over a vast land. For some thirty years after the Trek British policy fluctuated. There was no desire in Whitehall to annex territory, to paint the map red; this would be expensive and not very effective in so vast an area –

and where would it stop? On the other hand, the activities of small weak states of white men in a sea of native tribes could provoke bitter conflict and expose the frontiers of the Cape Colony to endless trouble. Moreover, the missionaries continued to press for action against the Boers because of their racial views. So in 1843 British forces annexed Natal, and most of those Boers who had in 1839 set up a republic there with its capital at Pietermaritzburg trekked out across the Drakensberg mountains again. In 1848 Britain proclaimed sovereignty over a second Boer state, the Orange River Colony. But within four years policy was reversed. The government by the Sand River Convention (1852) declared it had no intention of annexing the land beyond the Vaal River, the third trekkers' state of Transvaal; and in 1854 by the Bloemfontein Convention it declared the Orange Free State independent. During the 1860s there was much talk of a federation of the several South African states, but no action.

From the Trek to Majuba Hill The Great Trek was one major landmark in the history of modern South Africa. A second was the discovery of rich mineral wealth, first of diamonds at Kimberley in Griqualand West in 1868 and then of gold on the Rand in the Transvaal in 1886. These 'finds' transformed South Africa's place in the world, making a backward agricultural land into an area of supreme interest to capitalists and politicians. The diamonds were less important than the gold, though they provided the Transvaal Boers with a grievance. For the Transvaal government – as well as the Cape, the Orange Free State and native chieftains – claimed the area and was much offended when an English arbitrator awarded it to the Cape. In the later 1870s British attention turned to the problems of the Transvaal itself, where an unpopular government was in grave trouble. Its finances were in disorder, with the farmers refusing to pay taxes and the bank to make any more loans (the Postmaster General took his salary in stamps and the Surveyor General in land); while powerful African tribes, above all the Zulus under their chieftain Cetewayo, threatened them from several sides.

A remarkable series of events followed during the years 1877–81. In 1877 Britain persuaded the enfeebled Transvaal to allow itself to be annexed. Next year Sir Bartle Frere, Governor of the Cape, pursuing a 'forward' policy independently of the home government (Disraeli, then Prime Minister, had little idea of what was going on) sent an army to invade Zululand. In January 1879 the Zulu impis defeated a British army at Isandhlwana, killing 1600 men. This humiliation was avenged by the heroic defence of Rorke's Drift when a British force of 150 held off 4000 Zulu warriors, and by a decisive victory at Ulundi, Cetewayo's capital, which broke the Zulu military power. But this Zulu War, undertaken in part at least to save the Transvaal from the tribesmen, entirely failed to win its people's gratitude to Britain. By removing the Zulu threat it encouraged the Boers, now led by the tough and wily Paul Kruger, to demand freedom from British rule. They rose in rebellion, proclaimed a 'South African Republic', and defeated a British force under Sir George Colley at Majuba Hill (1881); whereupon Gladstone's government in the Convention of Pretoria duly gave them independence back, subject only to an ill-defined British suzerainty (p.173).

First Boer War

Gladstone's change of direction was decisive. For it meant that it was in the South African Republic, and not in the British Empire, that a great goldfield was found in 1886. The events which followed during the next twenty years, especially the Jameson Raid and the Boer War of 1899–1902, which brought South Africa into the Empire, have already been described as a central part of British history (pp.227–33). Another series of related developments of that time must be recounted here. These centred round the career of perhaps the most extraordinary of British imperial adventurers of the nineteenth century, Cecil John Rhodes (1853–1902), the delicate fourth son of a Hertfordshire clergyman. Sent to South Africa for his health at 17, he went to the diggings at Kimberley in 1871, and within the next twenty years had made immense fortunes both in diamonds and in the gold-mines of the Rand. By the 1890s his De Beers Company controlled the entire diamond production of South Africa (90 per cent of the world output), and his income from the two minerals together in the 1890s was between £300,000 and £400,000 a year. But what made him significant in British history was the use to which he put his wealth. For this astute capitalist, with his uncanny business flair and his extraordinary capacity for work, was a single-minded political idealist whose belief in the virtues of the British Empire knew no bounds. He pointed to the map of South Africa, saying 'all this to be painted red; that is my dream' – a dream based not on a simple lust for conquest but in a genuine belief that Anglo-Saxon values should be spread over as wide a part of the world's surface as possible. Africa in the 1880s and 1890s seemed to present a golden opportunity to make the dream reality. In 1880 Rhodes entered the Cape Parliament, and by 1890 he was Prime Minister of the Cape. His policy there was to work as closely as possible with the Dutch in the colony, in the hope of winning their confidence and making them partners in his imperial vision.

Cecil Rhodes

Meanwhile he was looking to the north and east. For these were the years of the 'Scramble for Africa', and in 1883 Germany laid claim to Angra Pequena and to a vast hinterland which became German South West Africa (modern Namibia). Here was a dangerous challenge to Rhodes' dream. He was prominent in pressing Salisbury's government to take control in 1885 of the great area of Bechuanaland, lying between the new German colony and the Transvaal – the smaller but more fertile southern part as a Crown Colony, the largely desert north as a Protectorate. Yet this was not enough for Rhodes, whose imperial vision extended hundreds of miles north and east, to the Zambesi and beyond. Having first secured from Lobenguela, chieftain of Matabele-

Rhodesia

land, the monopoly of all mineral rights in his lands in return for £100 a month, 100 rifles, 100,000 rounds of ammunition and an armed steamer on the Zambesi, he then in 1889 persuaded the British government to grant his newly-formed British South Africa Company a royal charter. This conferred upon it almost unlimited powers of government as well as of trade over a vast region from the Bechuanaland Protectorate northwards. This extension of British authority would cost the British government nothing. It was an astonishing achievement, with Cecil Rhodes acting like an independent power. It is scarcely surprising that in 1895 the name 'Rhodesia' was officially conferred by the British Crown on much of this huge territory.

The fall of Rhodes

But 1895 was the climax of Rhodes' power. These activities bring him into armed conflict with the black African peoples, with wars in Matabeleland and Mashonaland during the 1890s, inevitably won by white firearms. They also intensified Anglo-Boer hostility. As the map (p.228) shows, the extension of British authority went near to encircling the Transvaal. President Kruger understandably distrusted Rhodes from the time of their first meeting. For the two men represented opposing views of the way in which white people saw the development of South Africa: Kruger was dedicated to the independence of the Boer Republic whose creation he had led, Rhodes to the spread of British imperial supremacy. The Jameson Raid of 1895 (p.228) was an attempt planned by Rhodes to destroy Kruger's Transvaal. Its failure wrecked his political career. He resigned from the premiership of Cape Colony, even though he was exonerated – or whitewashed – by the British parliamentary enquiry. The outbreak in 1899 of the Second Boer War, for which his activities were in part responsible, seemed to shatter his vision of co-operation between British and Dutch in the development of South Africa. When the war broke out he was among those besieged in Kimberley. In 1902 he died, aged 49, two months before the war ended with the Treaty of Vereeniging.

The Union of South Africa

Yet surprisingly soon after the war there was co-operation. In 1906 Sir Henry Campbell-Bannerman, now Prime Minister, granted responsible self-government to the former Boer republics of the Orange Free State and the Transvaal; and in 1910, under his successor H. H. Asquith, the Union of South Africa, consisting of those two territories together with the Cape Colony and Natal, came into being as a self-governing dominion under the British Crown. Contemporary opinion, at any rate on the Liberal side (neither Balfour nor Milner approved) saw these events as a triumph for the principle of self-government. Later opinion has perhaps paid more attention to the fact that the whites of the two former Boer republics firmly declined to allow coloured people to vote: 'no colour bar, no union' was their line in negotiations. The British Liberals for their part accepted this, with regret: without this compromise, they said, 'the Union would be smashed'.

Conclusion

Britain went to war with Germany at the August Bank Holiday week-end of 1914. The majority of public opinion supported the government's decision, and crowds outside the Foreign Office greeted the official declaration with 'round after round of cheers'. By mid-September half a million young men had volunteered for the forces. It was widely assumed that the war would be 'over by Christmas', and the officially-encouraged slogan was 'business as usual'. But the conflict was known from the start as 'The Great War', and Lord Kitchener, appointed to the War Office, told the Cabinet straightaway that he expected it to last three years. Winston Churchill, as First Lord of the Admiralty, had the fleet fully mobilised before the outbreak of war; and the British Expeditionary Force created by Haldane went off to France at once.

By 1914 Britain had become a parliamentary democracy. The series of Reform Acts from 1832 onwards had given the vote to most men over 21 – though in practice the rules about residence meant that fewer than sixty per cent actually got on the register; but women were still excluded. With this widening of the franchise had come better-organized and stronger political parties. Conservatives and Liberals still dominated the field, as they had done since the days of the Gladstone-Disraeli duel. Yet now the Liberals in particular were challenged by an openly working-class Labour party, which in the last pre-war election won 42 seats. The Parliament Act of 1911 had broken the strength of the House of Lords; while George V had far less political power than George IV a century before. Yet thanks in great part to Victoria's long reign the monarchy was much more popular than in 1815 – and well fitted to serve as a symbol of unity in a great war.

The Crown was also an admirable focus of the loyalty of the 420 million people (some 350 million of them coloured) of the British Empire, which was virtually at its greatest extent in 1914. The war was to evoke a remarkable display of loyalty from the territories of the Empire, the more so in that none of them were asked whether they wished to go to war or not. About 2,400,000 troops from the overseas empire fought for Britain, and over 200,000 of them died; in these totals the figures for India were over 1,500,000 and 62,000. Nevertheless much contemporary opinion realised in 1914 that the climax of Empire was already past. The Boer War had done much to tarnish the imperial image, and in India, where about 70 per cent of the entire population of the British Empire lived, there were clear signs of a growing demand for self-government. Moreover Ireland, which most foreigners saw simply as a British colony, was in 1914 still an unsolved problem – indeed, further from solution than ever. For not only did the outbreak of European war put Home Rule into cold storage for the duration. Civil war threatened in both north and south, with Ulstermen preparing to fight against the creation of a united Ireland and the Sinn Fein republicans to fight for it.

In 1914 Britain was a rich country, thanks to the foundations laid in the earlier years of the Industrial Revolution and to great economic progress since. She was rich in population, almost 41 million in the census of 1911; in the varied skills of her people, in the scale and range of her territories, foundries and workshops, in the extent of her commerce. She was the world's greatest trading nation; since 1850 her exports had risen seven and a half-fold, her imports eight-fold. Sterling was the world's most important currency, London its financial capital. Britain's overseas investments were eight times bigger in 1914 than they had been sixty years before, and bigger than those of the rest of Europe put together. These things made the average standard of living of her people in 1914 high. Certainly great numbers of British people were still living in deep poverty. Yet supporters of the Liberals could claim, with some truth, that they had in their reforms since 1908 launched as vigorous an attack upon the ills of an industrial society as could be found anywhere on earth in 1914.

Yet it is also true that in 1914 Britain's economy was extremely vulnerable in several ways. Her share of world trade was declining; while her proportion of the world's industrial output, one-third in 1870, was down to one-seventh in 1913. Her dependence on imported goods was very great, and was growing. From overseas came most of her wool and timber, much of her iron ore, all her cotton, rubber, and petroleum[1] – as well as much of her food, including 55 per cent of her grain and 40 per cent of her meat. Only in coal was she self-supporting: her miners dug more coal in 1913 than ever before (or since) – yet her share of the world's coal trade was falling. In the greatest of all nineteenth-century British industries, cotton goods, British firms still had more than half the world's trade in 1914; but they were now being fiercely challenged not merely by European and American firms but also, in the huge market of Asia, by Japanese and Indian companies (the latter mainly financed by British investors). In the new science-based industries of the late nineteenth and early twentieth centuries – chemicals, electrical engineering, dye-stuffs, motor-cars, rubber – the British were outpaced from the start by Germans and Americans. Finally, even what appeared to be the ultimate mark of British

[1] Just becoming the vital fuel of the immediate future. The government became a shareholder in the Anglo-Persian Oil Company in 1909, and the Navy began to change over from coal to oil.

economic power, her role as investor overseas, was itself a source of potential disaster. Overseas investments brought in 10 per cent of her income in 1914; they provided a sizeable part of the 'invisible exports' which bridged the gap between what Britain imported and what she exported, and so kept her 'out of the red'. But these vast funds were peculiarly at risk in a large-scale war between the great nations (and were in fact largely liquidated between 1914 and 1918). So by 1914 there were already abundant signs that Britain's dominant economic role of the nineteenth century was over. Inevitably, economic supremacy in the world was passing into other – mainly American – hands. The outbreak of world war only accelerated and completed this change.

Time Chart of British History 1815-1914

Year	Imperial	Foreign	Ireland	Political	Economic and Social
1815		Waterloo. Congress of Vienna		The Corn Laws	1815
1816				Income Tax abolished	16
1817					17
1818		Congress of Aix-la-Chapelle			18
1819				Peterloo. The Six Acts	19
1820		Congress of Troppau		Cato Street Conspiracy	20
1821		Greek Revolt			21
1822		Congress of Verona		Death of Castlereagh	22
1823					Penal Code reform began 23
1824	South American Republics recognised			Combination Acts repealed	24
1825					Stockton-Darlington Railway 25
1826					26
1827		Navarino		Canning Prime Minister	27
1828			Clare Election		Neilson's Hot Blast / Dr Arnold Head of Rugby 28
1829				Catholic Emancipation	Metropolitan Police 29
1830		Belgian Revolt		Grey Prime Minister	Liverpool-Manchester Railway 30
1831					31
1832				Great Reform Act	32
1833	Abolition of Slavery	Treaty of Unkiar-Skelessi		Factory Act	Oxford Movement began / First state grant to education 33
1834				Poor Law Amendment Act	34

1835	Municipal Reform Act
1836	Great Trek began
1837	Accession of Victoria
1838	People's Charter
1839	Durham Report; Belgian Neutrality; Anti-Corn Law league founded; Nasmyth's Steam Hammer
1840	Treaty of Waitangi; Opium War; Penny Post
1841	Straits Convention; Peel Prime Minister
1842	Hong Kong annexed; Mines Act. Income Tax
1843	Natal annexed
1844	Rochdale Pioneers
1845	The Great Famine; Simpson used anaesthetics
1846	Oregon Treaty; Repeal of Corn Laws
1847	Ten Hours Act
1848	The 'Year of Revolutions'; Public Health Act; Bedford College for Women
1849	
1850	Don Pacifico
1851	Amalgamated Society of Engineers founded. The Great Exhibition
1852	Livingstone's first journey; Gladstone at Exchequer
1853	
1854	Crimean War began
1855	Palmerston Prime Minister

	Economic and Social	Political	Ireland	Foreign	Imperial
1856	Bessemer's Converter			Treaty of Paris	
1857					Indian Mutiny
1858			Fenian Society		
1859	*Origin of Species*				
1860		Cobden Free Trade Treaty		Garibaldi and the 1000	Maori War
1861		Prince Consort died		American Civil War began	
1862					
1863				Schleswig-Holstein Affair	
1864	London Sewerage system				
1865		Death of Palmerston			
1866	Open Hearth Process				
1867	Barnardo's Homes began	Second Reform Act			British North America Act
1868	First official T.U.C.	Gladstone Prime Minister			Diamonds at Kimberley
1869			Irish Church Act		
1870		Forster's Education Act	1st Irish Land Act	Franco-Prussian War	
1871	Universities Tests Act			German Empire founded	
1872	Girton, Cambridge	Ballot Act			
1873					
1874		Disraeli Prime Minister			
1875		Public Health Act Artisans' Dwellings Act		Purchase of Suez Canal shares	

1876	Bulgarian Atrocities
1877	
1878	Treaties of San Stefano & Berlin; Gilchrist-Thomas Process; Salvation Army founded
1879	Zulu War; Midlothian Campaign; Land League
1880	Roberts' march to Kandahar; Gladstone Prime Minister
1881	Majuba Hill; Death of Disraeli; Second Irish Land Act
1882	Married Women's Property Act; Phoenix Park Murders
1883	
1884	Death of Gordon; 3rd Reform Act
1885	Salisbury Prime Minister; Rover Safety Bicycle
1886	Gold on the Rand; 1st Home Rule Bill
1887	Balfour Chief Secretary
1888	Wilhelm II Kaiser; Local Government Act
1889	London Dock Strike
1890	Rhodes Prime Minister of the Cape; Fall of Bismarck
1891	Death of Parnell
1892	
1893	2nd Home Rule Bill
1894	Gladstone retired; Parson's Turbine Engine; Manchester Ship Canal
1895	Chamberlain Colonial Secretary; Jameson Raid
1896	Daily Mail founded

Year	Economic and Social	Political	Ireland	Foreign	Imperial
1897		The Diamond Jubilee			
1898				Fashoda Incident	Omdurman
1899					Boer War began
1900		Labour Party formed			
1901		Death of Queen Victoria			Commonwealth of Australia
1902		Balfour's Education Act		Anglo-Japanese Alliance	Treaty of Vereeniging
1903			Wyndham's Land Act		
1904				Dual Entente	
1905					
1906	Trade Disputes Act			Algeciras Conference	Transvaal and Orange Free State self-government
1907		1st *Dreadnought* Haldane's Army Reforms		Triple Entente	New Zealand a Dominion
1908	Old Age Pensions	Asquith Prime Minister			
1909		'People's Budget'			Morley-Minto reforms
1910					
1911		Parliament Act			
1912			3rd Home Rule Bill	First Balkan War	
1913				Second Balkan War	
1914			Curragh 'Mutiny'	Murder at Sarajevo First World War began	

Prime Ministers 1815-1914

Dates	Prime Minister	Party
1812–27	Lord Liverpool	Tory
1827	George Canning	Tory
1827–8	Lord Goderich	Tory
1828–30	Duke of Wellington	Tory
1830–4	Earl Grey	Whig
1834	Lord Melbourne	Whig
1834–5	Sir Robert Peel	Conservative
1835–41	Lord Melbourne	Whig
1841–6	Sir Robert Peel	Conservative
1846–52	Lord John Russell	Whig
1852	Earl of Derby	Conservative
1852–5	Lord Aberdeen	Coalition
1855–8	Lord Palmerston	Whig
1858–9	Earl of Derby	Conservative
1859–65	Lord Palmerston	Whig and Liberal
1865–6	Earl (formerly Lord John) Russell	Liberal
1866–8	Earl of Derby	Conservative
1868	Benjamin Disraeli	Conservative
1868–74	W. E. Gladstone	Liberal
1874–80	Benjamin Disraeli[1]	Conservative
1880–5	W. E. Gladstone	Liberal
1885–6	Lord Salisbury	Conservative
1886	W. E. Gladstone	Liberal
1886–92	Lord Salisbury	Conservative
1892–4	W. E. Gladstone	Liberal
1894–5	Lord Rosebery	Liberal
1895–1902	Lord Salisbury	Unionist
1902–5	A. J. Balfour	Unionist
1905–8	Sir Henry Campbell-Bannerman	Liberal
1908–15	H. H. Asquith	Liberal

[1]Disraeli became Earl of Beaconsfield in 1876

Index

Entries in **bold** indicate central topics and personalities